Antonov's Turboprop Twins

An-24/An-26/An-30/An-32

**Yefim Gordon and Dmitriy Komissarov
with Sergey Komissarov**

MIDLAND
An imprint of
Ian Allan Publishing

Antonov's Turboprop Twins
© 2003 Yefim Gordon, Dmitriy Komissarov
and Sergey Komissarov

ISBN 1 85780 153 9

Published by Midland Publishing
4 Watling Drive, Hinckley, LE10 3EY, England
Tel: 01455 254 490   Fax: 01455 254 495
E-mail: midlandbooks@compuserve.com

Midland Publishing is an imprint of
Ian Allan Publishing Ltd

Worldwide distribution (except North America):
Midland Counties Publications
4 Watling Drive, Hinckley, LE10 3EY, England
Telephone: 01455 254 450   Fax: 01455 233 737
E-mail: midlandbooks@compuserve.com
www.midlandcountiessuperstore.com

North American trade distribution:
Specialty Press Publishers & Wholesalers Inc.
39966 Grand Avenue, North Branch, MN 55056, USA
Tel: 651 277 1400   Fax: 651 277 1203
Toll free telephone: 800 895 4585
www.specialtypress.com

© 2003 Midland Publishing
Design concept and layout by
Polygon Press Ltd. (Moscow,Russia)
Line drawings by G.F.Petrov and S.D.Komissarov

This book is illustrated with photos photos by
Yefim Gordon, Dmitriy Komissarov, Sergey
Komissarov, Dmitriy Petrochenko, Sergey Panov,
Sergey Popsuyevich and Simon Watson, as well
as from the archives of Yefim Gordon, Sergey
Komissarov, the Russian Aviation Research Trust,
Kryl'ya Rodiny, *Airliner World* and *Air Forces Monthly*

Printed in England by Ian Allan Printing Ltd
Riverdene Business Park, Molesey Road,
Hersham, Surrey, KT12 4RG

Contents

Title page: A typical Soviet Air Force An-26 coded '60 Orange' on final approach. Air Force examples usually wore this uniform grey camouflage scheme.
Back cover, top: An-30A CCCP-30075 takes off from runway 30 at Moscow-Bykovo; bottom, Russian Air Force An-26 '01 Blue' at Kubinka AB near Moscow.

Below: An-24A CCCP-46723 (c/n 37300303) wearing an early pre-1973 livery. The aircraft was photographed at some kind of exhibition; note the cordoned-off area around the aircraft and the public address loudspeaker temporarily installed on top of the port wing.

Introduction

By the mid-1950s the restoration of the Soviet Union's war-devastated national economy was basically completed. The country's industry and agriculture resumed their growth; under these conditions the task of developing the transport system, including civil aviation, became of paramount importance. Nikita Sergeyevich Khruschchov, Chairman of the Council of Ministers and First Secretary of the Communist Party Central Committee, dreamed of achieving the Party's goal – the construction of the Communist society – within the lifetime of his generation and visualised the growth of well-being and life comfort of the country's citizens as the Party's task. He set the goal of catching up and outstripping the USA not only as regards the number of nuclear warheads but also as far as the living standards of the masses were concerned. One of the most important factors influencing the development of air transport in the USSR to a very high degree was a certain relaxation of intensity of the 'Cold War'. It was during that period that Aeroflot, the Soviet Union's sole airline, gained its own reliable and state-of-the-art wings.

Initially priority in the construction of civil aircraft was accorded to heavy turbine-powered aircraft intended for trunk routes. They were to represent the Soviet Union on the world arena, and international prestige was a matter of primary concern at that time. The Tupolev Tu-104, the first Soviet turbojet-powered airliner, made its maiden flight in 1955, and as many as four new airliners intended for trunk routes made their appearance in 1957. These were the Antonov An-10 *Ookraïna* (the Ukraine), the Il'yushin IL-18 *Moskva* (Moscow), the Tu-110 and the Tu-114 *Rossiya* (Russia). The West was caught unawares and much astounded by this giant leap in the development of Soviet civil aviation. Three of the four types entered series production.

Having thus solved the topmost-priority task, the Soviet aircraft industry proceeded to give serious attention to aircraft intended for local services.

The Kiev-based State Union Experimental Design Bureau No.473 (GSOKB-473 – *Gosoodarstvennoye soyooznoye opytno-konstrooktorskoye byuro*) initiated its independent activities in the second half of the 1940s in Novosibirsk. (The 'Union' bit indicated

that the OKB had national importance.) Its first task was the design of the An-2 utility biplane which was destined to become the main transport means in the Soviet regional air transport services for many years to come. Since that time the development of aircraft technology in the Soviet Union became closely connected with the name of Oleg Konstantinovich Antonov, an outstanding aircraft designer. Within a short space of time the Design Bureau headed by him developed into one of the country's leading design teams engaged in the creation of the most up-to-date specimens of aviation technology. At present, thousands of aircraft bearing the Antonov brand render efficient service in the field of both civil and military aviation in many countries of the world. This book will relate the story of a family of light passenger, transport and special-mission aircraft – the An-24, An-26, An-30 and An-32; aircraft that are operated in dozens of countries to this day, having proved their worth as a sufficiently fuel-efficient and cheap means of carrying passengers and cargo to distances of 1,000-2,500 km (620-1,550 miles).

The An-24 proved to possess characteristics which place it among the world's most fuel-efficient aircraft. By the end of 1977 aircraft of this type were used on about a thousand domestic routes and also flew missions delivering supplies to Arctic research stations set up on drifting icefields. The structure of the An-24 and its stablemates featured, for the first time in the world, the use of metal bonding in the fuselage and tail surfaces instead of traditional riveting. This new method was evolved in the Welding Institute named after Academician Ye. O. Paton. Thanks to this method, the man-hours involved in the manufacture of the aircraft were considerably reduced, the working conditions of the manufacturing personnel were improved and the airframe life was extended to 30,000 hours, or 25,000 cycles. The aircraft of this lineage won high appraisal on the part of specialists at aircraft exhibitions in France, Great Britain, Czechoslovakia, Denmark, Italy and so on. In the Soviet Union the An-24 was responsible for the transportation of up to 30% of the total number of passengers in the 1970s.

Development of this aircraft family has its interesting history. Once, speaking about the

main direction of work of his Design Bureau, Oleg K. Antonov said that every employee of the Design Bureau was obliged to see to it that a new aircraft should meet the needs of the country as fully as possible and be, to a certain extent, a machine capable of flying anywhere and pioneering new routes. This meant that Antonov machines were to be capable of transporting people and cargoes anywhere, especially to development regions where other aircraft would be unsuitable because of the lack of airfields with paved runways and modern maintenance facilities.

As mentioned above, GSOKB-473's first product was the multi-purpose An-2 which was later to gain renown. In the mid-1950s the OKB was tasked with developing large airliners and military transport aircraft. For some time this caused the work associated with the needs of local air services to be put on the back burner, but Chief Designer Antonov reverted to this work as soon as circumstances permitted it. To begin with, the OKB developed under Antonov's direction the An-14 *Pcholka* (Little bee) 'micro-airliner' capable of operating from just about any improvised 'airport' – as often as not a tiny stretch of land allotted for the purpose by the chairman of a collective farm. A logical sequel to this was the advanced development project (ADP) of the An-26 airliner (the first aircraft to bear this designation) intended for communication between regional centres (medium-haul routes). The design work was initiated in 1957 as the OKB's 'private venture' (ie, it was financed by the OKB from resources 'saved' on the officially sanctioned projects).

The aircraft's layout was a combination of traditional and original design features. In those years it was the low-wing monoplane that was considered to be the more attractive layout for a passenger aircraft because it offered a number of advantages. For example, in the event of a crash landing the strong wing centre section protected the passenger cabin from beneath, while in a high-wing layout the centre section, conversely, tended to break through the cabin roof. The undercarriage struts could be made shorter and lighter, the engines were more readily accessible, refuelling posed fewer problems etc. Significantly, the low-wing layout was utilised in the 'classic' Douglas DC-3 and its Soviet

Above: At the time when the An-24 was developed, the Soviet regional air transport scene was populated by piston-engined aircraft, such as this Lisunov Li-2P CCCP-06134 (note the small passenger door).

derivative, the Lisunov Li-2, as well as in the 'purely Soviet' IL-12, IL-14, IL-18, Tu-104 and many foreign passenger aircraft belonging to the mid-1950s generation.

However, shoulder-mounted wings offer better aerodynamic properties; in addition, they reduce the ground effect during take-off and landing. Last but not least, this layout makes it possible to place the powerplant higher above the ground, which is very important for aircraft having to operate from unprepared airfields and in dusty localities. When designing the An-8 military transport, An-10 airliner and An-12 transport, Antonov had a chance to fully appreciate both the advantages and disadvantages of the high-wing layout. Besides, he was fully aware of the tasks that were to be fulfilled by as multi-purpose aircraft. This also had its influence on the choice of layout – the configuration of the new machine resembled a scaled-down An-8 and would be quite suitable for a cargo aircraft.

The centre fuselage included a cylindrical section of considerable length making it possible either to mount rows of passenger seats affording sufficient comfort or to accommodate typical cargoes or mail. The fuselage section also met the requirements of both passenger comfort and typical cargo accom-

modation. There was had nothing to disrupt the clean contours of the fuselage – even the main landing gear struts, when retracted, were stowed not in 'draggy' lateral fairings as on the An-8/An-10/An-12 but in the extended aft sections of the engine nacelles. (Speaking of which, the landing gear and engine nacelle design were identical to those of the Dutch Fokker F.27 Friendship twin-turboprop airliner in the same class. The twin-wheel main units retracted aft to lie behind the engines, resulting in slender cigar-shaped nacelles with annular air intakes, while the nose unit had a single wheel and was inclined forward when extended, the nosewheel well doors remaining open.)

The high aspect ratio wings featuring a high-lift airfoil were optimised for cruising at a relatively modest speed. The propeller wash covered more than one-third of the wing area; this, in combination with the large-area double-slotted flaps, enhanced the aircraft's airfield performance.

The aircraft had a tail unit of unusual design. It featured triple fins and rudders; two vertical tails placed as endplates at the tips of the horizontal tail were supplemented by a centrally-mounted third fin. This is a relatively rarely used layout, the most notable example

being the famous Lockheed L-049/L-349/L-749/L-1049 Constellation airliner.

Soviet-produced turboprop engines were chosen as the aircraft's powerplant. In those years the relatively fuel-efficient (by Soviet standards) AM-5 turbojet designed by the Aleksandr A. Mikulin's OKB-300 could be regarded as a possible alternative; GSOKB-473 specialists had thoroughly appraised this engine. Consideration was also given to purchasing turboprop engines of the 'light' class in France or Great Britain. However, the final choice fell on an indigenous turboprop.

The year of 1951 saw the commencement of a most fruitful cooperation between the Antonov-led GSOKB-473 and the Engine Design Bureau No.478 of the Ministry of Aircraft Industry (MAP – *Ministerstvo aviatsionnoy promyshlennosti*) which had been set up in the town of Zaporozhye, also in the Ukraine. Its leader was Chief Designer Aleksandr G. Ivchenko. This enterprise's early activities could not be termed a success; actually, the poor performance of the TV-2T turboprop developed in Zaporozhye almost killed off the An-8 which was tested initially with this engine. However, the leaders of the two enterprises proved equal to the task of solving, through united efforts, the problems of extreme complexity that had arisen. Subsequently the new AI-20 turboprop, in a tough competition with the NK-4 engine designed by Nikolay D. Kuznetsov's OKB-276, won its place under the wings of series-produced aircraft such as the An-8, An-10, An-12, IL-18, the Beriyev Be-12 Chaika (Seagull) naval amphibian and other well-known Soviet aircraft. Since then the two design collectives proved to be firmly united by long-lasting common ties.

The An-26 project was calculated to accept two AI-20P engines placed in underwing nacelles. This was the version in which the output of the AI-20 turboprop (originally rated at 4,000 ehp for take-off) was boosted to the extreme, making use of all possible reserves of power. The AI-20P delivered up to 5,800 ehp for take-off, enabling the aircraft to gain altitude in a steep climb when taking off from a small airfield. Conversely, the power rating in cruise flight was not very high, which ensured a low fuel consumption per hour. The engine was equipped with a device for setting the propeller into reverse pitch, thereby dramatically reducing the landing run. Should the engine cut, the propeller was feathered automatically, thus minimising the drag.

This project was not destined to result in a machine that would become the main transport workhorse for the multi-million population of the country. Yet, the interest for this type of aircraft had been undoubtedly stirred not only in the Ministry of Aircraft Industry but among the Soviet Union's leaders as well.

The Il'yushin IL-14 was another typical Soviet short-haul airliner of the 1950s. This is IL-14P CCCP-48098 in 1973-standard Aeroflot livery.

Chapter 1

An-24

The Father of a Family

An-24 prototypes

On 18th December 1957 the Council of Ministers issued directive No.1417-656 tasking GSOKB-473 led by Chief Designer Oleg K. Antonov with developing, building and testing a 44-seat feederliner – or, as we would say today, a regional airliner.

Now that the project enjoyed official status, being included into MAP's new hardware development plan, the engineers were able to considerably refine the original PD project, enlisting the help of several aircraft and electronics industry research establishments. By then the Antonov design bureau was no longer a neophyte, having gained considerable experience with large aircraft in the development and testing of the An-8, An-10 and An-12.

The new twin-turboprop regional airliner received the designation An-24, with A. I. Shivrin appointed chief project engineer. The design team included M. G. Pinegin who headed the wing design group, engineer Limanskiy who was in charge of the fuselage design, engineer Litsook who was responsible for the propulsion group and engineer Semiryad whose responsibilities lay with the control system, avionics and equipment.

Maximum fuselage width was 2.9 m (9 ft 6⅛ in), which meant the seating could be four-abreast only. In contrast to the projected An-26's circular-section fuselage, the basic fuselage cross-section was now formed by two arcs of different radii; this resulted in a flattened underside, with characteristic chines running along the lower fuselage sides.

The Connie-style triple tails of the An-26 project gave way to a more conventional tail unit patterned on that of the An-10, except for the omission of endplate fins. The fin had a prominent root fillet. The stabilisers featuring 9° dihedral were set high on the aft fuselage.

The landing gear was totally reworked. All three units now retracted forward and the nose unit had twin wheels. As the mainwheels were now stowed under the engines when retracted, the engine nacelles became considerably shorter and deeper, making it possible to place the engines' oil coolers below the propeller spinners.

The greatest changes concerned the powerplant. With the AI-20P, the engineers of OKB-478 had pushed the AI-20 turboprop nearly to the limit of what it could deliver. This not only led to a high fuel consumption, espe-

cially during take-off and climb, but led to major reliability problems. Given the AI-20's high operating temperature and the inevitably low time between overhauls (TBO) at the start of mass production, engine changes would be so frequent that operating the airliner would be economically unviable. (Eventually, though, uprated versions of the AI-20 did appear and the TBO was vastly increased – but that's another story.)

What the An-24 needed was a 'clean sheet of paper' engine – a purely commercial turboprop designed with economic efficiency in mind. Calculations showed that available take-off power could be reduced by more than 50% over an AI-20P-powered version without causing an unacceptable reduction in climb and cruise performance. A derated engine would not only be more fuel-efficient but also have an adequate service life and TBO, costing less at the same time. This target could be attained by reducing the turbine temperature and engine speed, allowing the design of the gas flow duct to be simplified and cheaper materials to be used.

According to calculations, two engines rated at 2,500 ehp for take-off would be

The first prototype An-24, CCCP-Л1959 (ie, SSSR-L1959, c/n 0001), in an early test flight. This view shows clearly the lack of a ventral fin, the short engine nacelles and the marked tailplane dihedral. Note the ventral ADF strake aerials and the radio altimeter dipole aerials under the stabilisers.

Above and below: The first prototype at Kiev-Svyatoshino in December 1959 shortly before its maiden flight. Note the short, almost hemispherical nose radome, the cutouts in the main gear doors (the mainwheels were partly exposed when retracted) and the eight cabin windows on each side.

Above: One more shot of CCCP-Л1959 as first flown. The aircraft is mostly white with an orange cheatline and large Aeroflot titles. Note how the tails of the engine nacelles are split horizontally, the upper half being attached to the inboard wing flaps and sliding inside the lower half.

enough to achieve adequate performance; in this case, however, short take-off and landing (STOL) capability was no longer possible. With this powerplant the aircraft would operate from more or less well-equipped airports possessing concrete, perforated steel plate (PSP) or hard-packed dirt runways of sufficient length. The required nominal power for achieving a cruising speed of 400-450 km/h (250-280 mph) was determined at 2,000 ehp.

Calculations also showed that with a 2,500-ehp take-off rating the aircraft could maintain level flight on one engine at altitudes up to 3,000-4,000 m (9,840-13,120 ft) with no reduction in range. It was also possible to continue take-off safely in the event of an engine failure.

Aleksandr G. Ivchenko's OKB-478 started work on such an engine in 1958. Based on the core of the production 4,000-ehp AI-20K, the new 2,400-ehp turboprop was tailored for the future An-24; unsurprisingly therefore, it received the designation AI-24. Compared to the AI-20, the new engine had a slightly higher specific fuel consumption (SFC) at 0.24 kg·hp/hr (0.529 lb·hp/hr) versus 0.20 kg·hp/hr (0.44 lb·hp/hr); however, as there was no excess power, the cruise SFC and fuel consumption during take-off and climb turned out to be much lower. Later the AI-24 was

equipped with a water injection system maintaining the rated take-off power at high ambient temperatures.

The AV-72 four-blade reversible-pitch propeller of 3.9 m (12 ft 9½ in) diameter was specially developed for the AI-24 by the Stoopino Machinery Design Bureau (SKBM – *Stoopinskoye konstrooktorskoye byuro ma-shinostroyeniya*), alias KB-120, located in Stoopino near Moscow. (The enterprise is now called NPP Aerosila, = Aeropower Research & Production Enterprise.) The Antonov OKB was heavily involved in the development of the engine and propeller right from the start, wishing to make sure the new powerplant would be a success. Thus it converted an An-12 transport (identity unknown) into a testbed for the engine and the An-24's automated fuel management system. With the AI-24/AV-72 combination fitted instead of one of the AI-20 engines, the trials began in 1959 with the active participation of the Flight Research Institute named after Mikhail M. Gromov (LII – *Lyotno-issledovatel'skiy institoot*) in the town of Zhukovskiy south of Moscow.

Powerplant reliability and safety was the subject of special attention. In service the An-10 and An-12 had suffered several cases

Below: The first prototype caught by the camera moments before touchdown, still in its original colour scheme. Note that the rudder has been replaced and an L-shaped aerial added aft of the nose gear.

Above and below: The first prototype following a repaint; it is seen here during soft-field trials. Note the rod aerials of the PDSP-2N Proton-M theatre navigation system under the fuselage and wings, the modified main gear doors and the test equipment sensors above the wing trailing edge and on the centre fuselage.

Above: Another view of CCCP-Л1959 with a red cheatline, tan lower fuselage sides and 'feathers'. Note the camera holder in the No.1 cabin window to port.
Below: CCCP-Л1959 seen after 1961 with longer radome, pointed nacelle tails and a ventral fin. Note the forward position of the APU outlet in the engine nacelle.

Above: The second prototype An-24, CCCP-Л1960 (c/n 0002), was again registered to signify the year of completion. It is seen here as originally flown; note the different colour scheme from the first prototype.

of a propeller spontaneously going to fine pitch (ie, reversing) or refusing to feather automatically in the event of an engine failure/in-flight shutdown. The resulting strong drag and asymmetric thrust led to loss of control, causing the aircraft to crash, often fatally. The engineers were determined not to let this happen on the An-24. Hence the new airliner's powerplant featured three propeller pitch holding systems and an intermediate stop precluding uncommanded transition to fine pitch. Furthermore, there were two main propeller feathering systems with automatic and manual control, each of which had its own hydraulic pumps. As a last resort, there was also an emergency feathering system powered by the aircraft's main hydraulic system.

The fuel system featured both traditional bladder tanks (rubber fuel cells) and advanced integral tanks in the wing torsion box. Using single-point pressure refuelling, it was possible to fill 4,800-4,900 litres (1,056-1,078 Imp. gal.) of fuel and then top up the tanks via individual filler caps on the wings' upper surface, bringing the total to 5,100 litres (1,122 Imp. gal.). Normally the port and starboard engines' fuel systems were isolated,

but a cross-feed valve enabled either engine to draw fuel from any group of tanks.

For the first time in Soviet aircraft design practice the An-24 made use of a micro-ejector de-icing system for the wing, tail unit and engine inlet leading edges. This was a variation on the hot air de-icing system; bleed air from the engines' 10th compressor stage passed through a narrow gap between the inner and outer metal panels of the de-icer structure and was ejected outside. In comparison to traditional hot air de-icing systems the required amount of engine bleed air was estimated to be 30-40% less. The windscreen and the propeller blades were de-iced electrically.

It was just as well that the Antonov OKB paid so much attention to de-icing when developing the An-24. On 26th February 1960, barely two years after the beginning of the An-24's full-scale development phase, an An-10 operated by the Ukrainian Civil Aviation Directorate's Kiev United Air Detachment (CCCP-11180) crashed on approach to L'vov airport after losing control due to wing and tailplane icing, killing 40 people. Still, when the new airliner reached the hardware stage

its de-icing system was not quite what the designers had envisaged.

The aircraft featured an RPSN-2AN *Emblema* (Emblem, or Badge) weather radar (RPSN = **rah**diolokatsi**on**nyy pri**bor** sle**poy** navi**gaht**sii – blind navigation radar device). Unlike the radars fitted to contemporary Soviet airliners, this was a purely civilian weather radar – and was brand-new, which inevitably meant lots of teething troubles. The radar also had navigation and traffic collision avoidance system (TCAS) functions, allowing the aircraft's position to be ascertained by using familiar landmarks and ground radio beacons; additionally, it allowed true airspeed and drift angle to be determined. Together with gyroscopic, magnetic and radio navigation aids, the SP-50 *Materik* (Continent) instrument landing system ([*sistema*] *slepoy posahdki* – blind landing system) and state-of-the-art flight instrumentation the radar gave the An-24 day/night and poor weather operating capability. This was all the more remarkable because, unlike other Soviet airliners of the day, the An-24 was conceived for three-crew operations with two pilots and a navigator; no provision was made for a flight engineer or a radio operator.

The flight control system included an AP-28L1 autopilot. The Antonov OKB engineers were well familiar with this system, having utilised the broadly similar AP-28D1 autopilot on the An-12.

The projected airliner featured a very capable fire suppression system protecting the engine bays bay in the engine nacelles, as well as the bays housing the inner wing fuel cells. The system was designed to be activated manually or automatically. For higher safety the engines were separated from the main-wheel wells by airtight titanium firewalls.

GSOKB-473 had a tradition for maximising passenger and crew comfort. Thus for the first time in Soviet aircraft design practice the passenger cabin featured electroluminescent lighting. The flightdeck introduced red lighting on the instrument panels instead of the then-current ultraviolet night lighting; this feature reduced pilot fatigue during night operations. Interestingly, this red lighting was only about to be introduced on Soviet combat aircraft at the time.

The passenger cabin featured two emergency exits; passenger evacuation in an emergency was also possible via the forward baggage door and rear service door. The fuselage was designed for sufficient structural strength to withstand a belly landing or ditching; in the latter case the aircraft was capable of remaining afloat for a while, allowing the occupants to 'abandon ship'.

From the outset the designers had envisaged that the baseline An-24 would evolve into a wide range of advanced and/or spe-

Above: The second prototype following the same aerodynamic improvements as on the first prototype. The ventral fin appears to have been damaged in an overrotation. Note the main gear oleo fairings.

Three more views of the second prototype as originally flown, with ventral fin but still with a short radome and short nacelle tails. Note the different original colour scheme; Feathers'R'Us. The lower view illustrates the stabiliser dihedral and outer wing anhedral.

Before... and after. The upper picture shows СССР-Л1960 as originally built; note the exhaust-stained engine nacelles. The lower photo shows the same aircraft in modified form with pointed engine nacelles taxying at Kiev-Gostomel', the OKB's flight test facility; note the black panels making the soot less conspicuous.

Two more views of the updated second prototype as it makes a flypast, showing off the 'anti-soot' panels painted on the nacelles, the fully enclosed mainwheel wells and the anti-collision beacons in the fin leading edge and under the centre fuselage. Once again the TC-16M APU is located well forward in the nacelle.

Above and below: The third prototype with the non-standard five-digit registration CCCP-Л19603 (= year of manufacture 1960, 3rd airframe) featured the pointed nose and elongated nacelles from the start.

A crudely retouched photo (the tail has been retouched away!!) from an Aeroflot brochure, showing CCCP-Л19603 during service trials. Note the T-shaped photo calibration markings near the entry door.

cialised versions. This obviously included military uses, as revealed by the fact alone that two DOS-24 cassettes (*derzhahtel' osvetitel'nykh sredstv* – 'rack for means of illumination' were installed vertically aft of fuselage frame 40. These were to hold two 10-kg (22-lb) TsOSAB-10 colour marker/signal flare bombs (*tsvetnaya oriyenteerno-signahl'naya aviabomba*). The bombs were to be loaded nose-up, falling out when the cassette doors were opened and the locks released; alternatively, PR-8 parachute-retarded illumination flares (*parashootnaya raketa*) could be used.

The An-24 project included a host of innovative features. For the first time on an Antonov aircraft, chemically milled skins of varying thickness were utilised. Another 'first' in Soviet aircraft design practice was the large-scale use of bonding – specifically, bonded/riveted and bonded/welded joints – alongside traditional rivet and bolted joints. The new assembly techniques were developed in cooperation with the All-Union Research Institute of Aviation Materials (VIAM – *Vsesoyooznyy instituut aviatsionnykh materiahlov*), the Central Aerodynamics & Hydrodynamics Institute named after Nikolay V. Zhukovskiy (TsAGI – *Tsentrahl'nyy aero- i ghidrodinamicheskiy instituut*) and the Kiev-based Institute of Welding Technologies, then headed by Academician O. Ye. Paton. All this gave the projected airliner unprecedented weight efficiency while still keeping manufacturing complexity and production costs at an acceptable level.

Bonded/welded joints had the advantage of distributing the load evenly over the joint and were stronger than conventional welded or rivet joints. This technology was utilised on the fuselage and empennage, and the panels making use of bonded/welded joints made up 67% of the total skin area. Spot welding eliminated the need for more than 120,000 rivets! Bonded/riveted joints were capable of withstanding substantial deformations without incurring permanent structural damage, such as skin wrinkling or cracking. This allowed the airframe structure to be made elastic and lightweight, giving the aircraft a long designated service life. The use of monolithic (chemically milled) panels in the wing centre section instead of conventional riveted components gave a weight saving of 12% for this subassembly. Later, the designers' estimates of the An-24's service life were confirmed during fatigue tests.

As was the case with the An-12 (or indeed with any large aircraft), the An-24's airframe was split into several major subassemblies, each of which was manufactured in its own assembly jig. Thus, having invested once into a set of jigs and tooling, the factory building the type reduced unit costs dramatically during large-scale production. This subdivision was also necessary for ensuring high-quality bonding at locations where specific temperature conditions were required for the adhesive to set properly. Thus, a chunk of airframe could be cured in an autoclave where exactly the right temperature and pressure could be created.

Construction of the first prototype (construction number 0001 – ie, Batch 0, first aircraft in the batch) got under way at GSOKB-473's experimental production facility in Kiev as early as 1958. Aptly registered CCCP-Л1959 (ie, SSSR-L1959 in Cyrillic characters), the aircraft was rolled out and transferred to the OKB's flight test facility in September 1959. The prototype wore a smart white colour scheme with orange (later red and tan) trim and had a pug-nosed appearance due to the almost hemispherical radome.

(Note: Under the Soviet civil aircraft registration system used in 1922-1958 the CCCP-country prefix was followed by a letter designating the agency to which a particular aircraft was assigned, plus up to four figures. In this case the operator designator is an L (for *leeneynyy* [*samolyot*] – aircraft in airline service) denoting the Main Directorate of the Civil Air Fleet (GU GVF – *Glahvnoye oopravleniye grazhdahnskovo vozdooshnovo flota*) which operated scheduled passenger/cargo services. Cf. CCCP-Hxxx (the Cyrillic N) for the Main Directorate of the Northern Sea Route (GU SMP – *Glahvnoye oopravleniye severnovo morskovo putee*) which included the Polar Aviation branch, CCCP-Cxxxx (the Cyrillic S; derived from 'sport') for the Osoaviakhim sports organisation running Soviet air clubs, CCCP-Axxxx for the agricultural division, CCCP-Kxxx (derived from *krahsnyy krest* – red cross) for ambulance aircraft etc. The rendering of the registrations as actually applied is used throughout.)

On 20th December 1959, when the requisite ground checks and taxying tests/high-speed runs had been completed, the first prototype An-24 successfully performed its maiden flight from Kiev-Svyatoshino airfield. The crew consisted of captain G. I. Lysenko, first officer Yuriy V. Koorlin, navigator V. N. Popov, flight engineer A. A. Kroots, radio operator P. S. Mel'nichenko and test engineer Ya. I. Ryzhik. (Although, as already mentioned, the advanced development project did not provide for a flight engineer and a radio operator, these were included into the test crew; the pilots would have enough to do without managing the systems and communicating with the ground!)

It should be noted that the late 1950s and early 1960s were the 'dark ages' of the Soviet Union's aircraft industry, if not for the nation at large. This was due to the Soviet leader Nikita S. Khruschchov's famous 'missile itch', ie, his

Above: The fourth prototype (and the fifth airframe to be completed) was registered CCCP-Л19605. This was the first An-24 to feature twin ventral strakes which were later used on the An-24T/RT and An-24B/RV.

Three out of four flying prototypes make a pass in echelon starboard formation during an airshow in 1961. The first prototype (foreground) leads CCCP-Л19603, with CCCP-Л1960 rearmost.

predilection towards missile systems and his lack of faith in manned combat aircraft. In line with this new policy the funding of new military aviation programmes was curtailed dramatically, which inevitably had a knock-on effect on the industry as a whole – civil aviation also suffered. In 1957, when the An-24 entered full-scale development, the aircraft industry was subordinated to the Ministry of Defence Industry (MOP – *Ministerstvo oboronnoy promyshlennosti*); the Ministry of Aircraft Industry lost its ministerial status together with several other ministries and was 'demoted' to the State Committee for Aviation Hardware (GKAT – *Gosoodarstvennyy komi-tet po aviatsionnoy tekhnike*). Numerous ex-MAP enterprises were transferred to the nascent missile and space industry; those which survived as aircraft factories were now running on empty.

In this situation many aircraft had to be tested… well, not haphazardly (this costs lives!) but less extensively than they would have been before the reorganisation; the government would not have authorised extensive tests (and the expenditures associated therewith). The An-24 was one of these aircraft. True, the OKB still tried to be as thorough about the tests as possible; the manufacturer's flight test programme involved four flying prototypes. The second aircraft was again very aptly registered CCCP-Л1960 (ie, SSSR-L1960; c/n 0002), while the other two wore non-standard five-digit registrations – CCCP-Л19603 (c/n 0003) and CCCP-Л19605 (c/n 0005). Aircraft c/n 0004 was probably the static test airframe.

Early test flights revealed that directional stability was poor, so the second prototype introduced a single ventral fin tapering off towards the front. Also, in original form the An-24 could not meet its speed target due to excessive drag; to remedy this, on the second aircraft the radome was soon given a more pointed shape and the truncated engine nacelles were extended aft, the rear portions receiving an ogival shape in side view. These measures not only gave good results but changed the airliner's appearance, giving it a more racy look. Concurrently a TG-16M auxiliary power unit (APU) was introduced; located in the starboard engine nacelle, this small gas turbine driving a generator supplied electric power on the ground, easing the load on the DC batteries. These changes were incorporated from the third prototype onwards.

Due to the reasons stated earlier, the An-24's manufacturer's flight tests were relatively brief, ending in March 1961. After some minor modifications, including the aerodynamic refinements introduced on CCCP-Л1960, all four prototypes were submitted for State acceptance trials in April. The trials proceeded at the Civil Air Fleet Research Institute (NII GVF – *Naoochno-issledovatel'skiy institoot Grazhdahnskovo vozdooshnovo flota*) and the Soviet Air Force State Research Institute named after Valeriy Pavlovich Chkalov (GK NII VVS – *Gosoodarstvennyy krasnoznamyonnyy naoochno-issledovatel'skiy institoot voyenno-vozdooshnykh seel*) at Chkalovskaya airbase about 30 km (18.5 miles) east of Moscow. This institution tested all new civil aircraft in those days, assessing possible military uses.

(Note: GosNII GVF later became the State Civil Aviation Research Institute (GosNII GA – *Gosoodarstvennyy naoochno-issledovatel'-skiy institoot grazhdahnskoy aviahtsii*). The word *Krasnoznamyonnyy* in the Air Force Research Institute's name means it was awarded the Order of the Red Banner.)

The State commission's report clearing the aircraft for production and service was endorsed in August 1961, just one year and eight months after the An-24's first flight, marking the end of the rather brief test programme. By then aircraft factory No.473 at Kiev-Svyatoshino had already launched series production of the type.

(Note: The number of the Kiev factory which was the first to build the An-24 has also been reported as 62. While such a factory *did* exist and was likewise located at Kiev-Svyatoshino, this assertion is doubtful – see below.)

Apparently only the four prototypes were 'pure' An-24s with no suffix letters to the designation, or *sans suffixe*. These aircraft were retained by the OKB, the Kiev aircraft factory or other GKAT divisions as 'dogships' for use in various test and development programmes, as well as for cargo/mail carriage during the type's service tests with Aeroflot or for demonstration purposes.

An-24A airliner project (first use of designation)

Designated An-24A in alphabetical sequence, this project developed in 1960 envisaged the installation of two Kuznetsov NK-4 turboprops with a take-off rating of 4,000 ehp driving AV-68 four-blade variable-pitch constant-speed propellers of 4.5 m (14 ft 9⅛ in) diameter. The project died when the NK-4 was phased out of mass production in favour of the identically rated AI-20.

An-24A airliner (second use of designation)

Plant No.473 started tooling up for An-24 production back in 1959 when the first prototype had yet to enter flight test. Unlike Western aircraft companies, in the Soviet Union and post-Soviet Russia the OKBs had only very limited production facilities for prototype manufacturing. If and when a new aircraft was ordered into production, this took place at a formally independent production plant within the MAP (GKAT) framework.

The first production aircraft (c/n 27300101; probably registered CCCP-46711) was released by the factory in 1962. Outwardly the production version differed from the prototypes in having the APU nozzle moved aft to the tip of the nacelle.

(Note: The construction numbers of Kiev-built An-24s are deciphered as follows. For instance, An-24B CCCP-46817 manufactured on 28th July 1966 is 67302605 – ie, year of manufacture 1966, plant No.[4]73 (the first digit is omitted to confuse would-be spies), Batch 026, fifth aircraft in the batch. Th c/n is usually stencilled below the port stabiliser.

A very early-production An-24A on display in the Central Plaza of the Economic Achievements Exhibition (VDNKh) in Moscow in company with Tu-124V CCCP-45052 and IL-18B CCCP-75664.

Above: An-24A CCCP-46711 was probably the first production example (c/n 27300101?). It wore the same colour scheme as the prototypes. This aircraft stayed around long enough to see the demise of the USSR, becoming RA-46711 and then EK-46711. Note the main gear oleo fairings which were soon abandoned.

Another Aeroflot An-24A, this time in a different livery with a 'Blue Lightning' cheatline, a silver belly and a silver tail. A modified version of this colour scheme was later used for the An-24B and An-24RV, but a couple of other liveries were also tried. Note that the nose titles read 'An-24'.

The first 19 batches consisted of five aircraft; subsequent Kiev-built batches had ten aircraft each, except for the 108th and final batch which comprised 13 aircraft because it was considered inexpedient to begin a new batch for the last three production examples. Thus c/n 77310810 was followed by c/ns 77310810A, 87310810Б (a Cyrillic B) and 97310810В (a Cyrillic V).

(Note: The Soviet civil aircraft registration system was changed in 1958. The operator designator was deleted and the CCCP- prefix was now followed by a five-digit number. The first two digits were usually a sort of type designator introduced for flight safety reasons (this allowed air traffic control officers to identify the aircraft type by its registration and thus avoid placing excessive demands on the crew). This system is still in use today in Russia and most of the other CIS republics. Under the new system An-24s were normally registered in the 46xxx and 47xxx blocks.

There were also about a dozen registration blocks reserved for Aeroflot's Polar division (04xxx), the Ministry of Aircraft Industry (29xxx, 48xxx, 69xxx, 93xxx, 98xxx etc.), the Ministry of Defence (08xxx, 13xxx etc.) and so on. They do not correspond to any specific type and are a mixed bag of assorted aircraft.)

The state order for An-24 production meant that the Kiev aircraft factory needed to modernise its production facilities and master new manufacturing technologies. This was no easy task, and putting the An-24 into production required nationwide cooperation with other aviation industry enterprises. The landing gear, for instance, was supplied by an aircraft component factory in Kuibyshev (now renamed back to Samara) in central Russia; some large airframe subassemblies were 'subcontracted out' to aircraft factory No.116 in the town of Arsen'yev in the Soviet Far East and so on.

In the mid-1960s the official use of plant numbers in the MAP framework was discontinued (it should be noted here that MAP regained its former status in 1965, although it did not regain all of the factories it had lost). Thus the former plant No.473 came to be known as the Kiev aircraft factory (KiAZ – *Kiyevskiy aviazavod*). A few years later, when the Soviet government launched a large-scale reform of the national economy, the plant became the core of the Kiev Aircraft Production Association (KiAPO – *Kiyevskoye aviatsionnoye proizvodstvennoye obyedineniye*). This plant reportedly built 1,028 An-24s in various passenger versions, the final aircraft with the non-standard registration CCCP-08824 being manufactured on 29th March 1979.

Plant No.99 in the East Siberian city of Ulan-Ude (later U-UAPO – the Ulan-Ude Aircraft Production Association) joined in later, manufacturing 180 An-24Bs between 1965

and June 1971. For example, CCCP-47785 manufactured on 30th March 1968 is c/n 89901510 – ie, year of manufacture 1968, plant No.99, Batch 015, 10th aircraft in the batch. There were five aircraft per batch in the first ten batches and ten aircraft per batch in batches 11-23. This makes a total of 1,208 An-24s built in passenger and VIP versions.

Despite having its hands full with the high-priority task of developing heavy military transports – first and foremost the An-22 Antey (Antheus; NATO reporting name *Cock*), – the Antonov OKB started refining the baseline An-24 and adapting it to new tasks as soon as the manufacturing drawings were issued to the Kiev aircraft factory. (Speaking of which, GSOKB-473 had also undergone a change of name in the mid-1960s, becoming KMZ 'Trood' (*Kiyevskiy mashinostroitel'nyy zavod* – the 'Labour' Kiev Machinery Plant.)

The first major production version was again designated An-24A. Most of these aircraft were powered by 2,550-ehp AI-24 Srs II engines having a 0.15 kg/hp·hr (0.33 lb/hp·hr) lower SFC (early examples had 'pure' AI-24s, aka AI-24 Srs Is). This model remained in production up to and including Batch 21; however, the version was painted on the actual aircraft simply as 'An-24' (possibly because no other versions existed at the time). The NATO allocated the reporting name *Coke* to the An-24.

The An-24A officially entered service with a crew of two. However, at the customer's insistence provisions were made on all production An-24As and subsequent versions for a navigator, a flight engineer and a radio operator to reduce pilot workload. The flight engineer's sliding seat was installed on the centreline, just aft of the pilots. The radio operator sat at a slightly lower on the starboard side, facing the tail, while the navigator faced the starboard side, with the radarscope in front of him. If there was no navigator, the radarscope was mounted centrally on top of the pilots' instrument panel.

The An-24 had a functional interior layout. A baggage compartment with a 1.2 x 1.1 m (3 ft 11¼ x 3 ft 7⅜ in) door to starboard which slid inwards and upwards into the roof was located aft of the flightdeck. The cabin featuring 50 comfortable seats at 75 cm (29½ in) pitch occupied the greater part of the fuselage. All seats were double units featuring armrests and tall reclining backs. A galley module was located across the aisle from the rearmost pair of seats; in flight the stewardess would serve refreshments and coffee.

The cabin was separated by a bulkhead from the entry vestibule with an aft-sliding port side entry door of quasi-oval shape, built-in two-section airstairs and a toilet. Further aft were a coat closet and the rear baggage compartment accessed via a similar service door

on the starboard side; it terminated in the rear pressure dome. A single emergency exit was provided on each side of the cabin; thus the window arrangement was as follows: exit (with window)+7+door to port and 1+baggage door+4+exit+3+service door to starboard. The foremost window on the starboard side (ahead of the baggage door) was for the navigator and radio operator.

In cruise flight at 6,000 m (19,685 ft) the cabin pressure was equal to 2,140 m (7,020 ft) above sea level; this ensured acceptable passenger comfort and the pressurisation loads on the structure were fairly low. The pressure differential was 0.3 kg/cm² (4.28 psi).

The airframe and systems underwent constant refinement in the course of production. One of the first major changes concerned the flight controls. On the first 20 aircraft the ailerons terminated one rib short of the wingtip, with a small fixed portion outboard. Starting with c/n 37300301 (possibly CCCP-46721), the ailerons were extended all the way to the wingtips.

From c/n 37300901 (CCCP-46744?) onwards the amount of unusable fuel in the inner wing bladder tanks was reduced from 155 litres (34.1 Imp. gal.) to 65 litres (14.3 Imp. gal.). Previously built aircraft were upgraded accordingly during the next overhaul.

All sorts of changes were made to the systems and equipment. From Batch 16 onwards (ie, CCCP-46779?) all An-24s featured a curtain closing the forward baggage door aperture to prevent draughts and stop rain and snow from blowing inside. A more reliable landing gear emergency extension mechanism was introduced on Batch 18, starting with An-24A CCCP-46788 (c/n 57301801).

An-24A 'Salon' VIP aircraft

VIP versions of the An-24A designated An-24A 'Salon' ('*samolyot-salon*' being the Russian term for VIP aircraft) were introduced quickly, the first such aircraft leaving the Kiev factory in the early 1960s. Most of these aircraft were delivered to the Soviet Air Force which operated them in an airline-style colour scheme. Known examples were coded '11 Black' (c/n 37300601) and '01 Yellow' (c/n 47301305); one quasi-civil example was registered CCCP-46777 (c/n 47301504).

(Note: Unlike Western military aircraft (which have *serials* allowing positive identification), since 1955 Soviet/CIS military aircraft normally have two-digit *tactical codes* which usually are simply the aircraft's number in the unit operating it. Three-digit codes are usually worn by development aircraft, often tying in with the c/n or fuselage number (f/n or line number) – although some SovAF transports which were previously quasi-civil have tactical codes matching the last three digits of the former civil registration.)

Above: An-24A CCCP-46781 (c/n 47301603?) was a regular airline machine in the most common livery worn by the type until the mid-1970s.
Below: This An-24B with the non-standard registration CCCP-98104 (c/n 67302310) belonged to aircraft factory No.135 in Khar'kov and wore a different livery.

Above: This An-24B (identity unknown) illustrates yet another livery with a double pale blue cheatline.

An-24AT tactical transport/ troopship project

Giant transport aircraft were Soviet aviation's trademark in the 1970s, and none more so than the An-22, the flagship of the Soviet Air Force's transport element. However, the Air Force and Aeroflot needed inexpensive mass-produced transport aircraft comparable in payload to a five-ton lorry just as much as the unique giants. Such aircraft were to carry small items totalling 4 tons (8,820 lb), stretcher patients and walking wounded. They were also to paradrop small items of materiel or 33 paratroopers, or carry 37 fully equipped troops.

In 1962 the Antonov OKB developed a tactical transport derivative of the An-24A called An-24AT (*trahnsportnyy* – transport, used attributively) as a 'private venture'. The radically modified aircraft was to feature a rear cargo door equipped with a loading ramp. The powerplant was new, comprising two Izotov TV2-117DS coupled turboprops rated at 3,200 ehp for take-off and driving contra-rotating propellers of 4.0 m diameter.

The TV2-117DS was a coupled version of the 1,500-eshp TV2-117A turboshaft developed by Sergey P. Izotov's KB-117 in Leningrad for the Mil' Mi-8 multi-purpose helicopter. It had a fairly low SFC and a good power/weight ratio; the OKB's rich experience in developing main gearboxes for twin-engined choppers assured it success in designing the reduction gear. The coupled engines offered high reliability – if one core failed, the other 'half' of the engine would keep running, preventing total loss of power. (Interestingly, the British company Armstrong Siddeley used the same principle for its Double Mamba turboprop designed for the Fairey Gannet anti-submarine warfare aircraft. Two Mamba engines drove contra-rotating propellers via common reduction gear. In patrol mode one of the engines could be shut down to save fuel and one propeller row feathered.)

However, the An-24AT was ahead of its time. The extensive (and expensive) redesign did not win support from the potential customer and the project was not proceeded with.

An-24AT-RD tactical transport project

Auxiliary jet engines used as boosters, or for braking if fitted with thrust reversers, were common on American heavy aircraft in the 1960s. Hence Antonov tried to incorporate this feature on the An-24AT; two jet boosters of an unknown type and thrust were pylon-mounted under the outer wings. Designated An-24AT-RD (= *reaktivnyye dvigateli* – jet engines), the aircraft also featured a wider cargo hatch with a loading ramp. The ADP project was presented in 1966 but the aircraft was never built.

An-24AT-U tactical transport project

A more down-to-earth derivative called An-24AT-U featured three or five PRD-63 jet-assisted take-off (JATO) rocket boosters (PRD = *porokhovoy raketnyy dvigatel'* – solid-propellant rocket motor). The U suffix letter in the designation apparently stood for *ooskoriteli* – boosters. Three brake parachutes with a total area of 47 m² (505 sq.ft) were provided to slow the aircraft down on landing – a feature that would have been unique among propeller-driven aircraft, had the An-24AT-U reached the hardware stage. Like the An-24AT-RD, the freighter featured a wide cargo hatch/ramp.

Again, the project was submitted in 1966 but never got off the drawing board. Yet, both projects (the An-24AT-RD and An-24AT-U) were stepping stones towards the highly successful An-26 transport.

An-24B airliner

Designated An-24B, the next version was destined to be the most widespread variant of the type. The prototype was converted from a production An-24A, making its first flight on 16th November 1965; some sources suggest it was CCCP-46802 (c/n 57302102) which was originally released by the factory as an An-24A on 28th August 1965. Kiev production began in January 1966 with Batch 22, and the type was now properly marked on the tail (or nose). All An-24s manufactured in Ulan-Ude were 'Bs.

The easiest way to tell the B model from the An-24A was by counting the cabin windows. One window was added on each side ahead of the wings; thus the window arrangement was now 1+exit+7+door to port and 1+baggage door+5+exit+3+service door to starboard.Later, however, some An-24As were upgraded to this standard

The new version allowed numerous changes to be introduced on the production lines or in service to suit customer needs. Extending the range was a prime requirement; hence some An-24Bs featured four extra bladder tanks in the wing centre section increasing total fuel capacity to 6,180 litres (1,360 Imp. gal.) ±2%. These so-called 'eight-

An-24B CCCP-46257 (c/n 77303405), Central Regions CAD/Bykovo UAD/61st Flight machine, in the static park at Moscow-Domodedovo during the airshow on 9th July 1967.

tank' An-24Bs were completed according to special schedules as the orders came in.

Soon after the An-24B entered production the complex double-slotted inboard flaps, which were quite difficult to manufacture, gave way to simple slotted flaps. To compensate for their reduced efficiency and avoid compromising field performance, flap area was increased by extending the inner wing flap chord. Thus the overall chord inboard of the engine nacelles was increased from 3.2 m (10 ft 6 in) to 3.5 m (11 ft 5¾ in), resulting in a characteristically stepped wing trailing edge; total wing area rose from 72.46 m² (779.14 sq.ft) to 74.98 m² (806.23 sq.ft). This change was approved by Chief Designer Oleg K. Antonov on 14th July 1966 and incorporated from Batch 26 onwards; however, the first aircraft to incorporate it was an An-24V (see below).

An-24As and early An-24Bs had one ventral fin of 1.8 m² (19.35 sq.ft) area, but operational experience revealed poor directional stability in certain flight modes. Hence twin ventral fins were introduced on the An-24B from Batch 29 onwards. This feature had been tested on the fourth prototype An-24 *sans suffixe* (CCCP-Л19605) and then put into production on the An-24T built in Irkutsk (see below), the Kiev plant following suit. The diverging fins were splayed and were shallower than the original single fin; their total area was 2.02 m² (21.72 sq.ft). This arrangement proved effective and was also used on the An-10 which suffered from the same problem.

Refining the systems and equipment still called for a lot of effort. The changes may seem to be of minor importance but they were not. For instance, from An-24B CCCP-46556 (c/n 87304601) onwards the DP-702 switch in the landing gear locking circuit, which was troublesome, was augmented by a manual switch; this was centrally placed on the instrument panel and accessible to both pilots. All previously built aircraft were retrofitted eventually.

The baseline An-24B was still a 50-seater but had a seat pitch reduced by 3 cm (1⅛ in) versus the An-24A, allowing two baby cots to be installed at the back of the cabin; alternatively, two more seats could be fitted, raising the total to 52. The galley and the flight attendant's jump seat were moved aft to the entry vestibule. The coat closet was also moved, causing a reduction in rear baggage compartment volume, but this could be restored to 5 m³ (176.5 cu.ft) at the expense of coat storage space.

The An-24B enhanced passenger comfort by providing rigid overhead baggage racks, eliminating the need to check in small bags. The racks incorporated heating and ventilation air ducts and, on some aircraft, passen-

Above: This Ulan-Ude built An-24B 'Salon' coded '101 Red' (c/n 59900201) belonged to the 226th Independent Composite Air Regiment stationed in East Germany. It is seen here in its original colours.

Above: Another Soviet Air Force An-24B 'Salon' coded '47 Red' is seen on short finals to Moscow-Sheremet'yevo in the late 1960s. The aircraft wears basic Aeroflot colours as used for Batch 3 or 4.

A Russian Air Force An-24B 'Salon' coded '798 Black' (ex-CCCP-47798, c/n 09902302?) in basic 1973-standard Aeroflot colours climbs out from Kubinka AB in 1995.

ger service units (PSUs) featuring individual ventilation nozzles and reading lights. There was a stewardess call button for each pair of seats.

The 48-seat version offered the highest comfort, featuring a better equipped galley and two fight attendants to cater for the passengers instead of one (but no baby cots). A lightweight partition could be fitted at frame 15 or 20 instead of two rows of seats, requir-ing just 0.75 man-hours for installation. In tourist class layout the An-24B had 40 seats at maximum pitch (84 cm/33 in) and more galley storage space for soft drinks and such.

Alternatively, the An-24B could be easily reconfigured for all-cargo operations. The passenger seats, the galley and the cabin's forward bulkhead could be removed, requir-ing just five man-hours to create 38.6 m³ (1,363 cu.ft) of cargo space – enough to

Above: Bulgarian Air Force'/16th Airlift Regiment An-24B 'Salon' '040 Black' (c/n 07305810) on short finals. The blue cheatline is patterned on that of TABSO, the precursor of Balkan Bulgarian Airlines.

Appropriately marked An-24B TZ-ACT (ex-CCCP-46419?; c/n 87304104) of Air Mali. This aircraft was lost in a crash on 22nd February 1985.

accommodate 5.4 tons (11,900 lb) of cargo. In combi (passenger/cargo) configuration the rear cabin had 38 or 20 seats, depending on whether the partition was installed at frame 15 or 20, while the forward cabin was reserved for cargo.

An-24B 'Salon' VIP aircraft

The An-24B was also built as a VIP aircraft designated An-24B 'Salon' – again mostly for the Soviet Air Force and other air arms. The first VIP version (so-called 'de luxe' 20-seat version) had three cabins; the first two were separated by a partition with a curtained doorway. There were two pairs of facing seats with a table in between on either side in each compartment. The foremost compartment also featured a flight attendant's jump seat (facing the tail) and two galley modules. The rear cabin, being the farthest removed from the propellers' plane of rotation and hence the quietest place in the aircraft, was the VIP cabin (referred to as 'the main passenger's cabin', *salon glavnovo passazheera*). It was separated from the forward cabins by a bulkhead with a solid door – both for privacy and to keep the retinue from eavesdropping on the boss. There were four comfortable chairs with a table in between on the port side and a

couch separated by a curtain to starboard, with a small table featuring a reading lamp and a fan beside it. Further aft were a coat closet and a toilet, and then a baggage compartment (the forward baggage compartment was retained).

A more modest version had a 28-seat forward cabin for the retinue (with galley and flight attendant's seat) and an identical 'club-four' VIP cabin separated by a bulkhead. All cabins featured a deep pile carpet with a foam rubber base. On some aircraft the forward baggage compartment was replaced by a second toilet. Outwardly the VIP version can be identified by having the foremost cabin window on each side blocked by a metal plug; you have to look really closely to discover these non-functional windows.

An-24V airliner (An-24V-I, An-24V-II)

The successful An-24B evolved into the first export version which entered production in Kiev in 1962 (An-24s manufactured in Ulan-Ude were not exported for some reason). This aircraft was designated An-24V in Russian alphabetical sequence; since the Cyrillic letters B (Б) and V (В) are quite similar, there was considerable confusion in the West regarding these two variants.

The equipment fit of export aircraft was specified individually for each customer. For the Soviet Union's closest allies which were members of the Council for Mutual Economic Assistance (COMECON – the Eastern Bloc's answer to the EEC) and the Warsaw Pact defensive organisation the aircraft were delivered in the so-called 'version A'. This was identical to the An-24B in identification friend-or-foe (IFF), air traffic control (ATC) and communications equipment. 'Third world' nations received 'version B' featuring slightly downgraded avionics. (It was the same story with Soviet combat aircraft delivered to Warsaw Pact nations ('version A') and the rest of the world ('version B').)

Before offering the An-24 on the export market the OKB tested it thoroughly for four years on cargo/mail flights and then on passenger routes in all climatic zones from the Polar regions to the equator. Aeroflot crews flying at home and abroad (eg, in the United Arab Republic) carried more than 6 million passengers on a handful of initial production aircraft. Among other things, An-24Vs and An-24TVs carried urgent cargo and Soviet specialists to the site of the Aswan hydroelectric power station built by the Soviet Union on the Nile. These transport operations were a demanding task, which the aircraft coped with admirably.

Most production An-24Vs had the simpler avionics fit, which not only reduced unit costs but also increased the payload. The An-24B's payload was 5.0 tons (11,020 lb) or 5.4 tons (11,900 lb) in passenger or cargo configuration respectively; on the An-24V it was 5.4 tons and 5.7 tons (12,570 lb) respectively.

At the customers' request some An-24Vs were fitted with Western VOR/ILS instead of the Soviet SP-50 system. As a rule, such aircraft lacked the classified IFF transponder, featuring either the same ATC transponder as the An-24A or an early version of the An-24B's IFF. For instance, An-24Vs delivered to LOT Polish Airlines had two R-802GM (RSIU-5GM) UHF radios and an R-836 Neon VHF radio with a US-8K receiver. The avionics included an RPSN-2 Emblema weather radar, an ARK-11 automatic direction finder, an RV-UM low-range radio altimeter and a Privod-ANE compass system. Part of the fleet had the British Marconi AD-260 VOR/ILS. The An-24V had an AP-28L1D autopilot.

As noted earlier, in the summer of 1966 the An-24B and An-24V underwent a wing redesign, receiving wide-chord inner wings of increased area with simple slotted flaps. The first aircraft to incorporate the change was An-24V CU-T881 (c/n 67302601) delivered to the Cuban flag carrier Empresa Consolidada Cubana de Aviación in the late summer of 1966. In some sources early export aircraft with one ventral fin and double-slotted inner wing flaps are designated **An-24V-I**, while the late-model export version featuring the new wings and twin ventral fins is called **An-24V-II**.

Starting in January 1968, many An-24Bs and An-24Vs were built with uprated AI-24T (Srs II) engines delivering 2,820 ehp for take-off in international standard atmosphere (ISA) conditions, ie, at +15°C (59°F). At ambient temperatures of +30°C (86°F) the maximum take-off weight with this powerplant was 18.8 tons (41,450 lb) at 'dry power' and 20.7 tons (45,635 lb) with water injection; some AI-24T engines, however, lacked the water injection system.

The avionics fit was altered considerably during the time the An-24B/An-24V remained in production. Some aircraft featured a PSBN-2-34 radar instead of the usual RPSN-2AN weather radar. As the designation reveals (PSBN = *pribor slepovo bombometahniya i navigahtsii* – blind-bombing and navigation device), this was a navigation/bomb-aiming radar developed for the An-24T military transport aircraft (see below). Some production aircraft featured the then-new Koors-MP (Heading-MP) approach system replacing the Materik ILS. On aircraft still equipped with the old ILS the antiquated ARK-5 Amur first-generation ADF was replaced by the ARK-11 ADF working with a wider range of frequencies. The equally outdated RV-2 Kristall low-range radio altimeter

Above: Czechoslovak Air Force An-24B (An-24V-II) 'Salon' '5605 Black' (c/n 97305605) as originally delivered. This aircraft was transferred to the newly-formed Slovak Air Force in 1990.

copied from an American unit installed on the Boeing B-29A Stratofortress bomber gave place to the RV-3 (aka RV-UM), a state-of-the-art unit which was standardised for new civil and military aircraft alike.

An-24D airliner project

The advent of the Tumanskiy RU19A-300 turbojet booster/APU developed for the An-24RT tactical transport (see below) created the potential to increase the take-off weight of the passenger version when operating from paved runways of sufficient length. The main hindrances to creating a high gross weight version were the standard airframe's structural strength limitations and the limited fuel capacity and cabin volume.

Considering this, in 1967 the Antonov OKB brought out the advanced development project of an improved version designated

Hungarian Air Force An-24B 'Salon' '907 Black' (c/n 77303907) in landing configuration. This aircraft wears An-24B nose titles – but see next page!

Above: Air Ukraine An-24B UR-47266 (c/n 07306304) taxies in at Moscow-Bykovo after arriving on a flight from Kiev-Zhulyany on 8th April 1993.
Below: An-24V-II CU-T882 (c/n 67302602) was the seventh An-24 delivered to Cubana. It already has wide-chord inner wings but still retains the single ventral fin.

An-24D (*dahl'niy* – long-range). The aircraft featured the same powerplant as the future An-24RT and An-24RV, the two AI-24 turboprops being augmented by an RU19A-300 in the starboard engine nacelle. The fuselage was stretched by 2.8 m (9 ft 2¼ in) by inserting two 'plugs' fore and aft of the wings, thereby increasing seating capacity to 60. The fuel capacity was also increased to give a maximum range of 2,700 km (1,680 miles) and the airframe was suitably restressed to absorb the increased loads.

Antonov envisaged the An-24D as a much-needed replacement for the fuel-thirsty Tupolev Tu-104 twinjet on Aeroflot's domestic routes. However, the general belief at the time was that turboprop aircraft had no future and the An-24D was never built.

An-24T tactical transport prototype (first use of designation)

As noted earlier, the An-24AT tactical transport project of 1962 was axed. This was the time when Nikita S. Khruschchov, Soviet aviation's *bête noire*, was running the country. Two years later, however, the Soviet Air Force's fortunes changed when Khruschchov was unseated by his political enemies and Leonid I. Brezhnev became the new leader of the Communist Party and the Soviet state. Hence interest in a tactical transport derivative of the An-24 was revived.

True, despite the fact that the Air Force was now properly funded once again, light tactical transports were not allocated top priority – the reborn MAP assigned funds first and foremost to all-new supersonic jets (fight-ers, strategic bombers and a Mach 3 reconnaissance aircraft). Hence the military requested only a simple adaptation of the airliner for transport duties – nothing like the radically redesigned An-24AT; the basic airframe structure and the powerplant were to be retained.

The Ministry of Defence's Central Research Institute No.30 (TsNII-30 MO – *Tsentrahl'nyy naoochno-issledovatel'skiy institoot Ministerstva oborony*), an establishment responsible for formulating operational requirements for new military aircraft, specified that the transport version should have a crew of five. The two pilots were to be augmented by a navigator, a radio operator and a loadmaster.

Designated An-24T (*trahnsportnyy*), the prototype of the military transport version was converted from the third prototype An-24 *sans suffixe* (CCCP-Л19603, c/n 0003) in 1961. Outwardly it was almost identical to the passenger version, retaining a full complement of doors and windows at this stage; just about the only visible difference lay in several additional aerials. Changes were made to the centre and aft fuselage and the flightdeck layout was altered to accommodate the extra crew members. The aircraft was powered by two 2,550-ehp AI-24As and equipped with a TG-16M APU.

By September 1961 the aircraft had traded its red/yellow/white Aeroflot livery for an overall mousy grey colour scheme, receiving the tactical code '93 Blue' (which, unusually, was painted on the nose, not the rear fuselage or tail). Flight tests began on 4th September and were held jointly with the Parachute Delivery Systems Research and Experimental Institute (NIEI PDS – *Naoochno-issledovatel'skiy i eksperimentahl'nyy institoot parashootno-desahntnykh sistem*). The aircraft was flown by GSOKB-473 test pilots Yuriy V. Koorlin and A. M. Tsygankov. By 3rd January 1962 they had made 36 test flights, assessing the aircraft's performance and handling, as well as the possibility of paradropping personnel and cargo through the entry and cargo doors. Twenty-two more flights followed in the late spring and early summer of 1962 within Stage B of the manufacturer's flight tests which served to verify the aircraft's mission equipment (special avionics etc).

In July 1962 the An-24T prototype was submitted for State acceptance trials which were held jointly by the OKB and the Air Force between 17th September 1962 and 12th July 1963. For the duration the aircraft was based at Chkalovskaya AB which hosted the Military Transport Section of GK NII VVS. At this stage the An-24T was flown by a GK NII VVS crew captained by Lt. Col. V. S. Yeliseyev, with Maj. V. A. Anisimov as the engineer in charge of the trials; the latter man would be responsible for trials of other aircraft in the An-24 family for many more years yet.

(Note: The transport aircraft division of (ex-) GK NII VVS is still located at Chkalovskaya AB; combat aircraft, however, are tested at the main facility in Akhtoobinsk near Saratov in southern Russia since the 1960s.)

The State commission's report said that the An-24T basically met the requirements of

The prototype of the 'An-24T Mk II' (ex-An-24A c/n 37300602), the version which eventually entered production, wore a civil-style colour scheme. Note the blister fairing of the bombsight aft of the nose gear, the rod aerials of the PDSP-2N theatre navigation system and the photo calibration grid on the aft fuselage.

Above: A production An-24T in standard grey camouflage at Moscow/Sheremet'yevo-1. As the red band on the rudder reveals, this example coded '01 Red' is operated by the Border Guards.

A fine air-to-air of a very early-production An-24T (possibly c/n 6910101) during tests. Note the narrow-chord inner wings with double-slotted flaps; nearly all production examples had the wide-chord version.

the VVS and could be recommended for service. Yet Lt. Gen. I. A. Taranenko (Hero of the Soviet Union), the First Deputy Commander of the Soviet Air Force's military airlift arm (VTA – *Voyenno-trahnsportnaya aviahtsiya*), had different views. In the said report he wrote, '...*the An-24T is no match for the tasks which present-day military light transports are required to fulfil. [...] It is not capable of paradropping combat vehicles, and the side cargo door does not permit loading such vehicles. The ferry range of 1,890 km [1,170 miles] is inadequate; so is the combat radius in paradropping mode of 180-225 km [110-140 miles] at altitudes of 1,000 m [3,280 ft] and 6,000 m [19,685 ft] respectively. The aircraft cannot operate from unprepared tactical airstrips due to unsatisfactory field performance.*' The criticism concerning inability to paradrop materiel implied the lack of cargo handling equipment, primarily a transporter propelling the items of cargo towards the

hatch. Another obvious deficiency was that the An-24T retained the passenger aircraft's plywood floor panels which were easily damaged during cargo handling.

That said, it is hardly surprising that the original An-24T was rejected. The prototype subsequently assumed a civil identity, receiving the non-standard registration CCCP-29101; it ended its career as a ground instructional airframe at the Kuibyshev Aviation Institute. Yet that was not the end of the An-24T story – see next item.

An-24T tactical transport (second use of designation, aka An-34)

Taking due notice of the Air Force's complaints, the Antonov OKB proposed redesigning the An-24T to feature a ventral loading/paradropping hatch; additionally, the payload would be increased to 5 tons (11,020 lb) and extra fuel tanks installed to give a ferry range of 2,900 km (1,800 miles). MAP passed a

formal decision authorising development of such an aircraft on 13th February 1965. Soon the OKB's experimental shop at Kiev-Svyatoshino started conversion work on a production An-24A (registration unknown, c/n 37300602) which became the 'An-24T Mk II' prototype. Originally this aircraft was allocated a separate designation, An-34, to underscore the changes; however, since the big idea was to develop a derivative with minimum changes and not a new aircraft, this designation did not catch on. V. A. Soomtsov was appointed the military transport version's project chief.

The fuselage of the 'An-24T Mk II' (An-34) featured a ventral cargo hatch 2.85 m (9 ft 4¼ in) long between frames 33-40; its minimum and maximum width was 1.1 m (3 ft 7⅜ in) and 1.4 m (4 ft 7⅛ in) respectively. The hatch was closed by double doors opening inwards and upwards to lie flat against the sides of the freight hold, in a manner similar to the main cargo door segments of the An-12.

The result was a simple and lightweight structure, but the design obviously had serious shortcomings. For one thing, the height of the cargo hatch incorporated into the flattened underside of the fuselage was exceedingly small, precluding the loading of vehicles and complicating the paradropping of personnel. Secondly, bailing out in an emergency turned into a real problem. The former baggage door on the starboard side was unusable because it was immediately ahead of the starboard propeller. Hence an escape hatch measuring 1.155 x 0.7 m (3 ft 9½ in x 2 ft 3½ in) with a forward-hinged cover doubling as a slipstream deflector had to be provided aft of the nose gear, restricting usable freight hold length to 11.1 m (36 ft 5 in). A toilet was provided on the port side at the forward extremity of the freight hold.

The cargo cold be propelled from or towards the hatch by an overhead hoist with a lifting capacity of 1.5 tons (3,300 lb) or by a P-149 chain drive conveyor of identical capacity built into the freight hold floor; the conveyor was 11.0 m (36 ft 1 in) long. Tip-up seats for 37 paratroopers were installed along the freight hold walls; in paradrop configuration a special divider was fitted ahead of the cargo hatch, organising the drop so as to stop the paratroopers from colliding after leaving the aircraft.

The An-24T (An-34) had a take-off weight of 21 tons (46,300 lb) and was powered by uprated AI-24T engines delivering 2,820 ehp for take-off and 1,580 ehp at cruise power. Twin splayed ventral fins were installed aft of the cargo hatch (as already mentioned, these were later used on the An-24B *et seq.*).

To assess the efficacy of the new features and check the possibility of paradropping personnel through the ventral hatch the

Antonov OKB and NIEI PDS held a new round of trials between 7th December 1965 and 12th February 1966. The tests took place at Kiev and Fergana, Uzbekistan; the test crew was captained by GSOKB-473 project test pilot Yuriy N. Ketov. Unlike the 'An-24T Mk I' prototype, the aircraft wore an airline-style colour scheme with Air Force insignia. It had no tactical code but sported large grid-shaped photo calibration markings on the rear fuselage sides for paradropping experiments.

When the tests gave encouraging results, the Antonov OKB submitted the revamped An-24T for State acceptance trials which lasted from 16th June to 10th November 1966. Two GK NII VVS crews captained by project test pilots A. S. Timofeyev and I. Ya. Markov made a total of 73 flights in the prototype. This time the result was a thumbs-up: the military stated that the new aircraft met the requirements, except for a few performance figures. These included ferry range which fell short of the expectations, being 2,565 km (1,593 miles) instead of the stated 2,900 km. This and other shortcomings were to be rectified as the aircraft entered production.

Following what was fairly common practice in the USSR, Minister of Aircraft Industry Pyotr V. Dement'yev signed order No.181 clearing the An-24T for series production on 29th July 1965 *before the State acceptance trials had even begun*! MAP plant No.39 in Irkutsk was assigned to build the type. Having started life as NKAP factory No.125, an aircraft component supplier, in the pre-war years, this East Siberian plant was absorbed by aircraft factory No.39 which was evacuated from Moscow in 1941 in the face of the advancing German troops. (NKAP, the People's Commissariat of Aircraft Industry, was the immediate precursor of MAP.) Unlike some other factories, plant No.39 was not re-evacuated when the immediate danger to Moscow was past.

In the 1960s the plant manufactured bomber, reconnaissance, electronic countermeasures and trainer versions of the Yakovlev Yak-28 tactical twinjet. Being rather troublesome and awkward to fly, the Yak-28 was not among the Air Force's favourite types, which is why the VVS was wont to view the factory building it with a jaundiced eye. Hence the management of plant No.39 had long been looking for a new aeroplane to build which would change the attitude towards the factory, allowing funds for modernisation and for social needs to be appropriated. Although it brought new worries for the management and the workforce, the An-24T presented a welcome break, as it allowed some long-standing problems to be solved.

Having produced the An-12A in 1958-1961, plant No.39 was already familiar with the design features and manufacturing technologies of Antonov aircraft, and it did not take the factory long to launch An-24T production. The first production An-24T (identity unknown; c/n 6910101 – ie, year of manufacture 1966, plant No.[3]9, presumably *izdeliye* (product) 1, Batch 01, first aircraft in the batch) took off from Irkutsk-2 airfield in January 1966. The maiden flight was performed by a factory test crew comprising captain G. I. Starostenko, first officer Eduard N. Chel'tsov, navigator F. D. Onischchenko, radio operator M. Yu. Yoorov and flight engineer A. P. Razgoolyayev.

There are reasons to believe that production was suspended after one or two aircraft had been completed, pending the results of the State acceptance trials, and really got under way in early 1967 when the results proved good. Later production aircraft underwent their pre-delivery flight tests at the hands of Chel'tsov and other factory pilots, including V. S. Prantskeavicius, V. N. Troobnikov and S. M. Koorkay.

(Note: Some sources suggest that 91 was a new number (or rather code) for the Irkutsk aircraft factory introduced in order to avoid confusion with Irkutsk-built An-12s. However, this appears doubtful because, firstly, no confusion can arise if it is known for certain that different types are involved. In any document the aircraft type is stated first, and any fool can see that An-12 No.0204 is not the same as An-24 No.0204! Secondly, An-12 production in Irkutsk had long since ended by then.)

Outwardly the production An-24T differed from the passenger version in a number of details. The most noticeable difference was the reduced number of cabin windows and the lack of doors on the aft fuselage sides. The window arrangement was exit+1+1+1 to port and 1+door+1+exit+1+1 to starboard; the former forward baggage door now served as the entry door. There was also a fairly large astrodome in the flightdeck roof, which the An-24A/B did not have. A shallow spine ran from the fin fillet all the way to the wings.

Production An-24T freighters differed from the 'An-24T Mk II' prototype in cargo hatch design. Firstly, it was slightly shorter and wider, the length being reduced to 2.72 m (8 ft 11 in) while minimum width at frame 40 was increased to 1.25 m (4 ft 1¼ in). Secondly, the cargo doors were now split into forward and aft sections instead of port and starboard; the aft section was hinged at the rear, opening upwards.

For accurate navigation to the drop zone the An-24T featured an upgraded PSBN-3N Emblema radar (a derivative of the civil RPSN-2N with enhanced ground mapping capability) and a PDSP-2S Proton-M receiver (*para**shoot**no-de**sahnt**naya sis**tema** pelen-**gah**tsii*) identifiable by characteristic double rod aerials under the forward fuselage and triple aerials under the outer wings. To ensure accurate delivery the aircraft was equipped with a World War Two-vintage NKPB-7 night-capable collimator bombsight (*noch**noy** kolli**mah**tornyy pri**tsel** bombardi**rov**ochnyy*) and an AIP-32 optical bombsight (an OPB-1R with an infra-red imaging adapter). The bombsights were located on the port side of the flightdeck; for take-off and landing their protruding lenses were protected from flying stones by a segmented cover which had a hemispherical shape when closed.

The production An-24T had a payload of 4,120 kg (9,080 lb); the cargo handling and paradropping equipment weighed 430 kg (950 lb). The number of paratroopers was increased to 42. Alternatively, 24 stretcher patients or 37 walking wounded accompanied by a medical attendant could be carried. The P-149 roller conveyor enabled the loading/unloading or paradropping of seven PGS-500 cargo pallets equipped with a five-canopy parachute system (PGS = *para**shoot**naya groozovaya sis**tema*** – parachute cargo system). Other airdroppable load options were 20 to 27 PDUR-47 packages or 16 PDSB-1 containers for ammunition or other materiel.

The freight hold floor was made of reinforced foam plastic to save weight; the upper side was faced with corrugated duralumin while the lower side resting on the transverse floor beams was faced with heavy-duty plywood. An electric winch was installed in the freight hold.

An-24T deliveries commenced in early 1967; by early 1971 the plant had manufactured 164 An-24s in three cargo versions (An-24T, An-24TV and An-24RT – see below), and the former version made up the greatest proportion by far. Batches 1 and 2 consisted of five aircraft each; the others had ten aircraft per batch, except for Batch 18, the final one, which had four.

On 31st March 1967 the Irkutsk aircraft factory manufactured the fourth production An-24T (c/n 7910104) in a special 'civilianised' configuration devoid of theatre navigation systems and bombsights. Registered CCCP-46280 and wearing a predominantly ochre colour scheme developed at General Designer Oleg K. Antonov's request (whoever was the author, he sure lacked taste), the aircraft was displayed at the 26th Paris Air Show in June with the exhibit code 234 in the hope of securing export orders. Despite the rather garish colour scheme, the An-24T failed to attract any major interest at Le Bourget; nonetheless, in May 1969 CCCP-46280 was on display again at the 27th Paris Air Show.

Like all other Soviet Air Force transports, the An-24T could be used as an auxiliary bomber; this was in line with the OTTT VVS-58

Above and below: A production An-24T coded '21 Red' on final approach to Moscow-Vnukovo in the late 1960s Interestingly, this example lacks the PDSP-2N theatre navigation system; the position of the tactical code on the tail is also noteworthy.

general operational requirements of 1958 (**Ob**schchiye **tak**tiko-tekh**nich**eskiye **trebo**vaniya) which insisted that a transport aircraft absolutely had to be capable of dropping bombs. To this end two specially developed BD3-34 bomb racks (BD = **bah**lochnyy der**zhah**tel' – beam-type rack) could be installed in tandem on each side of the lower centre fuselage. As the '3' in the designation implies, these were Group 3 racks capable of carrying ordnance up to 500 kg (1,102 lb) calibre; interestingly, the '34' refers to the aircraft's original designation (An-34)!

Apart from general-purpose or flare/marker bombs, the BD3-34 racks could carry special items, such as paradroppable radio beacons used during major airborne operations, providing their dimensions did not exceed those of the FAB-500M54 bomb (FAB = foo**gah**snaya avia**bom**ba – high-explosive bomb). These included the Shtyr'-3 (Rod-3) and Ogonyok (Little light) radio beacons.

State acceptance trials of the bomb armament proceeded at Kirovskoye AB in March-April 1969, involving An-24T c/n 7910309 (tactical code unknown). A GK NII VVS crew captained by A. S. Sooshko made 18 flights in this aircraft, including ten live bombing sorties. The test report read that '...the An-24T's bomb armament enables bombing attacks, given direct visibility of the target, [...] at speeds of 260-480 km/h [160-300 mph] and altitudes of 600-6,000 m [1,970-19,685 ft]; the BD3-34 racks permit carriage of bombs [...] of up to 500 kg calibre.'

Since the An-24T was intended primarily for the Soviet Air Force and the air forces of 'friendly nations', very few were delivered to civil operators. Only one aircraft is confirmed as being truly in airline service with Aeroflot; this was the aforementioned CCCP-46280 which was operated by the Kursk United Air Detachment of the Central Regions Civil Aviation Directorate. Other civil examples mostly belonged to MAP or the Ministry of General Machinery (MOM – Mini**ster**stvo **ob**schchevo ma**shin**ostro**yen**iya), the agency responsible for the Soviet space and missile programmes. These included CCCP-46336 (c/n 8910709) operated by aircraft factory No.135 in Khar'kov and CCCP-98116 (c/n 7910403) operated by the 'Polyot' (Flight) Production Association in Omsk. (The latter enterprise was one of the victims of Khruschchov's 'missilisation', being formerly MAP's aircraft factory No.166.)

Speaking of which, some Soviet Air Force An-24T transports were quasi-civil, wearing full Aeroflot colours. These included CCCP-46458 (c/n 9910810), CCCP-46700 (c/n 7910402) and CCCP-46849 (c/n unknown).

An-24T/RT production may well have continued into the 1970s, but it was 'tripped up' by a more important order. In 1970 plant

Above: An-24T '53 Blue' (c/n unknown) operated by the Russian AF's 978th Military Airlift Regiment at Klin-5 AB north of Moscow is unusual in having an Aeroflot-style colour scheme. It was broken up in 2001.

No.39 was ordered to gear up for building the Mikoyan/Gurevich MiG-23UB combat trainer, the 'two-stick' version of the most advanced Soviet fighter of the day. The MiG-23 enjoyed support in high places, being launched under the auspices of the Air Force General Headquarters and the Communist Party Central Committee's Defence Industry Commission. This order was of course good for the Irkutsk factory but bad for the An-24T which was ousted to free up production capacity.

The An-24T saw service with VVS units stationed in all climatic zones of the Soviet Union's vast territory. Interestingly, civil examples were operated chiefly in Siberia and Central Asia – the coldest and the hottest regions of the country, as distinct from the passenger versions which were scattered far and wide. The pressurised An-24T offered much better conditions than the familiar An-12 with its unpressurised freight hold (only a small personnel compartment aft of the flightdeck was pressurised on the latter type). The new transport's air conditioning system (ACS) maintained interior temperature at a comfortable +20°C (68°F) in any weather and season. The cabin air was exchanged completely 25 times an hour – the same as in a well-aired room. Importantly, the ACS could function with the engines inoperative, using ground power or power supplied by the TG-16 APU.

An-24TV export tactical transport

A small number of An-24T transports was built for export to Congo-Brazzaville, Iraq, Romania and possibly Sudan (the Sudanese examples may be in the later An-24RT version, see below). In some documents these aircraft

Another An-24T in basic Aeroflot colours. This one, coded '03 Red' (c/n unknown), belonged to the Central Aero Club and was based at Moscow-Tushino. It is believed to be ex-'61 Red' in a grey colour scheme.

were designated An-24TV by analogy with the An-24V, and the difference from the version for the home market was basically the same, being confined to IFF equipment.

Deliveries began in 1968. Export aircraft had a different c/n system (so-called 'Aviaexport c/ns', the Aviaexport All-Union Agency being the sole national exporter of aircraft in those days). These were intended to conceal the batch number and the number of the aircraft in the batch so as to avoid revealing how many had been built (and hence how many could be in service with the Soviet Air Force). For instance, a Romanian Air Force example registered YR-AMS is c/n 1021911 – ie, *izdeliye* 102, version 1 ('variant A' as regards IFF etc.), year of manufacture 1969, 11th An-24T exported to all customers. Such aircraft also had *fuselage numbers* (line numbers) consisting of the batch number and the number of the aircraft in the batch but no c/n to f/n tie-ups are known.

The An-24TV had the distinction of being the first aircraft in the large family of An-24 derivatives to participate in an armed conflict. In 1969 Iraqi Air Force An-24TVs were used for bombing raids against Kurdish rebel positions in northern Iraq.

An-24RT tactical transport
While the An-24T was a useful airlift asset, the standard TG-16 APU could not provide enough power in certain situations. Besides, GSOKB-473 was facing the task of improving the An-24T's short-field and hot-and-high performance. Improving the efficiency of the de-icing system was another high-priority task. The micro-ejector de-icing system used a lot more air than anticipated. At maximum power the required amount of engine bleed air equalled 5% of the compressor output; this caused an unacceptable 15% drop in the engines' take-off power, which is why switching on the de-icing system during take-off was expressly forbidden. (By comparison, on the Il'yushin IL-62 four-turbofan long-haul airliner the de-icing system used 3.5% of the compressor output, reducing take-off thrust by a mere 4%.)

Meanwhile, back in 1960 Sergey K. Tumanskiy's OKB-300 had developed the 900-kgp (1,980-lb st) RU19-300 axial-flow turbojet for the Yakovlev Yak-30 (Yak-104) advanced trainer. Intended as a replacement for the obsolete Mikoyan/Gurevich UTI-MiG-15, the Yak-30 passed its trials with flying colours but was victimised by a political decision to adopt the inferior Aero L-29 Delfin as the standard advanced trainer of the Warsaw Pact nations in order to give the Czechoslovak aircraft industry some work to do. Since the L-29 was powered by a Czech-built Walter M-701 turbojet, there was no application for the RU19-300.

Not wishing to let this good engine be wasted, OKB-300 developed it into a jet booster/APU for a heavy transport aircraft – which was just what the Antonov OKB needed for the An-24T. Derated to a static thrust of 220 kgp (485 lb st), the new version could supply enough bleed air and electric power to operate the An-24's de-icing system at maximum power in all flight modes. The available thrust could be used to shorten the take-off run or provide a valuable power reserve in the event of an engine failure. The compact turbojet could be easily accommodated in the rear portion of the starboard engine nacelle instead of the existing TG-16M APU, breathing through a fixed-area intake on the inboard side and exhausting through a jetpipe in the tip of the nacelle. The entire rear end of the engine nacelle hinged upwards for access to the turbojet.

Designated RU19A-300 (the A standing for Antonov), the modified engine entered production in 1966 at the Tyumen' engine factory which was MAP's northernmost enterprise. Accordingly the 'mixed-power' version of the An-24T was designated An-24RT, the R denoting *reaktivnyy ooskoritel'* – jet booster. (It is tempting to decipher the letters RU in the jet engine's designation likewise as *reaktivnyy ooskoritel'* – but then, the original 900-kgp turbojet also has them, and it was no 'booster' but the main engine!)

The An-24RT prototype was converted from the aforementioned fourth production An-24T, CCCP-46280. The new version entered production in 1967 and was manufactured alongside the original An-24T rather than replace it completely; a total of 62 had been built when production ended in 1971. Again, most examples were delivered to the Soviet Air Force and a few were exported to Bulgaria, Romania and possibly Sudan. One example was possibly delivered to Aeroflot, namely the East Siberian CAD/Ust'-Kut UAD (CCCP-47250, c/n 9911304). Others were operated by MAP enterprises, including an aircraft with the non-standard An-26 style registration CCCP-26187 (c/n 0911308) which was retained by the manufacturer, CCCP-26189 (c/n 1911803, operator unknown) and CCCP-47251 (c/n ?911305) belonging to the Beriyev OKB in Taganrog. Quasi-civil examples include CCCP-46709 (c/n 0911310).

In April 1969 An-24RT CCCP-46280 started off on a promotional tour of India on behalf of Aviaexport. Indian Air Force representatives were aboard in many of the demonstration flights which involved paradrops of various loads at low level and operations from mountain airfields located more than 4,000 m (13,100 ft) above sea level. Flown by an experienced crew under B. V. Stepanov, the aircraft performed excellently; still, the Indian Air Force was not convinced that the aircraft had

enough power reserves for safe operation in mountainous areas. This conclusion ultimately led to the development of the An-32 tactical airlifter aimed specifically at the Indian market; this is described later in this book.

Apart from the nations listed above, the An-24T/An-24RT was operated by the People's Democratic Republic of Yemen Air Force. Other reported (but unconfirmed) users include the air arms of Bangladesh, Cuba, Laos, Mongolia, Somalia and Vietnam. Of the 165 examples built, 139 were still operational in 2001, including 12 aircraft outside the former Soviet Union. In post-Soviet times a number of An-24T/An-24RT transports was disposed of by the military, and 20 such aircraft were in service with Russian, Ukrainian and Armenian airlines in 2001.

An-24RV airliner
Operational experience with the An-24V in 'third world' nations, many of which still lacked a proper airfield network and associated infrastructure (or had them destroyed in the course of armed conflicts which are common in such places), demonstrated the need to increase available engine power in order to improve hot-and-high/short-field performance. The solution was obvious – to install an RU19A-300 auxiliary turbojet in the same fashion as on the An-24RT. The resulting 'trimotor' passenger version was accordingly designated An-24RV.

The added thrust of the jet booster allowed the An-24RV's payload to be increased to 4,620 kg (10,185 lb). Rate of climb in the event of an engine failure on take-off was at least 2.9 m/sec (570 ft/min) in ISA conditions or at least 1.5 m/sec (295 ft/min) in 'hot and high' conditions

Production started in Kiev with Batch 66 in late 1970. As the RU19A-300 was also used to power the An-24RT and the An-26 transport (which latter had entered production in 1970), the Tyumen' engine factory could not furnish enough engines to equip all three types. Hence An-24RVs were interspersed with An-24Bs on the production line; it was not until January 1973 that the new version took over completely from Batch 83 onwards. (Even so, some sources report An-24Bs were manufactured occasionally for several more years.) On the other hand, some aircraft originally built as An-24Bs were upgraded to An-24RV standard during refurbishment. An-24RVs were delivered both to Aeroflot and to foreign customers. A few even found their way to the Soviet Air Force.

On the first production An-24RVs the existing engine nacelle structure was retained for the sake of simplicity and cost reduction. However, this meant that the jetpipe was angled to starboard, the jet booster creating considerable yaw when running. Hence the rear portion of the starboard nacelle was redesigned so that the booster's thrust line was parallel to the fuselage axis.

In 1982, when the An-24RV was… well, not quite a vintage aeroplane yet but not a new one either, it surprised the world by demonstrating that 'the old girl still has got some spunk'. Soviet female pilots Marina L. Popovich and Galina G. Korchooganova established no fewer than 39 world records for women in an An-24RV. Among other things, they climbed to 9,540 m (31,300 ft) with a 5-ton (11,020-lb) payload and to 11,050 m (36,250 ft) in an unladen aircraft with an all-up weight of 16,000 kg (35,270 lb). The two aviatrices logged an average speed of 519.2 km/h (322.48 mph) over a 500-km (310.5-mile) closed circuit and reached an altitude of 6,000 m (19,685 ft) within 14 minutes 23.45 seconds. Finally, they succeeded in lifting a payload of 24,038 kg (52,993 lb) – more than five times the An-24's specified payload! – to an altitude of 2,000 m (6,560 ft).

An-24RV 'Salon' VIP aircraft

A few An-24RVs were completed in VIP configurations designated An-24RV 'Salon'. Usually they were export aircraft, but two examples found their way to the Soviet (Russian) Air Force. Known examples are Bulgarian Air Force '030 Red' (c/n 37309103), Chinese People's Liberation Army Air Force '51051 Red' (c/n 37309106), Hungarian Air Force '401 Black' (c/n 37308401), Hungarian Air Force '402 Black' (c/n 37308402), Soviet Air Force '699 Black' (ex-CCCP-46699, c/n 47309910) and CCCP-13344 (former tactical code unknown, c/n 37308310).

The An-24B and An-24RV proved to be an easily adaptable platform for all manner of special mission equipment, spawning a multitude of specialised versions. The spacious pressurised cabin and capable air conditioning system rendered it well suited for this role, ensuring comfortable working conditions for the mission crew, while the APU (especially on the An-24RV) provided power for the mission equipment without overtaxing the engine-driven generators.

An-24PS experimental SAR aircraft

In the late 1960s the Antonov OKB brought out a search and rescue (SAR) version of the An-24B designated An-24PS (*poiskovo-spasahtel'nyy* – SAR, used attributively). The aircraft was intended for both overland and maritime SAR operations, using the radar and three optical search systems to locate people in distress. The optical systems were housed in three prominent lateral blisters distinguishing the An-24PS from regular airliners.

The aircraft was equipped with four BD3-34 racks on the lower centre fuselage sides

Voronezhavia An-24RV RA-46690 (c/n 47309901) sits on a snow-covered ramp at Moscow-Domodedovo on a bleak day in mid-November 1998. Many of Russia's new air carriers retained basic Aeroflot colours.

RA-47362 (c/n 67310706), a very late-production An-24RV owned by Ryazan'aviatrans, rests between flights at Moscow/Vnukovo-1 on 18th June 2002.

The large forward baggage/cargo door allowed the An-24 to be used for cargo operations. Here, mailbags and crates are loaded aboard an Aeroflot An-24RV.

The An-24 was operated even by those former Soviet republics which are not part of the CIS. This is Latavio Latvian Airlines An-24B YL-LCF (c/n 27308105), formerly CCCP-46487 with the Latvian CAD/Riga UAD/106th Flight/2nd Squadron. It was later sold to Cubana as CU-T1294.

A single An-24A (OD-AEN, c/n 57301604) was delivered to the Lebanese flag carrier MEA (Middle East Airlines) in 1965. It was subsequently sold to Air Guinée, becoming 3X-GAS and then 3X-GCD.

An-24RV YR-BMN (c/n 77310808) displays the latest livery of the Romanian flag carrier TAROM. It was later sold to the Kyrghyz airline Aerovista as EX-24808.

for carrying rescue equipment capsules or flare/marker bombs. Three types of the latter were envisaged. The NOSAB night marker/signal flare bomb (*nochnaya oriyenteerno-signahl'naya aviabomba*) created a bright torch with a long burn time marking a threat or a drop zone for a rescue team. Maritime operations involved the use of OMAB maritime marker bombs (*oriyenteernaya morskaya aviabomba*). The OMAB-25-12D designed for daytime use (*dnevnaya*) left a bright-coloured spot on the water surface which stayed for at least 75 minutes and was visible at 10-26 km (6.2-16 miles) range. The night version designated OMAB-25-8N (*nochnaya*) created a luminous spot which stayed for 60-80 minutes and was visible at 32-58 km (19.8-36 miles) range. Rescue means could be dropped to the people in distress through the side door; the aircraft could also carry a team of rescue workers equipped with parachutes.

The prototype (identity unknown) completed State acceptance trials successfully in 1969 but was rejected in favour of a slightly modified version based on the An-24RT (see next entry).

An-24PRT SAR aircraft

While the An-24PS prototype showed good results, it was decided that the production version should be based on the An-24RT featuring an RU19A-300 jet booster. Eleven of these transports were built in SAR configuration, receiving the designation An-24PRT.

An-24LP forestry protection aircraft

1971 saw the advent of another special mission version, this time a purely civil one. As the designation reveals, the An-24LP (*lesopozharnyy*) based on the An-24RV was designed for fighting forest fires. The aircraft was equipped with optical systems for detecting smoke and flames; provisions were also made for installing a thermal imager. Such systems, which were undergoing trials at the time could not only determine the limits of a fire zone but even detect a dangerous rise of the temperature within layers of peat; the latter was invaluable, as peat fires are among the most difficult and dangerous to fight.

A water tank with a ventral outlet was installed along the centre of the cabin. It may be said straight away that tests gave an astounding result: despite having an internal water tank of four times smaller capacity, a suitably equipped An-2 utility biplane could dump more water within an hour than the An-24LP due to the latter type's longer turn-around time! However, the An-24LP took fire-fighting technology to a new level. Four BD3-34 racks were fitted to the centre fuselage for carrying streamlined pods with flare dispensers. These fired 26-mm (1.02-in.) PV-26 cartridges with rainmaking chemicals for cloud-seeding, allowing the fire-fighters to call upon Mother Nature to help them. Also, compared to the An-2, the An-24LP could carry four times as many fire-fighters to be paradropped in the area of the blaze, fighting the fire at ground level.

Compared to the Mil' Mi-6PZh and Mi-6PZh-2 (fire-fighting versions of the Mi-6 heavy-lift helicopter), the An-24LP could get to the scene more quickly. (Despite the reputed ability of choppers to operate from any clearing that's big enough, experience showed that Mi-6PZh helicopters had to operate from permanent airports, usually located a long way from the fires.) Importantly, the An-24LP was cheaper to operate than the Mi-6PZh and was more reliable.

A total of three An-24s were converted into the fire-fighting version, including An-24RV CCCP-47819 (c/n 17307108) operated by the Far Eastern CAD/1st Khabarovsk UAD/289th Flight. This aircraft also featured metal plugs incorporating additional quadruple flare dispensers in some cabin windows (four units per window). Later the aircraft was apparently reconverted to passenger configuration, serving with Dalavia Far Eastern Airlines as RA-47819.

An-24RR NBC reconnaissance aircraft

Since it was generally assumed that future wars would be fought in a nuclear/biological/chemical contamination (NBC) environment, in the 1960s the Soviet Air Force ordered the development of aircraft equipped for NBC reconnaissance duties so as to min-

An-24RR '05 Red' caught by the camera on approach to its home base, Kubinka AB west of Moscow.

imise the harmful effects on friendly troops. These aircraft included a derivative of the An-24B designated An-24RR ([*samolyot*] *radiatsionnoy razvedki* – radiation reconnaissance aircraft). Really, it should have been called An-24RKhR ([*samolyot*] *radiatsionno-khimicheskoy razvedki*).

Outwardly the An-24RR could be identified by special cradles low on the forward fuselage sides for carrying two RR8311-100 standardised air sampling pods. Originally developed in 1964 for the Yak-28RR radiation reconnaissance aircraft, these pods had a nose intake closed by a movable cone and a paper filter which arrested dust particles, enabling their radiation level to be measured. A small cigar-shaped pod with air intakes was

installed on a horizontal pylons on the port side immediately aft of the flightdeck; this housed air sampling sensors for detecting toxic agents. A special device on the fuselage underside allowed soil samples to be taken after landing (this was done without exiting the aircraft). The cabin, which was carefully sealed against NBC contaminants, housed the mission equipment operators' workstations.

The An-24RR prototype underwent trials in 1967. Three more aircraft were converted to this standard the following year; two of them, coded '03 Blue' (c/n 89901901) and '05 Red' (c/n unknown) were based at Kubinka AB west of Moscow. Originally the An-24RR 'snoopers' were used to measure radiation

Another view of the An-24RR, showing the port side sensor pod (which has since been removed) and the two RR8311-100 air sampling canisters.

Above and below: The An-24LR *Toros* ice reconnaissance aircraft was characterised by lateral pods housing SLAR antennas and a camera fairing on the aft fuselage underside. Note the Antonov logo.

Above: Another view of An-24LR *Toros* CCCP-46211 (c/n 67302901). Note the Polar Aviation logo.
Below: CCCP-46395, the other known An-24LR *Toros* (C/n 07306209), wore a different colour scheme.

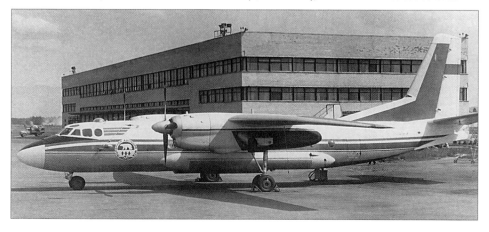

levels at Soviet nuclear test ranges and places where single nuclear devices had been detonated. Later, they performed ecological monitoring in areas where several dozen nuclear explosions had been performed for peaceful purposes. These included locations in the Bashkirian Autonomous Soviet Socialist Republic, the Komi ASSR, the Kalmykian ASSR, the Kazakh SSR (Azgir and Mangyshlak), the Uzbek SSR (Urta-Burlak and Pamuk), the Turkmenian SSR (Maryy), as well as the Tyumen', Murmansk, Perm', Orenburg and Stavropol' Regions of Russia. In due course part of the equipment and the associated port side pod were removed.

An-24RT (An-24Rt) communications relay aircraft

A few An-24T and An-24RT transports were converted into communications relay aircraft for supporting the operation of Soviet Army headquarters. Confusingly, such aircraft were still designated An-24RT; in this case, however, the suffix letters stood for *retranslyator* – relay installation. (To avoid confusion some sources give a different graphic presentation, An-24Rt.) The aircraft remained in service until the advent of the purpose-built An-26RT described later in this book.

An-24ShT airborne command post

A tactical airborne command post (ABCP) version of the An-24B designated An-24ShT (*shtabnoy* – staff or headquarters, used attributively) was developed for exercising command and control of troops at army level. Its equipment enabled army commanders to maintain constant communication with (and control of) the forces during offensive or defensive operations involving movement of troops over large distances.

Another important function of the An-24ShT and similar aircraft was brought into play when a tactical nuclear strike was impending. At such times the communication between army headquarters at various levels became more intensive, and establishing new lines of communication which were not yet discovered and monitored by the enemy became of crucial importance.

The An-24ShT could provide communications both in the air and on the ground; external aerials connected to the aircraft by long cables were used in the latter case. No aircraft have been identified in this version.

An-24LR *Toros* ice reconnaissance aircraft

A large number of An-24s were operated in the interests of the Soviet government agencies responsible for developing the northern regions of the USSR. These included a specialised version designated An-24LR *Toros*, an ice reconnaissance aircraft designed to support shipping operations along the Northern Sea Route (the LR stood for *ledovyy razvedchik* – ice reconnaissance aircraft).

The aircraft could be identified by two fairly large streamlined fairings grafted onto the centre fuselage sides. These were almost entirely dielectric, with small dorsal cooling air intakes at the rear, and housed the twin antenna arrays of the *Toros* (Ice hummock) side-looking airborne radar (SLAR). The radar, which mapped a strip 75 km (46.5 miles) wide in any weather, not only showed clear water areas and measured the width of passages in the icefields but could also measure the thickness of the ice, guiding the icebreakers leading ship convoys towards weak spots. A vertical camera of unknown type was housed in the rear fuselage, the lens being closed by a prominent teardrop fairing with clamshell doors located between the ventral fins. Observation blisters were provided in the foremost cabin window on each side, and the flightdeck roof featured an astrodome.

At least two An-24Bs, CCCP-46211 (c/n 67302902) and CCCP-46395 (c/n 07306209), were converted to An-24LR *Toros* configuration. Despite their mission and associated bright orange colour scheme for high definition against white backgrounds (complete with Polar Aviation badges), the aircraft were based in Moscow, deploying to the High North only as required. By April 1993 both aircraft had been stripped of their mission equipment.

An-24RV *Nit'* (An-24LR *Nit'*) multi-role survey aircraft

In 1978 a single An-24RV – well, actually a converted Kiev-built An-24B with the out-of-sequence registration CCCP-47195 (c/n 07306202) – was converted into a multi-mission survey aircraft. (This example should have been CCCP-46389, but it is not known if the aircraft had been reregistered before 1978 or the registration had been allocated but not taken up. As for CCCP-47195, theoretically this registration should have been allocated to an Ulan-Ude built An-24B with a c/n something like 99902102.)

The mission equipment suite of CCCP-47195 was built around a Nit'-S1 (Thread-S1) SLAR which gave the aircraft a rather bizarre appearance: the SLAR fairings were truly huge, drooping below the lower fuselage contour, and were angled slightly nose-down. 'Devil's pitchfork' arrays of triple fore-and-aft rod aerials were mounted in tandem under each SLAR fairing. Observation blisters were provided in the No.2 cabin window on each side. The cabin housed the researchers' workstations, as well as data processing and recording equipment.

Known as the An-24RV *Nit'*, the aircraft was used for prospecting natural resources,

Above: The other ice reconnaissance version, the An-24LR *Nit'*, featured much larger SLAR fairings. This is the sole An-24LR *Nit'* (RA-47195, c/n 07306202) parked at Pushkin on 8th August 2001.

Close-up of the fairings housing the *Nit'* SLAR on RA-47195. Note the pitchfork-like antenna arrays below the fairings.

including those of the World Ocean. However, the powerful SLAR could be used with equal success for measuring the thickness of icefields; hence CCCP-47195 was also referred to as An-24LR *Nit'*. (Incidentally, the same Nit'-S1 radar was fitted to the IL-24N long-range ice reconnaissance aircraft, a derivative of the IL-18D four-turboprop long-haul airliner.) Since it was to operate in the Polar regions, the aircraft wore Aeroflot's red/white polar colour scheme (also used by regular transport aircraft flying in the northern areas of the USSR, not only by Polar Aviation aircraft) for high definition against white backgrounds; the Polar Aviation badge was painted on the nose.

The An-24RV *Nit'* (An-24LR *Nit'*) was used in several major scientific programmes, working in concert with several dozen other aircraft, the smallest of which was an An-2; Soviet cosmonauts aboard the Salyut-6

space station also made their contribution. Unlike most other Soviet ice reconnaissance aircraft, the An-24LR *Nit'* remained in service after the demise of the Soviet Union, gaining the Russian registration RA-47195.

An-24RV propeller testbed

In 1979 a production An-24RV in 1973-standard Aeroflot colours was fitted with experimental eight-blade propellers of an unknown model replacing the standard AV-72s. The new propellers were intended to reduce external noise levels by reducing propeller speed.

The registration has been quoted as CCCP-46271 but this is doubtful. The aircraft had been converted from an early-production An-24B with one ventral fin, whereas CCCP-46271 (c/n 77303604?) should have twin ventral fins. The aircraft is now preserved as a 'gate guard' at the NPP Aerosila facility in Stoopino.

An-24USh navigator trainer

In 1970 the Antonov OKB brought out the An-24USh navigator trainer (*oochebno-shtoormanskiy* [*samolyot*]) to meet an order placed by the Ministry of Civil Aviation. The cabin featured five trainee workstations with radio navigation aids (three to port and two to starboard), with four standard rows of seats further aft for trainees waiting their turn. Bulged observation windows were provided at the trainee workstations, distinguishing the An-24USh from the standard An-24B.

Seven An-24Bs (mostly Ulan-Ude built) were converted to An-24USh trainers for the Kirovograd Higher Civil Aviation Flying School. Five aircraft registered CCCP-47155 (c/n 89901607), CCCP-47179 (c/n 99901904), CCCP-47711 (c/n 69900501), CCCP-47743 (c/n 79901106) and CCCP-47781 (c/n 89901506) have been identified so far. Apart from navigators, they were used to train air traffic controllers.

An-24B navigator trainer (Chinese version)

At least one An-24B delivered to the People's Liberation Army Air Force (PLAAF) and serialled '71291 Red' (c/n 17307104) was converted locally for training Tupolev Tu-16 medium bomber crews. The aircraft featured a large ventral radome housing a bomb-aiming/navigation radar, large faired lateral observation blisters looking like halves of the Tu-16's nose glazing and elongated lateral bulges housing part of the mission avionics. '71291 Red' now resides in the PLAAF Museum at Datang Shan AB near Beijing.

An-24ALK navaids calibration aircraft

In the 1970s several production An-24s were converted for calibrating the instrument landing systems and ATC radars of major airports. One such aircraft was RA-46395 (c/n 07306209), a former An-24LR *Toros*, which upon conversion received a new designation, An-24ALK (*avtomatizeerovannaya* [*sistema*] *lyotnovo kontrolya* – automated flight check system).

Painted in 1973-standard blue/white Aeroflot colours, this aircraft could be identified by a fairly large lentil-shaped fairing attached by two streamlined struts to the port side of the extreme nose (just aft of the radome); this housed a powerful retractable light for phototheodolite measurements allowing the glideslope angle to be checked. An optical sensor protected from flying stones by a segmented hemispherical cover (not unlike that of the An-24í) was mounted ventrally in line with the rear emergency exit, offset to starboard. Finally, small ILS aerials of the kind dubbed *Teufelsgabel* ('Devil's pitchfork') by the Germans because of their shape were installed under the radome and the tail-

cone. The aircraft was operated by the Central Regions CAD/Bykovo UAD/61st Flight.

Other calibrators include An-24B CCCP-46296 (c/n 77303808), An-24RV CCCP-47364 (c/n 77310709) which was also operated by the Central Regions CAD/Bykovo UAD/61st Flight but later reconverted to standard, and An-24RV YR-BMK (c/n 77310803) which belonged to the Romanian Civil Aviation Authority. The latter aircraft was 'killed in the line of duty', crashing near Baia Mare, Romania, on 7th April 1992.

An-24RT automatic approach system calibration aircraft

The many assorted aircraft involved in the development of the Buran (Snowstorm) space shuttle included an An-24 converted for calibrating the orbiter's automatic approach and landing system. This was in all probability An-24RT CCCP-26192 (c/n unknown) which was characterised by a strut-mounted faired light identical to that of An-24ALK RA-46395 and a blue/white striped radome. Interestingly, for the first time in the Soviet Union the aircraft featured an on-board digital data processing and recording system built around several Gamma-1101 computers.

The first automatic approach and landing system for the Buran was set up at Zhukovskiy airfield, the seat of the Flight Research Institute named after Mikhail M. Gromov (LII – *Lyotno-issledovatel'skiy institoot*), in 1983. Trials continued until 1986, involving more than 200 flights. The good results obtained at this stage were corroborated by the numerous flights of the three Tu-154LL control configured vehicles (CCCP-85024, -85083 and -85108) and the BTS-002 jet-powered version of the Buran used for horizontal flight tests (CCCP-3501002). The programme culminated in the first and only orbital flight of the 'real' Buran in 1989 which proceeded in automatic mode from beginning to end. CCCP-26192 was still used for calibration duties at Zhukovskiy in mid-1994 – still wearing the Soviet prefix and flag.

An-24LL flying meteorological laboratory

A single An-24 (identity unknown) was outfitted with a measurement suite for checking the conformity of other aircraft to current airworthiness standards. This aircraft has been referred to as the An-24LL (*letayuschchaya laboratoriya* – lit. 'flying laboratory'). This Russian term is used indiscriminately and can denote absolutely any kind of testbed or research/survey aircraft; in this case, however, the literal translation fits because the aircraft was a flying meteorological laboratory. The An-24LL was used in the early stages of a large-scale flight test programme managed by M. Kotik, a notable researcher at LII.

An-24T Troyanda avionics testbed

In the mid-1960s the US Navy was bolstered by new nuclear-powered submarines having a much lower acoustic signature compared to traditional diesel-electric subs. The Soviet Union countered by launching development of new anti-submarine warfare (ASW) systems using new principles of submarine detection. These systems were to be installed on new heavy ASW aircraft; the Antonov OKB, for one, proposed an ASW version of the An-22 heavy transport.

Meanwhile, the mission equipment had to be tested, and the assorted testbeds involved included a highly modified An-24T allocated the codename *Troyanda* (the word is Ukrainian for 'rose'). The aircraft's mission avionics were developed by the Leningrad-based All-Union Electronics Research Institute (VNIIRA – *Vsesoyooznyy naoochno-issledovatel'skiy institoot rahdioapparatoory*), aka LNPO Leninets (Leninist; LNPO = *Leningrahdskoye naoochno-proizvodstvennoye obyedineniye* – Leningrad Scientific & Production Association). This enterprise, which was one of the Soviet Union's leading avionics houses, is now the Leninets Holding Company.

Unlike most aircraft of a similar nature, the bizarre An-24T Troyanda was not converted from a standard An-24T; it was custom-built to a specification drawn up by VNIIRA and delivered 'green' for outfitting at the institute's flight test facility in Pushkin, Leningrad Region.

The fuselage featured major structural changes. Huge teardrop fairings were grafted onto the forward fuselage sides, making the aircraft look like a chipmunk which has stuffed its cheek pouches full of food; the undersides of these fairings incorporated large circular antenna panels associated with infra-red sensors. Since the starboard fairing would have obstructed the entry door, this was eliminated completely, access to the aircraft being solely via the ventral cargo hatch.

The wing/fuselage fairing was extended aft, resulting in a large flat-topped structure whose top was level with the top of the wing airfoil; it mounted a 'towel rail' aerial and incorporated hinged access panels. Camera windows were provided in the fuselage underside. The cabin housed six mission equipment operators working the IR sensor system, cameras and the sonobuoy receiver (SPARU – *samolyotnoye preeyomnoye avtomaticheskoye rahdioustroystvo*, 'airborne automatic radio receiver device') which detected and processed signals generated by sonobuoys.

Coded '04 Red' (c/n unknown) and wearing the overall medium grey camouflage which was standard for the An-24T, the aircraft underwent a lengthy test programme. However, only part of the equipment tested on the An-24T Troyanda eventually found its way to operational ASW aircraft.

Above: This An-24RV (converted from an An-24B) was used by the Stoopino Machinery Design Bureau for testing experimental eight-blade low-noise propellers. Here, maintenance work is under way on the aircraft, with a special vehicle providing hot air. One of the two original AV-72 propellers rests on a ground handling dolly close at hand.

Right: Close-up of the starboard propeller, showing the cropped blade tips. Note the single ventral fin.

An-24B avionics testbed

A late-production Kiev-built An-24B with the non-standard registration CCCP-26196 (c/n 17307303) was another avionics testbed operated by LNPO Leninets, featuring some kind of antenna or sensor array on the port side immediately aft of the wings and a camera fairing identical to that of the An-24LR *Nit'*. It is not known what purpose this aircraft served.

An-50 airliner project

In the mid-1960s the 'Progress' Zaporozhye Engine Design Bureau (*Zaporozhskoye motorno-konstrooktorskoye byuro 'Progress'*), as Aleksandr G. Ivchenko's OKB-478 was known since 1965, began development of a small commercial turbofan designated AI-25. Rated at 1,500 kgp (3,300 lb st) for take-off, this was the first Soviet engine in this category; its design relied both on the American Pratt & Whitney JT7 turbofan and on the Soviet

Kuznetsov NK-8 turbofan. The AI-25 emerged as a highly successful design, the team which created it being awarded the coveted Lenin Prize by the Soviet government; it was the first Soviet aero engine to be certificated to international standards.

The new engine immediately caught the attention of the Antonov OKB. Even as the AI-25 was undergoing trials, the Antonov OKB proposed the An-50 airliner. This was a deriv-

ative of the An-24V powered by four AI-25s; the engines were housed in paired nacelles carried on sharply swept pylons ahead of the wing leading edge *à la* Boeing B-52.

However, Aleksandr S. Yakovlev, head of the Moscow-based OKB-155 (aka MMZ-115 *Skorost'*, 'Speed' Moscow Machinery Plant), used his influence as Deputy Minister of Aircraft Industry to convince the Soviet leader Leonid I. Brezhnev that his Yak-40 trijet –

Above: The An-24ALK navaids calibration aircraft (RA-46395) on a snow-covered ramp at Moscow-Bykovo on 16th March 1993. Note the optical sensor closed by a protective cover under the centre fuselage.

This front view illustrates the An-24ALK shows the podded high-powered light used for checking glideslope angles; it can be seen at far longer range than the aircraft's normal landing lights.

powered by the same AI-25 turbofan – was the only viable option as a jet feederliner. The An-50 remained a 'paper aeroplane', and it was not until the advent of the An-74TK-200 in 1993 that jet-powered Antonov airliners became a reality.

Xian Y7 airliner/transport

Despite the fact that Sino-Soviet relations were deteriorating on ideological grounds, mainland China had been importing the An-24 since the early 1960s. In 1966 the Chinese government negotiated a licence to build the An-24T and its powerplant. The intention was that the An-24, which would be manufactured in both cargo and passenger configurations, would replace the obsolete Lisunov Li-2, Il'yushin IL-12 and IL-14 piston-engined aircraft in PLAAF service.

The first An-24T assembled in China took off on its maiden flight on 25th December 1970 at the hands of test pilot Li Ben-shung. The aircraft factory in Xian (sometimes spelled Xi'an or Sian), the capital of Shensi (Shaanxi) Province, launched production of the type in 1977 while still building the Tu-16 bomber (known locally as the H-6) at the same time. The Chinese-built version was designated Y7 (Yunshuji-7 – transport aircraft, Type 7).

The attempt to produce the An-24 came at a most inopportune time when China was in the throes of the Cultural Revolution, an ambitious political programme of the Chinese government which backfired, leading to untold chaos and devastation in the aircraft industry and the country at large. Many of China's leading aviation specialists, especially those

who had had contacts with the Soviet Union (which was now in disfavour), were purged and sent to jail or executed. As a result, the Y7's production entry period dragged on for an incredible 13 years – probably a world record. A pre-production aircraft was unveiled to the general public at Nanyuan airbase near Beijing on 17th April 1982. The first production aircraft (identity unknown, c/n 01701 – ie, Batch 1, Y7, first aircraft in the batch) was not rolled out until 1983, entering flight test in February 1984. Actually the initial Chinese-built version conformed to the An-24RV, not the An-24T/RT, featuring a full complement of windows and passenger doors.

The AI-24 turboprop was built by the Dong'an Engine Factory as the WJ-5A (Wojiang-5 – turboprop engine, Type 5). The RU19A-300 was also built in China. Curiously, it was referred to in Chinese advertising materials as PY19A-300 (obviously a corruption of the Cyrillic transcription); the actual Chinese designation is Baoding J16-G10A.

Y7 production picked up pace rather slowly. Most of the initial production aircraft were delivered to the PLAAF; most of them were transports, though a few aircraft were built in 52-seat airline configuration at this early stage for delivery to the 'Chinese Aeroflot' – the Civil Aviation Administration of China (CAAC).

Xian Y7-100 airliner

The first version of the An-24 originating beyond the Great Wall was the Y7-100 developed in cooperation with the Hong Kong Aircraft Engineering Co. (HAECO) in 1984. (Hong Kong, as the reader remembers, was then an independent entity, read: an island of Evil Capitalism in Truly Communist China.) Outwardly it differed from the standard early-production Y7 (An-24RV) mainly in having winglets; these were supposed to reduce drag in cruise flight by 4%, giving a 5% reduction in fuel burn – a claim which later proved to be somewhat exaggerated. The aircraft also featured a flightdeck configured for three, an all-new cabin interior developed by the US company Nordam specialising in aircraft components, new Western avionics (among other things, their installation was revealed by a protruding white dielectric panel between the ventral fins in the manner of the camera fairing of the An-24LR), an oxygen system and an upgraded air conditioning system.

The prototype Y7-100 was converted from a stock Y7 registered B-3499 (c/n 03702) which arrived at Hong Kong-Kai Tak airport for conversion on 27th December 1984 and was redelivered on 16th August 1985. Full-scale production commenced in 1986 and the Y7-100 was built (or refitted) chiefly for export.

Above and below: The bizarre An-24T Troyanda ('04 Red') was purpose-built for testing new anti-submarine warfare systems. The huge 'cheek pouches' house infra-red sensors for detecting submerged nuclear submarines. Note also the extended wing/fuselage fairing housing more mission equipment.

This full frontal of the monstrous An-24T Troyanda emphasises the size of the lateral fairings. 'A rose is a rose is a rose', you say ('troyanda' is the Ukrainian word for 'rose')? Garn! An ugly mug is an ugly mug is an ugly mug!

Above: A typical Y7 operated by one of China's many airlines. The baseline version is outwardly identical to the An-24RV.

Xian Y7-100C freighter

An all-cargo version of the Y7-100 (with no large cargo door or rear loading ramp) was developed as the Y7-100C (C for cargo). This version was built both for the home market and for export; for instance, one Y7-100C was ordered by Lao Aviation (the Laotian flag carrier) and three more by the Laotian Air Force.

Xian Y7-200 airliner

This version based on the Y7-100 was powered by WJ-5A-1 turboprops derated to 2,040 ehp. This was a forced measure aimed at improving engine reliability; thanks to a slightly lower turbine temperature the WJ-5A-1 offered a lower fuel burn and a longer TBO. It is debatable, though, whether the accompanying deterioration in payload and field performance were an acceptable tradeoff for this.

Xian Y7-200A and Y7-200B airliners

Broadening cooperation with the Western world in the late 1980s put China in a position to upgrade its commercial aircraft designs. Thus the substandard Y7-200 underwent a major redesign in the early 1990s; the result was the emergence of the much-improved Y7-200A and Y7-200B. The former was powered by Pratt & Whitney Canada PW127C turboprops driving four-blade Hamilton Standard propellers. It also featured a recontoured drooped nose of remarkably similar shape to the Bombardier (de Havilland Canada) DHC-8 Dash 8, a modest fuselage stretch, enlarged emergency exits, a two-crew flightdeck and a restyled cabin in 'wide-body look'. The seating capacity was increased to 60 but the maximum take-off weight remained unchanged at 21.8 tons (48,060 lb).

Wearing the test registration B-570L, the Y7-200A prototype was unveiled at Airshow China '96 held at Zhuhai-Sanzao airport in November 1996. The version entered production in 1999, with launch customer Chang'an Airlines (formerly ACA Air Changan Airlines) taking delivery of the first two aircraft – B-3720 (c/n 200-0001) and B-3721 (c/n 200-0002) – in March.

Xian Y7E

Mention has been made in the popular press of an advanced version designated Y7E. Unfortunately no details are available.

Xian MA-60 airliner

A further Westernised derivative of the Y7-200A is the MA-60 (the letters stand for 'Modern Ark'). The aircraft is powered by uprated PW127Js; the seating capacity is reduced to 56 in order to increase seat pitch, providing greater comfort. The MTOW is once again 21.8 tons.

The prototype, B-3425 (c/n 0101), entered flight test in 2000 and was delivered to launch customer Sichuan Airlines in August of that year. Twelve more were on order from China Northern Airlines, Sichuan Airlines and Wuhan Airlines in 2002, and the manufacturer estimated that as many as 400 MA-60s could be manufactured for the home market by 2018. Given proper mid-life updates, the type is expected to remain in service until 2040 or 2050.

Xian MA-60MPA Fearless Albatross maritime patrol aircraft

A version of the MA-60 adapted for maritime patrol duties was unveiled in model form at Airshow China 2002. Designated MA-60MPA and bearing the popular name Fearless Albatross – the Chinese do have a tradition of giving lofty names to aircraft and what-not – the maritime version differed from the standard airliner in having an extended and drooped nose housing a search radar with a 360° field of view. Pylons were installed under the outer wings, allowing anti-shipping missiles or other stores to be carried.

Despite all the efforts undertaken by Xian Aircraft Company (XAC), An-24 production in China never reached the intended scale. Only 62 'straight' Y7s and a little more than 50 Y7-100s had been manufactured by the turn of the century (even though, as already mentioned, there is a backlog of orders for the latest versions).

The reason may be that the Y7 was a comparatively low-priority programme, the Chinese aircraft industry being more concerned with producing the An-12 (without the benefit of a licence) as the Shaanxi Y8. The Chinese policy of reverse-engineering Antonov designs did not help either; people are touchy about copyright issues, and the Antonov Aviation Scientific & Technical Complex (ANTK imeni Antonova – the current name of the Antonov OKB) and associated enterprises were justifiably alarmed and irritated about the Chinese copying and modifying their designs without as much as a by your leave. In 2000, however, the copyright problem was finally resolved and a good working relationship re-established, enabling the Chinese aircraft industry to work with Antonov on a perfectly legal basis.

Y7-100 B-3707 (c/n 12701) in the rather gaudy livery of ACA Air Changan Airlines.

Chapter 2

Air Force Workhorse

An-26 transport aircraft prototypes

All its virtues notwithstanding, the An-24T with its simple ventral cargo hatch was not renowned for its convenience of loading/ unloading, as noted in the previous chapter. Still, the aircraft was also intended – in theory at least – for paradropping personnel and materiel; the existing fuselage design did not allow this to be performed with the required efficiency. The Soviet airborne troops (VDV – *Vozdooshno-desahntnyye voyska*) made use of the An-12 medium transport aircraft and the heavy-lift An-22, while the An-24T light transports were mostly used for delivering various urgent cargoes ranging from food supplies to ammunition. They carried mail sent by the servicemen and letters from home, as well as medical supplies and all manner of materiel when Soviet Armed Forces units redeployed to new locations.

The Vietnam War gave convincing evidence of the advantages offered by the de Havilland Canada C-7 Caribou and Fairchild C-123 Provider light military transports. Successful use of these aircraft heightened the interest of the Soviet military top brass to machines of this class, prompting the designers to seek ways and means of improving the An-24T. Therefore, as early as 1964 the Antonov OKB came up with the project of a new version of the aircraft. Inheriting the designation of the stillborn An-26 project, the new tactical transport featured a new forward and rear fuselage design. It was decided to incorporate a new navigator's station in a glazed nose similar to that of the An-12. The tail section featured a cargo hatch closed by three doors; they opened inwards for paradropping and the forward door segment doubled as a ramp for loading on the ground. The new aircraft could transport and airdrop not only cargoes but also the combat vehicles of the VDV, such as light self-propelled guns.

However, the Air Force command was of the opinion there was no need yet for such a machine. Nevertheless, the successful operation of the An-24T from unprepared airstrips and the lack of a full-fledged light military transport aircraft in the Armed Forces inventory stirred up the interest in the An-26 on the part of the military. Being aware of that, GSOKB-473 decided not to wait for an official order; in 1966 it started further development of the aircraft at its own initiative. A new tail

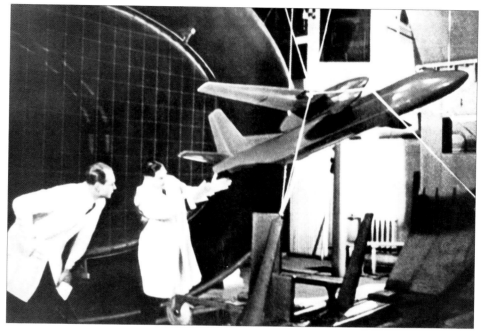

A large-scale model of the An-26 undergoing wind tunnel tests.

section was designed, featuring a large cargo hatch closed by a ramp of an unorthodox design. This ramp represents the Antonov OKB's know-how and merits a more detailed description.

The issue of designing a cargo ramp had already been studied in the OKB sufficiently well in the course of designing the An-8 and An-12 medium transports. It would seem that one could simply make use of the available positive experience and adapt a ramp taken from these aircraft to the new, lighter machine. However, the designers opted for a different approach.

A year prior to the events described here the OKB floated the project of the An-40 medium transport. Engineers V. T. Chmil', V. A. Maksimov, V. T. Shvedov, V. I. Orekhov and M. Ye. Babkin developed a new ramp for this aircraft. It ensured airtight sealing of the cargo hatch in flight, allowing the cargo hold to be pressurised. Besides loading wheeled vehicles in the usual way, the ramp could be slid beneath the fuselage, allowing straight-in loading from a truck bed or airdropping of cargoes. This design of the ramp was patented in eight countries, including the USA, France and Great Britain.

A large volume of theoretical studies and wind tunnel tests was conducted. The new ramp for the An-26 was based on the design features incorporated in the An-40 project. In order to receive a go-ahead from MAP for the official work on the An-26, the Antonov OKB's scale model specialists V. M. Onufrienko, V. P. Shapovalov, I. D. Radchenko, F. A. Ovchinnikov and R. L. Shteinberg built a working mock-up of the aircraft's cargo hatch to 1/12th scale. This mock-up was demonstrated to Minister of Aircraft Industry Pyotr V. Dement'yev when he visited the Antonov OKB at the end of 1967. The Minister was so impressed by the functioning of the cargo ramp, which seemed to him to be a promising design, that he immediately instructed the director of the Kiev aircraft factory No.473 accompanying him to build such an aircraft and put it into series production. A few months later, on 12th March 1968, an official MAP/Air Force joint decision was issued, giving the go-ahead for the development of the An-26 light transport aircraft.

The baseline An-24 had a relatively large ground clearance as compared to its predecessors. This made a traditional cargo door design irrational in terms of weight. A special

Above: The uncoded first prototype An-26 (c/n 0201) during an early test flight.

feature of the new-style cargo door was that its main element designed to close the cargo hatch doubled as a ramp for loading and unloading of pallets, platforms and wheeled vehicles. The threshold of the cargo door turned out to be roughly at the same level as the cargo platform of an average lorry. Hence it was decided that the massive cargo door/ramp should be slid down and forward to stow beneath the fuselage. The mechanism required for this turned out to be fairly complex but it simplified the work of the loadmaster considerably.

This design feature made it possible to solve one more paramount problem. During airdropping the cargo slides aft, covering some distance from the place where it was tied down to the cargo door threshold. This entails a shift of the aircraft's CG that may affect longitudinal stability to an unacceptable degree. To keep the CG within acceptable limits the cargo has to be dropped as quickly

as possible. If a part of the cargo door is used as a ramp for loading wheeled vehicles into the fuselage, during airdropping the aircraft's CG would shift backwards to a distance equal to the length of the ramp. Such a shift might be very dangerous for a light aircraft. To solve this contradiction, one would have to resort either to using additional massive ramps stored on the ground for loading wheeled vehicles, or to stowing the ramp that forms part of the cargo doors under the fuselage. The second approach turned out to be more advantageous in economic terms.

It was decided to equip the cargo hold of the new An-26 light transport derived from the An-24T with a mechanical conveyor. Designated P-157 in production form, the latter enabled mechanised loading/unloading of the aircraft on the ground and ensured the possibility of airdropping single cargoes weighing up to 1.5 tons (3,300 lb). The transporter was built integrally with the cargo floor

and was electrically powered. The cargo hold had a volume of 60 m³ (2,119 cu.ft) and accommodated up to 4.5 tons (9,920 lb) of cargo.

An overhead hoist travelling along a monorail was installed between fuselage frames 28 and 40 for lifting items of cargo from the ground or a truck bed and moving them inside the cargo hold; the winch of the hoist was rigidly installed in the cargo hold roof at frame 28. Unlike heavier transport aircraft, the An-26 had no powerful winch buried in the cargo floor for loading and unloading non-self-propelled wheeled vehicles – probably because the limited underfloor space (due to the flattened fuselage underside) left no room for such an installation. However, a set of pulley blocks and a long, strong cable enabled a tractor parked behind the aircraft to haul such vehicles aboard by pulling in the opposite direction. The complement of cargo handling equipment included tie-down nets, belts, cleats, cables etc.

Cables for hooking up parachutists' static lines ran the full length of the cargo hold. In medevac configuration the aircraft could be equipped with 24 stretchers arranged in three tiers; there was also a seat for one medical attendant.

The maximum width of the cargo hatch reached 2.34 m (7 ft 8 in), which necessitated a complete redesign of the adjoining structure. The new upswept rear fuselage was flattened and broad at the tip; it may well be said at this stage that the Germans bestowed the nickname *Biberschwanz*, 'beaver tail', on the An-26's rear fuselage because of its shape. The length of the rear fuselage was increased by 0.27 m (10⅝ in). Now the height of the

The first prototype in front of one of the KiAPO assembly hangars at Kiev-Svyatoshino. The cargo ramp is partially open. Note the circular navigator's blister (characteristic of early examples up to and including batch 10 at least) and the BD3-34 bomb racks low on the centre fuselage.

Above: This view of the first prototype (already civil-registered) shows the cargo ramp hinged fully open for loading vehicles or personnel.

cargo hatch aperture was almost equal to that of the cargo hold.

Wind tunnel tests revealed that the flattened rear fuselage generated strong turbulence, increasing drag dramatically. The design bureau's aerodynamics specialists headed by Yu. F. Krasontovich suggested fitting ventral strakes flanking the cargo door opening; they not only cut drag by eliminating harmful vortex interaction but also catered for enhancing directional stability. *'This device will perform the same role as a policeman in a crowd'* said O. V. Florinskiy, a leading specialist of the OKB's aerodynamics team.

'It will organise the flow coming from the wing and streaming along the fuselage [...] with minimum losses. This will ensure a considerable reduction of the aircraft's overall drag.'

The shape and the size of the strakes and their location were determined by trial and error during wind tunnel tests in which veneer

'Bird's eye view' of an An-26 with the non-standard registration CCCP-27205 (c/n 0804) at Moscow-Sheremet'yevo. This aircraft sporting the same colour scheme as the two prototypes was displayed at the 1971 Paris Air Show. Interestingly, the registration was later reused for a Soviet Air Force An-30.

The first prototype was earmarked for participation in the 1969 Paris Air Show, hence the exhibit code 831. Eventually, however, the second prototype was displayed instead.

The first prototype during single-engine handling tests. The propeller of the starboard engine is feathered.

plates attached to the model by modelling clay (!) were used. A beneficial side effect was that the strakes protected the parachutists and cargoes from the turbulent airflow around the rear fuselage, creating their own vortex system.

The new tail section radically altered the machine's appearance, endowing it with an elegance rarely seen in a transport aircraft. The overall area of the two strakes was 2.57 m² (27.7 sq.ft), which was 0.52 m² (5.6 sq.ft) greater than the area of the An-24T's twin ventral fins. The vertical tail remained unaltered; as for the horizontal tail, the redesign of the rear fuselage increased stabiliser span by nearly 1 m (3 ft 3⅜ in) and overall horizontal tail area from 17.23 to 19.83 m² (185.5 to 213.5 sq.ft) due to the increase of the part overlapping with the fuselage.

One of the designers' objectives was to retain maximum commonality with the production An-24RT. Therefore the existing productions breaks at frames 11 and 40 (which were the pressure bulkheads) were supplemented by one more at frame 33. The entire fuselage structure aft of it was new, the section between frames 33-40 being cut away from below to feature the large opening or the cargo door; despite this, the cargo hold remained fully pressurised. Changes were also made to the forward fuselage. The An-24RT's square-shaped upward-sliding entry door gave way to a quasi-oval door measuring 0. 6 x 1.4 m (1 ft 11⅞ in x 4 ft 7⅛ in) which swung inwards and aft. The ventral blister guard of the bombsight vanished; instead, the An-26 featured a hemispherical observation/bomb-aiming blister of 700 mm (27½ in) diameter on the port side of the nose for the navigator, and the sight was relocated there, swinging into position when required.

The take-off weight of the An-26 was to be increased to 24 tons (52,920 lb); hence the designers had to reinforce the wings and make use of AI-24VT engines with a take-off rating of 2,820 ehp driving AV-72T propellers. Like the An-24RT, the An-26 was equipped with an RU19A-300 APU/booster. To improve rough-field capability, experimental KT-157 wheels with fat low-pressure tyres were fitted on the main gear units.

One more task to be tackled by the aerodynamicists was to determine the forces to which the ramp was subjected in flight when slid forward under the fuselage. Research conducted in the OKB enabled the designers select an optimum placement of the ramp in which the stresses acting on it were minimum – even when the aircraft was side-slipping at an angle of up to 20°.

Deputy Chief Designer V. A. Garvardt, Oleg K. Antonov's closest aide, was appointed the An-26's chief project engineer. Detail design of the aircraft was handled primarily by teams led by Ye. A. Shakhatooni, V. Z. Bragilevskiy, N. P. Smirnov, A. P. Soshin and V. N. Ghel'prin. The creative spirit, enthusiasm and mutual understanding characteristic of these teams enabled them to issue the design documentation within a brief period (January to May) and transfer it to the production plant.

For the purpose of testing the Kiev aircraft factory initiated the manufacture of three An-26 airframes; the first of them, the sole aircraft in Batch 1 (c/n 0101), was the static test article. The two machines of the second batch were intended for joint State acceptance trials which it was considered expedient to conduct in a single stage instead of the usual two stages.

Wearing a grey/white colour scheme with a thin black cheatline and Soviet Air Force insignia but no tactical code, the first prototype (c/n 0201) was completed on 20th December 1968 but its final acceptance by specialists was protracted until 30th March 1969 (which is thus the manufacture date). In April Ya. G. Orlov became the new An-26 project chief, while A. K. Sereda became the engineer in charge of the trials.

On 21st May 1969 an Antonov OKB crew comprising captain Yuriy N. Ketov, co-pilot V. A. Bogdanov, navigator S. P. Kravchenko, radio operator M. A. Tupchiyenko, flight engineer P. D. Ignatiyenko and test engineer V. P. Lynovskiy took the first prototype An-26 to the air on her maiden flight. The flight passed uneventfully, despite high winds gusting at 15m/sec (30 kts) and more.

A week later the second prototype painted in the same colour scheme and registered CCCP 26184 No.1 (c/n 00202; the aircraft carried the c/n in a five-digit presentation) joined the flight test programme. A decision was taken to unveil the An-26 at the 27th Paris Air Show which was to open in a matter of days. Three flights were urgently performed to prepare the machine for its Paris trip; they were used for determining the speed range and fuel consumption per kilometre, checking stability and handling and checking the operation of the piloting and navigation equipment. Actually both prototypes were prepared for the event, receiving the exhibit codes 831 and 830 respectively; eventually it was CCCP 26184 that went to Le Bourget.

The international debut of the An-26 was quite successful. Foreign specialists were particularly intrigued by the cargo ramp design; a team of KiAPO technicians accompanying the aircraft changed the ramp's position every night. After Le Bourget the An-26 received the NATO codename Curl.

Almost all test flights of the two prototypes proceeded under the State Acceptance trials programme. They were performed by Antonov OKB and GK NII VVS crews headed by project test pilots V. A. Bogdanov and Colonel I. Ya. Markov respectively; Air Force test pilots Col. A. Bryksin, Col. V. N. Shibayev and Maj. Marina L. Popovich also took part in the trials. The most complex and crucial elements of the programme, such as determining the stability and handling at high angles of attack, were performed by the crew from Kiev on the first flying prototype. At this stage the second prototype traded its civil registration and Aeroflot titles for VVS red star insignia; both aircraft still wore their Le Bourget exhibit codes which thus became serials. (The registration CCCP-26184 was subsequently re-used for a Kamov Ka-26 utility helicopter. Later still, when An-26 c/n 00202 regained a civil identity, it was CCCP-261**94**.)

One of the main problems that cropped up in the course of testing was connected with the fact that maximum speed at the cruising altitude of 6,000 m (19,680 ft) fell short of the expectations by 15 km/h (9.3 mph). Antonov specialists set about refining the An-26's aerodynamics. For example, a transparent fairing was fitted aft of the navigator's blister, giving it a teardrop shape; however, this change was not introduced on production aircraft until Batch 11 at the earliest.

Special attention was paid to the cargo ramp/door whose attachment fittings drew a 'vote of no confidence' from the crews. Initially there were some apprehensions about opening it in flight; therefore, on the recommendation of structural strength experts, a whole system of steel cables was installed to hold the ramp more firmly in place. Thus, in the first flight when the ramp was opened the flight engineer performed the following procedure: he slackened the cable a bit, then opened the ramp slightly, walked over to the cargo hatch to check if everything was all right, then slackened the cable again and re-checked. This went on until he messed up the cables which eventually snapped! The ramp, however, remained securely in place on its attachment fittings and opened fully without anything untoward.

In subsequent flights the cargo ramp opened normally but failed to lock in the up position. It took a while to determine the cause of this. The reason was discovered by pure chance during the testing of the ventral escape hatch – the ramp slammed violently shut of its own accord when the hatch was opened; it was excess pressure in the hold that hindered it. Therefore initially small suction relief windows were incorporated which, when opened, facilitated the closing of the ramp; later a more powerful hydraulic actuator was installed for sliding the ramp under the fuselage and the links of the ramp drive chain were strengthened.

Above: The second prototype, CCCP 26184 (c/n 00202), wearing the exhibit number 830 with which it was unveiled to the world at Le Bourget in 1969.

The second prototype seen during State acceptance trials. Note that the aircraft has been retrofitted with the PDSP-2N theatre navigation system, as revealed by the ventral rod aerials.

In the course of the State acceptance trials the paradropping potential of the An-26 was thoroughly studied. The airborne part of the programme was performed at altitudes of 800-1,000 m (2,625-3,280 ft) and speeds of 270-350 km/h (168-218 mph). As is customary in such cases, dummies were dropped before any real parachutists could risk their lives. When the first dummy was pushed overboard, the static line of its extractor parachute began dangling in the cargo hatch, hampering the 'jump' of the next dummy. To determine the cause of the problem a model of the cargo hatch was placed in a wind tunnel where a parachute jump was simulated. Caught in the slipstream, the static line began performing circular movements in the hatch aperture. Then the researchers drove a nail into the model where the static line came closest to the fuselage. Further experiments showed that now, when a group of dummies 'performed jumps', every static line was caught by the nail, leaving the opening unobstructed. The solution thus found was quickly implemented in hardware; the cargo hatch of the An-26 was equipped with static line catchers resembling 'canine teeth' protruding inwards and up at an angle from the inner faces of the rear fuselage strakes. Subsequent drops of dummies were conducted successfully; next came the turn of test para-

chute jumpers from GK NII VVS headed by Lt. Col. Ye. N. Andreyev, Hero of the Soviet Union, who performed 320 jumps. The test also included dropping four UPDMM-65 bags (*ooniver**sahl**'nyy para**shoot**no-de**sahnt**nyy myah*kiy me*shok* – versatile non-rigid paradropping bag) with weapons.

Due attention was accorded to airborne landings. During this test stage assault troopers boarded a stationary An-26 on the ground and disembarked from it, loading and unloading operations were performed with ASU-57 and SD-85 self-propelled guns, GAZ-69 jeeps, a 120-mm (4.75-in.) mortar and military cargoes in standard PGS-500, PDUR-47 and PDSB-1 type packages. The functioning of the P-157 chain conveyor was assessed. To check the reliability of the cargo tie-down equipment, the aircraft performed taxying and high-speed runs at up to 100 km/h (62 mph) with subsequent harsh braking. The test pilots also performed 'bumpy ride' flights in which the pilot simulated the aircraft's behaviour in adverse weather conditions by pushing and pulling the control column back and forth. A crew captained by OKB test pilot V. A. Zalyubovskiy conducted the testing of the An-26 in hot-and-high conditions. The tests took place in Armenia and included flights from the unpaved airfield in Akhalkalaki (1,600 m/5,250 ft above sea level) which was close to the Turkish

An-26 '01 Blue' belonging to the Russian Air Force's 929th Flight Test Centre was photographed when visiting Klin-5 AB in 2000. The 'low-visibility' star insignia are noteworthy, as is the unit badge on the nose with a flying eagle and the inscription *Otechestvo, Doblest', Chest'* (Fatherland, Glory, Honour).

The first prototype An-26 coded '92 Red' was used for de-icing system tests at Chkalovskaya AB in 1971, as revealed by the striped wing and tail unit leading edges for icing visualisation and the camera under the starboard wingtip. Note the fairing added aft of the navigator's blister.

been revealed. The final report of the State Commission read: *'The transport capabilities of the An-26 aircraft as compared to the An-24T with a take-off weight of 21 ton [46,300 lb] have been extended, namely: transportation of materiel has been ensured, including the ASU-57 [SP gun], the GAZ-69 [jeep], 120-mm mortars, the SD-85 [SP gun] etc. Effective range when transporting people and cargoes, and the effective radius in the case of paradropping have been increased by approximately 50%. Piloting the aircraft when airdropping single cargo items, groups of cargoes or a series of cargoes with a total weight of up to 4,650 kg [10, 250 lb] presents no difficulties. As regards handling techniques, the An-26 can be flown by average-skilled pilots.'*

Subsequently the An-26 prototypes were used for special tests. Thus, de-icing system tests were conducted on the first prototype between 22nd April and 10th May 1971. A GK NII VVS crew captained by I. Ya. Markov performed flights from Chkalovskaya AB to Vorkuta via Syktyvkar, from Syktyvkar to Ukhta and back, from Vorkuta to Pechora and back. Test results revealed that the system ensured protection of the aircraft at ambient temperatures down to –20°C (–4°F) at altitudes of 1,200-3,000 m (3,940-9,840 ft) and speeds of 350-400 km/h (220-250 mph); the duration of continuous flight in an icing area should not exceed 20 minutes. The navigator's blister proved vulnerable to icing and had to be provided with a liquid de-icing system featuring a 2.6 litre (0.57 Imp. gal) alcohol tank.

In 1971-72 the same machine flown by a GK NII VVS crew captained by project test pilot S. Kipelkin performed 81 flights for the purpose of studying field performance and measuring structural stresses and vibrations when operating from unpaved and snow-covered runways. The tests were conducted at Chkalovskaya AB, Chernyakhovsk (Kaliningrad Region), Zyabrovka (Gomel' Region,

border. It was from this airfield that a flight was performed for assessing the aircraft's behaviour in the case of a single-engine failure on take-off. The flight nearly ended in tragedy. After lift-off it became obvious that the machine was accelerating very slowly, and there were mountains straight ahead. The crew had no choice but to start up the second engine, whereupon the An-26 pulled away

from the mountain ridge in a banking turn literally above the borderline zone.

The State acceptance trials continued until 21st September 1970. During the preceding period the first prototype performed 176 flights totalling 302 hours; the second aircraft logged 130 hours 52 minutes in 83 flights. The tests were interrupted twice in order to eliminate shortcomings that had

A bustle of activity on the flight line of a Soviet Air Force unit equipped with An-26s – very probably the Balashov Military Pilot College.

Belorussia), Sovetskiy (near Vorkuta), Zadoobov'ye (Vitebsk Region, Belorussia) and Zhasmin (Astrakhan' Region). As a result, the An-26 was cleared for operation from unpaved runways with a specific strength not less than 6 kg/cm² (85 lb/sq.in) or snow strips with a the density of the rolled-down snow not less than 0.5 g/cm³ (0.018 lb/cu.ft).

The first prototype was also used by the military for verifying the bomb armament. For this purpose the aircraft was equipped with four BD3-34 racks on pylons (two on each side of the fuselage between frames 15-16 and 21-24), a bomb release mechanism and an NKPB-7 bomb sight. The testing revealed that 40 combinations of various external stores could be carried by the An-26, including assorted bombs of up to 500 kg (1,102 lb) calibre, as well as Shtyr'-3 and Ogonyok radio beacons. After that, tests were conducted in April 1972 with the second prototype to determine the aircraft' performance in bombed-up condition. In so doing a crew captained by V. A. Zalyubovskiy performed 14 flights from the OKB's flight test facility at Kiev-Gostomel' in which the An-26 carried four FAB-500 high-explosive bombs or four OFAB-100 high-explosive/fragmentation bombs. It was established that the external stores reduced the aircraft's rate of climb and maximum speed but had virtually no adverse effect on stability and handling.

Two years later a further series of interesting tests was performed on An-26 '830 Grey' (c/n 00202). Thus, OKB and GK NII VVS crews captained by B. Stepanov and I. Bel'skiy performed 53 flights to determine the effectiveness of a negative thrust prevention system (ie, propeller auto feathering system). The tests took place in August-September 1974 in Chardzhou, Turkmenia, where day temperatures exceeded +33°C (91°F), and in December 1974 – January 1975 in Yakutia where the temperatures sank to –53°C (–63°F). The tests showed that the system functioned reliably in all operational modes, substantially enhancing flight safety.

More tests were conducted in October-November 1974, in the course of which recommendations were evolved for taking off with the RU-19A-300 APU inoperative. They were also conducted with the participation of crews from Kiev and GK NII VVS (crew captains Yuriy V. Koorlin and N. Shibayev). The results of these tests led to the conclusion that a safe take-off with the APU inoperative can only be ensured with a take-off weight not exceeding 20,700 kg (46,640 lb).

Tests of the An-26 prototypes showed that the designers had taken due regard of the operational experience accumulated with the An-24T/RT. Among other things, several key structural components were strengthened, and the avionics suite was updated.

Above: This Russian Air Force An-26, '25 Red' (c/n unknown), was seconded to the command of the Russian peacekeepers in Georgia, as revealed by the 'OK KMS' badge (*Operativnoye komandovaniye Korpoosa mirotvorcheskikh sil*). Note also the 'International Committee of the Red Cross' sticker on the fuselage and the Russian flag just aft of the tactical code; the latter practice originated in the early 1990s.

Seen here at its home base of Kubinka on 8th August 1997, An-26 '15 Red' (c/n 9303) of the Russian Air Force's 226th Mixed Composite Air Regiment used to be stationed at Sperenberg AB near Berlin.

An-26 military transport

The Kiev aircraft factory started gearing up for series production of the An-26 in 1968. At that time the enterprise was going through a period of intensive development, building up production of the An-24, and had no special difficulties in mastering the new machine, given the two types' high degree of commonality. The first production example (identity unknown, c/n 0301) rolled off the production line on 29th August 1969. In the first half of September it performed four flights according to the programme of testing the first production machine; on 27-30th September a GK NII VVS crew captained by I. Ya. Markov performed two more acceptance flights, after which the An-26 was cleared for operational use in a service unit.

Full-scale production of the type got under way in 1970 in accordance with MAP order No.301. The manufacture of the An-26 proceeded at a rate of 14 to 16 aircraft per month – an impressive figure, considering that the plant continued turning out An-24s and An-30s at the same time. The Powers That Be realised this, and in August 1970 the plant was awarded the Order of the Red Banner of Labour for its achievements.

In the course of An-26 production GK NII VVS conducted various tests of this machine.

Thus, in 1975 a crew captained by female test pilot Marina L. Popovich took part in the testing of the PGS-200 parachute cargo system on the An-26. 24 flights were performed, in which the PGS-200 was dropped 14 times with mock-ups of the cargo simulating its weight and dimensions; in addition, test parachutists made 44 jumps. The results showed that the system was suitable for service introduction but also revealed that it was not quite safe for the paratroopers to jump directly after the cargo had been dropped.

Additionally, the following items were tested. An-26 c/n 0901 (identity unknown) was used to test the upgraded Groza-26D radar. An example with the non-standard MAP registration CCCP-83966 No.1 (c/n 1006) served as a testbed for an altered avionics/flight instrumentation suite developed for the export version. (This An-26 wearing a prototype-style colour scheme was later converted into the first prototype of the An-32; see Chapter 5.) An-26 c/n 1506 (identity unknown) was used to verify the R-802V and R-832M radios, while the ARK-UD ADF/short-range search equipment underwent testing on An-26 c/n 1410 (identity unknown).

Production of the An-26 continued until 1986; the 1,398th and final example, An-26B CCCP-26214 (c/n 14403) was manufactured

Above: An-26 '30 Blue' was 'inherited' by the Ukrainian Air Force after the break-up of the USSR and the red star insignia were crudely overpainted and replaced with UAF shield-and-trident insignia.

on 24th January 1986. The leading test pilots of the plant, including Merited Test Pilots (an official grade reflecting experience and expertise) Boris Z. Popkov and S. I. Savchenkov, took part in the pre-delivery tests of the production machines.

(Note: Normally An-26s have four- or five-digit construction numbers showing only the batch number and the number of the aircraft in the batch (up to Batch 99 a zero was occasionally added to the batch number, as exemplified by the second prototype). Some aircraft, however, carry an extended An-24 style c/n showing the year of manufacture and the plant number (minus the first digit). In these cases the c/ns do not coincide completely because of the time gap between An-24/An-26 production, which was usually seven or eight years. Cf. An-24B CCCP-47828 manufactured on 20th September 1971 is c/n **17307210** while An-26 *sans suffixe* RA-26528 manufactured on 30th October 1978 is c/n **87307210**; interestingly, the c/n was painted

on simply as 7210 when the latter aircraft was still in Aeroflot markings as CCCP-26528.

Of the 144 batches built, the second and third consisted of two machines each; Batches 4 and 5 had five aircraft each, while the final batch had three. All other batches consisted of ten aircraft each.)

Various modifications were introduced in the course of series production; previously built machines also were subjected to improvements. This was effected *in situ* by factory teams, or in the course of an overhaul. For instance, major repairs and refurbishment of Soviet/Russian Air Force An-24B/T/RT and An-26 aircraft were performed by the Ministry of Defence's Aircraft Repair Plant No.308 (ARZ – *aviaremontnyy zavod*) at Ivanovo-Severnyy AB. Typical improvements applied to production machines included increasing the deflection angles of the aileron trim tab from ±7° to ±15°, which made it possible to bring the control forces in the roll control channel into accordance with the then-current airwor-

thiness standards. The 'Ground/Air' switch in the emergency engine starting system proved to be useless and was deleted.

Of the 1,398 An-26s manufactured in the Soviet Union (ie, not counting Chinese production), 564 machines were produced for the Soviet Armed Forces and various 'don't-mess-with-me' agencies, such as the Ministry of the Interior and the notorious KGB. 420 machines were exported to other countries, and the rest were delivered to the Ministry of Civil Aviation and other ministries, including MAP, MOM and the Ministry of Electronics Industry (MRP – *Ministerstvo rahdioelektronnoy promyshlennosti*). As of 2001, 1,168 machines of the type were listed as operational.

'An-26T' transport

This was the unofficial designation allocated by the East German Air Force to the regular transport-configured An-26s operated by the 24th Transport Squadron (*Transportfliegerstaffel* 24 or TS 24) at Dresden-Klotzsche.

An-26A transport/assault aircraft prototype

The first modified version of the An-26 was the An-26A optimised for airborne landing operations. In 1971 a production machine (c/n 0901) was modified into the An-26A prototype. In the process of modification it was stripped of the paradropping equipment, the NKPB-7 bombsight and a number of special systems; the navigator's blister was replaced by a plug with a regular window of 390 mm diameter, and the 'Emblema' radar was replaced by the Groza-26A radar. The combined effect of these measures cut empty weight by 966 kg (2,130 lb).

Between 17th August and 6th September 1971, OKB and GK NII VVS crews captained by V. A. Bogdanov and A. S. Mineyev respectively performed 14 flights within the programme of joint checkout tests. They showed that the An-26A had somewhat better performance as compared to the standard aircraft, possessing a higher top speed and service ceiling and a reduced fuel consumption per km. Still, the aircraft remained a one-off.

An-26 *shtabnoy* ('An-26S', 'An-26ST', An-26 'Salon') staff transport

Some of the An-26s delivered to the Soviet Armed Forces and the East German Air Force were modified to support the operations of army/fleet headquarters. This involved installation of a partition with a door separating the forward part of the cargo hold, which was turned into a passenger cabin with floor panels covering up the P-147 chain conveyor, and three four-abreast rows of seats borrowed from the An-24. The first two rows faced each other, with tables in between. The

Another An-26 in Aeroflot-style colours from Kubinka, '01 Blue'. A characteristic feature of military An-26s are the small blisters on the sides of the nose and the rear fuselage extremity associated with IFF.

rest of the cargo hold remained as it was, permitting carriage of different cargoes, including a GAZ-24 Volga D-class saloon car or an UAZ-469 (UAZ-3151) jeep. The aircraft could be easily reconverted to standard configuration by removing the 'cabin' trappings.

Such aircraft were officially designated An-26 *shtabnoy* (= staff transport); unofficially, however, they were dubbed An-26S (or An-26 'Salon'), while East German sources have gone so far as to call the two EGAF examples An-26ST! Although the staff transport versions were not 'real' passenger aircraft, the small number of passenger seats created the impression of enhanced comfort – even though the cabin was undoubtedly a bit claustrophobic because of the limited number of windows.

An-26Sh navigator trainer
The An-26Sh (*shtoormanskiy*) was a navigator trainer version broadly equivalent to the civil An-24USh and intended for training of navigators for the Soviet Air Force's airlift arm (VTA). The cargo hold housed equipment for training ten workstations for the navigator trainees and one for the instructor. Each workstation included a table and a double seat, as well as a panel with instruments and radio equipment. The An-26Sh was equipped with additional pitot tubes and power supply units. Three windows on starboard side and two on port side were replaced by blisters.

The aircraft was built in series at the Kiev plant. Production of this version totalled 36 machines which were operated both in military colleges and, later, in some civil aviation schools. Unfortunately none have been identified so far.

An-26RT (first use of designation; An-26RTR, An-26RR) ELINT aircraft
In the 1970s and 1980s a whole series of aircraft in the Soviet Air Force was adapted for conducting general-purpose or detailed electronic intelligence (ELINT). One of them was the An-26RT – confusingly, the first An-26 version to be thus designated. In the service units it has also been called, more appositely, An-26RTR ([*samolyot*] *rahdiotekhnicheskoy razvedki* – ELINT aircraft) or, even more confusingly, An-26RR (which might create the false impression this is an NBC reconnaissance aircraft!). Furthermore, Western sources have misidentified it as the 'An-26M'!

The An-26RT ELINT aircraft carries various electronic intelligence devices and radio equipment for prompt direction finding. The aircraft is intended primarily for detecting radio transmitters working illegally and the enemy's permanent radio engineering means of communication. The An-26RT can spot low-power radio transmitters, including radiotelephone devices of Western manufacture intended for personal, industrial and military use; spot electronic means of communication fitted with devices which enhance their ability to avoid detection; sort out and record the spotted sources of radio emissions and take their bearings. There are several interchangeable equipment fits; these were accommodated in the cargo hold and in small pods which could be suspended on standard BD3-34 bomb racks. Outwardly the An-26RT ELINT aircraft is characterised by numerous large blade aerials positioned dorsally and ventrally fore and aft of the wings.

During the Afghan War the Soviet troops used one An-26RT ELINT aircraft with the unusual three-digit tactical code '152' (c/n unknown); it could well be the most secret aircraft in the 40th Army, as the Soviet task force in Afghanistan was known. This aircraft was fitted with the *Tarahn* (Ramming attack) equipment suite capable of detecting the enemy's means of field communication, take their bearings and record radio traffic. Even the air squadron commander did not poke his nose into the work of the aircraft's crew, and only a few selected officers were permitted to come aboard. The machine was used primarily for intercepting radio exchanges between Mujahideen groups; the obtained information was immediately reported to the intelligence section of the 40th Army headquarters. The work was conducted in real time, for which purpose specialists having a command of the local languages were included into the crew for every sortie.

When performing missions in areas adjoining the borders with Iran and Pakistan, the mission crew listened to the communication channels of these countries' Air Forces and Air Defence units – with good reason, as Pakistani Air Force fighters frequently intruded into Afghan airspace to attack Soviet aircraft. On one occasion, having intercepted radio traffic between a pair of PAF General Dynamics F-16As and their forward air control station, the intelligence specialists gave timely warning to an An-30 patrolling the area that the Pakistanis were about to attack it.

A 'civilian' aspect of the work of the An-26RT ELINT aircraft included seeking out illegal radio transmitters which could pose a danger to flight safety by hampering the work of air traffic control means.

An-26RT communications relay aircraft (second use of designation)
Another version likewise designated An-26RT fills an altogether different role. This time the RT stands for *retranslyator* (relay installation), signifying this is a communications relay version. Its cargo hold accommodates the potent *Inzheer* (Fig, the fruit) radio relay suite making it possible to extend the range of radio communication between army units in mountainous areas or at over-the-horizon ranges; the latter is necessary primarily for ensuring the work of the UHF radios that work only within direct vision distances. Again the

An An-26RT communications relay aircraft coded '02 Red' sits under wraps at Chkalovskaya AB in the winter of 1995/96. The huge blade aerials characterising this version are clearly visible.

This poor but interesting shot depicts one of the two An-26M *Spasatel'* (aka An-26 Skalpel')flying hospitals which saw action in Afghanistan. The Red Cross markings on the fuselage and wings are clearly visible.

aircraft sports several huge blade aerials positioned dorsally and ventrally fore and aft of the wings; however, while the aerials are of the same type as on the other An-26RT, they are located differently and it is pretty hard to tell which is which!

Service units received a total of 42 An-26RT comms relay aircraft converted from production An-26s at ARZ No.308 in Ivanovo. The equipment installed in these aircraft was compatible with most types of radios that were in current use in the Soviet Armed Forces; these included both stationary equipment and portable radios used by tanks, movable troop command posts and other self-propelled vehicles, including aircraft.

Eight An-26RT relay aircraft coded '04', '11', '12', '14', '18', '21', '22' and '64' were used by Soviet troops during the Afghan War. These machines catered for reliable communication between the headquarters of the 40th Army and the garrisons scattered all over the country, helping to maintain control of combat activities and search-and-rescue operations. The An-26RT's were actually 'hovering' over Kabul all the time, relieving one another in the air. The usual norm of time on station for every crew was five flying hours per every 24 hours, but in the days of major combat operations, when several relay aircraft were airborne simultaneously, the airmen had to stay airborne for double the usual time.

Several of these aircraft were lost to enemy action. On 26th December 1986 An-26RT '22 Red', a 50th OSAP (*otdel'nyy smeshannyy aviapolk* – Independent Composite Air Regiment)/2nd Squadron aircraft, was hit consecutively by two Stinger missiles while cruising at over 8,000 m (26,250 ft). The crew bailed out.

At least one An-26RT was supplied to Syria. Curiously, this aircraft was civil-registered and painted in the smart colour scheme of Syrianair (!) for appearance's sake.

The comms relay version could also be engaged in various peaceful tasks. On numerous occasions it rendered services to geological prospecting parties, hunters in Siberia, and merchant and fishing vessels.

An-26REP electronic countermeasures aircraft

In 1974, in keeping with resolution No.76 of the Military Industrial Commission under the Presidium of the Soviet Council of Ministers dated 29th March 1972, the specialists of several research institutes within the MRP framework converted a Soviet Air Force An-26 into the prototype of an electronic countermeasures aircraft. Designated An-26REP (*rahdioelektronnoye protivodeystviye* – ECM), the uncoded aircraft (c/n 2101) was equipped for individual protection from surface-to-air and air-to-air missiles.

Mounted low on both sides of the fuselage between frames 16-21 were two large cylindrical pods whose ogival front and rear portions with lateral bulges were dielectric. They housed SPS-151 and SPS-153 active jammers (*stahntsiya pomekhovykh signahlov* – lit. 'interference emitter') for retaliatory ECM. The hefty pylons carrying the pods incorporated two ASO-2I-E7R flare dispensers, each of which contained 64 PPI-26 infra-red countermeasures (IRCM) flares. (ASO = *avtomaht sbrosa otrazhahteley* – automatic chaff/flare dispenser; PPI = *peeropatron infrakrahsnyy* – infra-red [countermeasures] cartridge.) The mission avionics also included an SPO-10 radar homing and warning system (*sistema preduprezhdeniya ob obloochenii* – lit. 'irradiation warning system') which gave warning about the aircraft being painted by enemy radars, as well as an experimental *Bar'yer* (Barrier) RHAWS.

Between 17th December 1975 and 24th June 1976 the aircraft was tested at GK NII VVS with N. A. Lyovushkin and M. L. Popovich as project test pilots and O. K. Ovchinnikov as engineer in charge). 39 flights were performed, including 19 flights with the participation of Sukhoi Su-15 and Su-15TM interceptors; the latter 'attacked' the An-26REP, making simulated launches of R-98, R-98M and R-3S missiles equipped with infra-red seeker heads. To counteract them, the aircraft fired PPI-26 flares; the total expenditure amounted to 700 such flares. The tests were filmed from a MiG-21U two-seat fighter trainer acting as chase plane. The effectiveness of the SPS-151 and SPS-153 jammers against HAWK ('Homing All-the-Way Killer') surface-to-air missile was assessed, using mathematical analysis.

The An-26REP was recommended for service, but not a single example was ever delivered to the Air Force. The prototype was reconverted to standard configuration, subsequently becoming a navaids calibration aircraft. Nevertheless, some Soviet Air Force An-26s, An-30s and An-32s did receive ASO-2I IRCM flare dispensers.

An-26M *Spasatel'* (An-26 *Skal'pel'*) flying hospital

In 1977 the Antonov OKB, in a joint effort with the Kiev Aircraft Production Association's own design bureau, created a version of the An-26 equipped as a flying surgery ward and intensive care unit. Designated was An-26M *Spasatel'* (Rescue worker), the aircraft was the first of its kind in the USSR; the M stood for *meditsinskiy* (medical).

The An-26M's cargo hold was divided into two compartments. The rear compartment was intended for giving urgent therapeutic aid to four patients (heavily wounded persons); the other one was an operating room provided with equipment for anaesthesia, blood group determination and blood transfusion, an 'artificial lung' apparatus, cardiographic appliances etc. The medical personnel could have a rest in a special small compartment with comfortable seats. A Stoopino Machinery Design Bureau TA-9 APU was installed in the port engine nacelle, supplying power to the medical equipment on the ground when the engines were shut down.

Two production An-26s (identities unknown) were converted into this version and transferred to the Military Medicine Directorate of the Soviet Ministry of Defence. During trials the first An-26M wore Aeroflot livery, and its pictures were repeatedly published in the press. After delivery to the military the aircraft was repainted into the overall light grey colour scheme which was standard for SovAF An-26s. (Note: Some sources suggest that the first An-26M was registered CCCP-26602 but it was *not* – see An-26B section below.)

On 25th December 1979 Soviet troops entered Afghanistan and the ten-year Afghan War broke out. Already during the first months the losses turned out to be so heavy that urgent measures had to be taken to organise medical aid to troops placed far from their permanent bases. The hot climate and insanitary conditions led to situations when even lightly wounded personnel died because of the unavailability of prompt medical assistance. In these conditions a decision was taken to use both An-26M 'flying hospitals' on the Afghan TO. Coded '07 Red' and '09 Red' and wearing huge Red Cross marking on the fuselage and wings – a measure meant to stop the aircraft from being fired upon – the two An-26Ms began airlifting heavily wounded personnel from Afghanistan to Tashkent, a major staging point for Soviet forces during the war. Interestingly, in Afghanistan these aircraft were dubbed *Skal'pel'* (Scalpel) and *Tabletka* (Pill); the former nickname stuck and got wider currency among the military than the official name *Spasatel'*.

An-26P water bomber

In 1987, in response to the task set by the Soviet Council of Ministers and in accordance with specifications issued by the Leningrad Institute of Forestry, the Antonov OKB teamed up with GosNII GA to develop the An-26P water bomber intended for fighting forest fires (P – *protivopozharnyy*, fire-fighting). After this KiAPO converted a production An-26, CCCP-26661 (c/n 8009), into the An-26P prototype.

Above: The starboard water tank of An-26P CCCP-26542 displayed at MosAeroShow-92. Note the sway braces, the filler hatch with locking handwheel, the ventral drop doors and the observation blister.

The An-26P was characterised by two cigar-shaped 2,000-litre (440-Imp. gal) external tanks scabbed onto the fuselage sides for dropping water or fire retardant on a fire. The tanks were attached to the standard fuselage hardpoints and additionally secured by four sway braces to fuselage frames 15, 17, 20 and 22. They featured dorsal filler caps and triple ventral discharge doors; the whole contents of the tanks could be emptied in no more than two seconds. Alternatively, the aircraft could be fitted with ASO-2I dispensers holding 384 PV-26 silver iodide flares for making rain. An observation blister was provided in the third cargo hold window on each side.

It was presumed that one An-26P could extinguish a fire at a site with an area of 3 hectares, with a radius of action up to 430 km (267 miles). In reality, forest fires took on far larger dimensions; hence the main task of the An-26Ps consisted in preventing the fire from spreading or creating defensive lines. Tests performed with the aircraft made it possible to evolve methods of its operational use; these included discharging the liquid from low altitude (right down to 50 m/160 ft) at a speed of 230-240 km/h (143-150 mph). In addition, the aircraft could be used for paradropping 30 fire-fighters and ten packages of equipment, each weighing 100 kg (220 lb), and for extinguishing fires by provoking a heavy rainfall.

Five machines were converted into the An-26P version. They were used in earnest only in 1991, when the Arkhangel'sk detachment of the Forestry Protection Service was engaged in extinguishing fires in Yakutia, near the town of Lensk. Then they stood idle for several years and finally were reconverted to the original transport version, because in the difficult economic situation of mid-1990s the forest protection organisations were not in a position to use these aircraft for fire-fighting.

An-26P CCCP-26542 (c/n 2708) dumps its load of water on the runway at Zhukovskiy on 12th August 1992, the second trade day of MosAero Show.

Don't be fooled by the Aeroflot colour scheme and the 'An-26B' nose titles. The small IFF blisters just aft of the radome and the blue-tipped propeller spinners reveal that CCCP-26-something is actually a Soviet Air Force aircraft masquerading as a bona fide civil airliner!

On 11-16th August 1992 an An-26P fire-bomber registered CCCP-26542 (c/n 2708) was demonstrated statically and in flight at the MosAeroshow-92 in Zhukovskiy. This aircraft and An-26P CCCP-26551 (c/n 3102) belonged to the Arkhangel'sk CAD/2nd Arkhangel'sk UAD/392nd Flight.

An-26LP fire-fighting aircraft

Another fire-fighting version of the An-26 is designated An-26LP. Known examples are registered RA-26000 (c/n 07309604, Dalavia Far East Airlines), RA-26001 (c/n 9705, Dalavia Far East Airlines), RA-26002 (c/n 9706, North-Eastern Forestry Protection Base), RA-26003 (c/n 9707, Igarka Airlines), RA-26005 (c/n 9809, Yeniseysk Air Enterprise), RA-26006 (c/n 9810, Baikal Airlines), RA-26037 (c/n 10608, Sakha Avia), RA-26039 (c/n 10702, Tomsk Avia) and RA-26040 (c/n 10703, Yeniseysk Air Enterprise).

An-26B civil cargo aircraft

In the 1970s the Unified Transportation System of Containerised Cargo Carriage in the People's Economy was developed in the USSR. It ensured mechanised and automated delivery of a vast range of standard cargoes 'from warehouse to warehouse'. (We nearly wrote 'door to door', but the term was unheard-of in the Soviet Union.) The new system followed international standards and could be introduced on all kinds of transport, including air transport. In the course of implementing this system several types of aircraft and helicopters that had been developed primarily for the Air Force were modified to suit the new requirements.

Thus, in 1980 a civil version of the An-26, designated An-26B (simply in alphabetical

order after the An-26A), came into existence. The aircraft was provided with communications and navigation equipment optimised for operation on civil air routes. Of the whole complement of the military version's cargo handling and paradropping equipment, only the overhead hoist remained on the civil version.

A cargo hold floor of lightened design was installed, permitting carriage of wheeled vehicles with a maximum axle load of 1,500 kg (3,300 lb) versus 3,100 kg (6,835 lb) for the An-26 sans suffixe. The floor incorporated locks for three PA-2.5 cargo pallets and tiedown cleats for carrying packaged cargoes with an overall weight of up to 5,500 kg (12,130 lb). Some machines featured roller conveyors to facilitate the loading/unloading of palletised goods. Separate air conditioning systems for the flightdeck and the cargo hold were provided, making it possible to use the cargo hold as a refrigerator for the transportation of perishable goods. The cargo hold was also fitted with two seats for the cargo attendants, pockets for life vests and a pallet for an additional emergency supply of food. The onboard equipment enabled two cargo handlers to do the job of loading three standard 1.5-ton pallets within 30 minutes.

Outwardly the An-26B could be discerned from the military An-26 sans suffixe (some of which were quasi-civil) by having appropriate nose titles and a plug incorporating a regular-sized window instead of the port side blister at the navigator's station – just like on the ill-fated An-26A. The performance remained unchanged as compared to the baseline version.

The An-26B prototype was converted from a standard An-26, CCCP-26602 (c/n

4407); built in mid-1976, this machine was one of the Antonov OKB's 'dogships'. Series production at KiAPO continued until 1985, totalling 116 units. Though adapted to carrying containerised and palletised goods, unfortunately An-26Bs were often operated by Aeroflot without making full use of their advantages.

An-26B mobile hospital version

Sometime in the 1980s the An-26B prototype was converted into a medevac or 'flying hospital' version, causing some people to mistake it for the An-26M Spasatel' prototype; actually it was the civilian equivalent of the latter. Outwardly the aircraft could be identified by the huge Red Cross markings on the fuselage between the third and fourth cabin windows, which required the CCCP- prefix to be removed. As distinct from the military An-26M Spasatel', it lacked the TA-9 APU in the port engine nacelle – not to mention the fact that both An-26Ms were being used operationally before the An-26B even appeared!

An-26KPA (An-26 Standart, An-26 Kalibrovshchik) flight checker

In 1986 a special version of the An-26 was created for checking the functioning of airfield navigation aids (instrument landing systems and air traffic control radars). Designated An-26KPA (kontrol'no-poverochnaya apparatoora – checking and calibration equipment), it is sometimes referred to as the An-26 Standart (Standard; this obviously is a reference to operating standards, not to the aircraft itself which is definitely non-standard!) or An-26 Kalibrovshchik (calibrator or flight checker). Twenty production machines were converted to this version.

In connection with the introduction of more modern equipment at some airports during the recent years, some An-26KPA aircraft were upgraded – presumably to the An-26ASLK version.

An-26L (An-26BL) flight checker

A single flight checker coded '14 Orange' (later recoded '27 Blue', c/n 00607) served with the 16th Air Army's 226th OSAP stationed at Sperenberg AB near Berlin until the early 1990s. Referred to , in Western sources as the An-26L (*laboratoriya* – laboratory) or An-26BL, this particular aircraft was related to the An-26KPA described above but presumably had a simplified set of equipment. It featured small 'devil's pitchfork' ILS aerials under the radome and the flattened tip of the 'beaver's tail' rear fuselage, three slot aerials in the fin and a prominent astrodome above the flightdeck.

An-26ASLK (An-26 *Kalibrovshchik*) flight checker

One more flight checker variant of the An-26 possessing a more up-to-date equipment suite is designated An-26ASLK (*avtomatizeerovannaya sistema lyotnovo kontrolya* – automated flight check system). It is readily identifiable by the largish fairing located low on the port side of the forward fuselage, just aft of the navigator's blister. The flat underside of this fairing incorporates a powerful retractable light for phototheodolite measurements which is protected by a movable visor when retracted. The aircraft also features four slot aerials in the fin and the aforementioned 'pitchfork' ILS aerials.

This version was operated both by Aeroflot and the Soviet/Russian Air Force. Known examples include CCCP-26521 (c/n 7102), CCCP-26526 (c/n 7208), CCCP-26531 (c/n 7403), CCCP-26571 (c/n 67303909), CCCP-26625 (c/n 5203), CCCP-26631 (c/n 5503), CCCP-26640 (c/n 3504), CCCP-26642 (c/n 2101, the former An-26REP ECM aircraft), CCCP-26673 (c/n 97308408) and Russian Air Force '29 Blue' (c/n unknown). The latter example differs from the civil examples in featuring additional antenna pods under the wing leading edge at half-span, while quasi-civil CCCP-26642 had a strake aerial along the top of the forward fuselage.

An-26RL (An-26BRL) ice reconnaissance aircraft

The An-26RL or An-26BRL is a multi-purpose version intended for spotting fish shoals and marine mammals, conducting ice reconnaissance and patrolling the 200-mile economic exclusion zone.

The prototype of this version was converted by KiAPO from a production An-26 in 1987. The aircraft was fitted with an aerial camera

Above: An-26ASLK RA-26625 (c/n 5203) under threatening skies in the smart colour scheme of Aviastar at Moscow-Domodedovo on 3rd November 1998. Note the fairing below the navigator's blister.

and special equipment developed by Leningrad-based VNIIRA (LNPO Leninets). The equipment was housed inside the cargo hold and in external fairings. The latter presumably housed a SLAR; thus the designation prefix may be deciphered both as *razvedchik ledovyy* (ice reconnaissance aircraft) and as *rahdiolokahtor* (radar – ie, side-looking radar).

The crew included observers whose work stations were provided with blisters. An additional fuel tank holding 4,000 litres (880 Imp. gal) was installed in the cargo hold, increasing endurance to 8 hours 36 minutes; the aircraft could remain on station for six hours when flying at an altitude of 200-400 m (650-1,300 ft).

Six aircraft, including An-26Bs CCCP-26008 (c/n 9902) and CCCP-26104 (c/n 12002), were converted to An-26RL (An-26BRL) configuration.

An-26 *Nel'mo* survey aircraft

In 1990 one more An-26 (identity unknown) was modified at the KiAPO for the same purposes. It was designated An-26 **Nel'mo** after the name of the equipment suite (the meaning of this word is unknown). The mission avionics were housed in a compact cubicle,

leaving the rest of the cargo hold free for carrying cargoes. Thus the An-26 *Nel'mo* could earn revenue when off duty.

An-26D military transport prototype

Operational experience with the An-26 revealed some shortcomings. Among other things, the aircraft's range proved insufficient in some cases. Hence an extended-range version designated An-26D (**dahl'niy** – long-range) was developed by the Antonov Design Bureau in 1995 to meet an order from the Russian Air Force.

It proved impossible to accommodate more fuel inside the wings or fuselage (without reducing usable internal space anyway). The solution was to fit semi-conformal fuel tanks to the sides of the centre fuselage, strapping them on to fuselage mainframes 17 and 20, the way it had been done before on the An-30D (see Chapter 4). The streamlined non-detachable fuel tanks were connected to the wing tanks by external fuel line conduits. Each tank held 1,500 litres (330 Imp. gal), the extra fuel increasing the range to 3,600 km (2,240 miles).

In 1996 the Aviant factory made appropriate modifications to a Russian Air Force An-26 *shtabnoy* staff transport coded '21 Yellow'

An-26ASLK calibrators were also operated by the Soviet/Russian Air Force. This example coded '29 Blue' seen at Pushkin on 18th August 1991 features additional podded aerials under the wing leading edge.

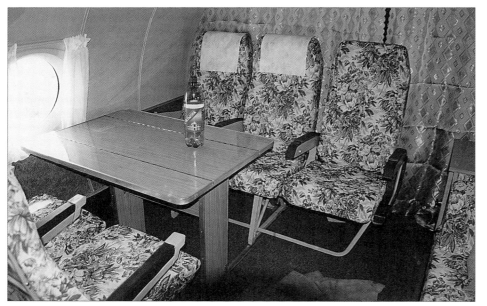

Above: The An-26-100 and An-26B-100 feature a convertible interior. This is the rear cabin section of An-26B-100 UR-BXV; the space behind the curtain is the baggage compartment set up on the cargo ramp.

Above: The Ukrainian Air Force's An-26 *Vita* flying hospital ('25 Blue', c/n 5406) displayed at Kiev-Svyatoshino on 15th September 2002 during the Aviasvit-XXI airshow.

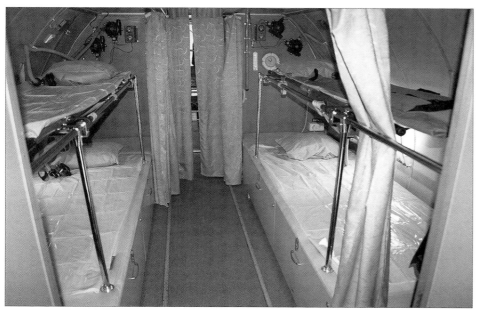

The rear section of the An-26 *Vita* is configured as a sick bay with room for four stretcher patients. Further forward is the operating room and a rest room for the medical team.

(c/n 13806). The aircraft was then flown to the Russian Air Force's 929th State Flight Test Centre named after Valeriy P. Chkalov (formerly GK NII VVS) at Chkalovskaya AB to undergo trials. On 19-24th August 1997 the An-26D was demonstrated at the MAKS-97 airshow in Zhukovskiy, but no more orders for this upgrade have been forthcoming.

An-26S VIP aircraft

In 1997 a new VIP version of the An-26 was created in response to an order from the Ukrainian Ministry of Defence. This is the aircraft which is officially designated An-26S ('Salon'). It is fitted with new-generation cabin equipment, improved thermal insulation and soundproofing and a flight/navigation avionics fit enabling flights on international routes.

An-26-100 and An-26B-100 convertible passenger/cargo aircraft

In accordance with joint resolution No.26 signed by the Ukrainian State Aviation Administration and the Antonov Aviation Scientific & Technical Complex (ANTK Antonov) on 12th July 1999, Aircraft Repair Plant No.410 in Kiev started converting low-time An-26s military transports and An-26B civil freighters into quick-change 43-seat passenger/cargo aircraft to meet customer demands. Depending on the original version, the resulting aircraft are designated An-26-100 and An-26B-100 respectively.

The conversion involves cutting additional windows (four on each side of the fuselage) and emergency exits with external reinforcement plates around them in order to ensure adequate natural lighting, give the passengers a good field of view and comply with the prescribed passenger evacuation times. The existing port side emergency exit is substantially enlarged, the opening being about three times higher than usual, and features a window of 30 cm (11⅞ in) diameter. The window arrangement is thus 1+large exit+3+small exit+2 to port and 1+door+4+exit+2 to starboard. The entry door is equipped with An-24 style integral airstairs stowed forward of it.

The cabin features all necessary amenities, including seats designed by ANTK Tupolev (the Tupolev Design Bureau) and manufactured by the 'Aviastar' aircraft factory in Ul'yanovsk, Russia. A curtained-off area next to the cargo ramp is set aside for the passengers' baggage. Provisions are made for an in-flight entertainment system, a refrigerator and other 'creature comforts'. Cabin noise levels are reduced by using advanced heat insulation/soundproofing materials plus a vibration-damping coating based on the 'Firest-1' and SKLG-6020M materials. The seats and extra flooring panels may be easily removed if an all-cargo configuration is required.

The first aircraft to undergo such a conversion was An-26B UR-26672 (c/n 11409) owned by ARP 410 Airlines, the flying division of Aircraft Repair Plant No.410, which was demonstrated at many airshows. Next came Avialiniï Donbasu/Donbass – Eastern Ukrainian Airlines An-26B UR-BXV (ex-UR-26113, c/n 12110); this aircraft was on display at the MAKS-99 airshow. An-26-100s include RA-26518 (c/n 7009) belonging to the Russian carrier Tomsk-Avia. By March 2002 ten production An-26s had been upgraded to An-26-100/An-26B-100 standard at the aircraft repair factories in Kiev, Rostov (No.412) and Irkutsk (No.403).

An-26 'combi executive' version (project)

The Kiev Aircraft Repair Plant No.410 has prepared a project for converting production An-26s and An-26Bs into an executive version for corporate customers. The aircraft will offer a high degree of comfort to 19 passengers and carry an automobile in the rear portion of the hold. In short, this is a civilised version of the An-26 *shtabnoy*.

The An-26 *Vita* medical and transport aircraft

In 2001 a single Ukrainian Air Force An-26 coded '25 Blue' (c/n 5406) was converted into a mobile surgery/intensive care unit, a present-day Ukrainian counterpart of the An-26M. The conversion was performed by UAF specialists under orders from the Ukrainian Armed Forces' Military Medical Centre. The aircraft was dubbed An-26 *Vita* (Life).

The aircraft's medical equipment complement is somewhat simplified in comparison with the An-26M. The An-26 *Vita* can transport five stretcher cases; one of the berths can be adapted for performing resuscitation or a surgical operation. Painted in a smart white/blue/yellow colour scheme, it was displayed at the Aviasvit-XXI airshow at Kiev-Svyatoshino on 14-18th September 2002.

Numerous An-26s have been converted into all sorts of testbeds and research/survey aircraft to suit the needs of various research establishments. The spacious pressurised cargo hold rendered the aircraft ideally suited for the installation of the systems to be tested, the test and recording equipment and the test engineers' workstations. Depending on the complexity of the conversion and the sensitivity of the programme, the aircraft were either sent to KiAPO or overhaul plants for modification or converted in-house – sometimes without approval from the Antonov OKB.

While a complete listing of the test and development versions of the An-26 cannot be given here for reasons of space, a small selection follows.

An-26B *Tsiklon* weather research aircraft

In 1987 an Aeroflot An-26B in red/white Polar colours (identity unknown) was converted into the An-26B *Tsiklon* (Cyclone) by KiAPO for the Central Aerologic Observatory named after V. I. Voyeikov. The c/n has been quoted as 14208 but this aircraft was exported to East Germany as '373 Black'.

Actually, unlike the other aircraft in the *Tsiklon* series, the An-26B *Tsiklon* was a 'sky cleaner' intended for treating clouds with special chemicals for the purpose of artificially increasing the rainfall and protecting designated areas from rain.

The machine was identifiable by two slab-sided pods mounted on BD3-34 pylons and by the eye-catching *Tsiklon* emblem applied aft of the flightdeck. The pods housed six ASO-2I-E7R flare dispensers each; the latter held PV-26 flares with silver iodide. The cargo hold housed a heat-insulated container for disseminating granulated carbon dioxide. A local discharge of a large amount of carbon dioxide into the atmosphere caused the temperature to fall, and microscopic particles of silver iodide became the centres of concentration to which moisture clung, turning into raindrops. One gram of silver iodide produced on average one billion raindrops.

An-26 *Pogoda* weather research aircraft

For tackling the same weather control tasks one more unidentified aircraft was modified in Kiev in 1988 to become the An-26 *Pogoda* (Weather). By comparison with the An-26 *Tsiklon* it featured a simpler set of mission equipment.

An-26 *Sfera* aerological research aircraft

In 1991 a single production An-26 (identity unknown) was outfitted for studying the physical properties of the atmosphere in response to an order from the Ukrainian Academy of Sciences. The machine was designated An-26 *Sfera* (Sphere), the name obviously deriving from the word 'atmosphere'.

The An-26LL-PLO avionics testbed

The 1970s saw a new generation of US Navy *Ohio* class nuclear-powered submarines and British *Resolution* class submarines armed with Trident sea-launched ballistic missiles; each missile could carry ten warheads and cover a distance of 10,000 km (6,200 miles) from the launch site to the target. These missile subs posed so serious a threat to the Soviet Union that a crash programme was initiated with a view to upgrading the Soviet ASW arsenal. In the period of 1972-1993 an avionics testbed based on the sole An-26A (c/n 0901) took part in that work.

(Note: The description that follows, together with photo evidence to match, suggests that An-26 c/n 0901 was registered CCCP-29113. However, this registration is consistently quoted in the Western press with the c/n 1301!)

Designated An-26LL-PLO (*letayuschaya laboratoriya protivolodochnoy oborony*, ASW testbed), the aircraft was used primarily for developing new ultra-sensitive magnetic anomaly detectors (MAD). It was believed that these devices, which until then had not been characterised by high precision and discriminating ability, would be able to replace the extremely costly sonobuoys (one Soviet RGB-3 sonobuoy, for example, cost more than a Volga car in terms of 1973 prices!).

The operation of onboard MADs which detected the magnetic field of a submarine moving at a great depth and took its bearings, was hampered by the aircraft's own electromagnetic field. For that reason the MAD sensors detector were to be placed as far from eventual sources of interference as possible. Hence the An-26LL-PLO was equipped with two double-kinked booms, each 5 m (16 ft 5 in) long, mounted beneath the cargo ramp; one of them housed the sensor of a reference MAD, while the other boom carried an experimental system. The sensors of two other MAD systems were towed on cables 170 m (560 ft) long. During the test flights three systems functioned in combat mode and one, as noted above, was used as a standard for comparison.

The aircraft was converted by the Taganrog Machinery Plant named after Gheorgiy Dimitrov (TMZD) with the participation of LII and the organisation responsible for the equipment, NPO Roodgheofizika. The testing continued from the mid-1980s until the early 1990s, but the onset of *perestroika* (restructuring), when the funding for a number of military programmes was reduced to a trickle, made it impossible to complete the work. The whole fleet of the main Soviet ASW aircraft – the IL-38 and Tu-142 – was placed in difficult situation. Moreover, it was pointless to continue the programme because the plans to launch production of the new Beriyev A-40 Albatross ASW amphibian were abandoned. Subsequently the An-26LL-PLO was used for ecological monitoring.

An-26P (*Prozhektor*) avionics testbed

In the late 1960s the USSR initiated development of guided weapons intended to replace the not overly successful Kh-66 and Kh-23M missiles with a radio command guidance system in the arsenal of the Soviet Air Force's tactical arm. New air-to surface guided missiles were to be fitted with a semi-active laser homing warhead, and their carriers were to be equipped with laser target designators.

In 1973 the An-26P avionics testbed was converted from a production aircraft by common efforts of LII (Flight Research Institute) and NPO Gheofizika. The P suffix stood for *Prozhektor* (Searchlight), as the new weapons programme was code-named. Mounted on board the aircraft were the *Prozhektor* podded laser designation system based on the use of a quantum generator (laser) and the Type 24N1 laser homing warhead from the Kh-25 missile. Test flights conducted in 1973-1974 served to studying the peculiarities of the laser ray's reflection from typical underlying surfaces and maritime and land objects, including road and railway bridges, and for studying the system's ability to work during sandstorms. In-flight experiments with weapons suspended under the aircraft enabled the researchers to study the ability of the laser homing warheads to withstand interference and investigate the possibility of guiding the Raduga Kh-25 and Kh-29 missiles to targets illuminated by a ground laser designator.

The work was conducted for the benefit of the Sukhoi Design Bureau with a view to developing a weapon system for the Su-17MKG fighter-bomber. Although the target designation system proved to be not quite up to the mark, it was, nevertheless, introduced into service and adopted for the production Su-17M2.

An-26K (*Kaira*) avionics testbed
Soviet combat aircraft equipped with a laser rangefinder/target designator of the Klyon (Maple) family could use the thing only in a dive because, if released in level flight, the guided bomb quickly began to lag behind the aircraft, entering a 'blind spot' out of reach of the ray of the aircraft's quantum generator. To solve this problem, development of the Kaira-23 (Great Auk) and Katoon'-BI laser/TV sighting systems (Katoon' is the name of a Russian river) was initiated. This was a radically different kind of equipment. Its development involved, among other things, the An-26K testbed (the K initially stood for *Kaira*, the name of the programme).

This time the main customer was the Mikoyan Design Bureau which was working on the MiG-27K fighter-bomber. The Kaira-23 (16S-1) laser ranger/target designator was accommodated under the nose of the An-26K in a fairing; two Kh-25 or Kh-29 missiles were carried on both sides of the fuselage.

The conversion job ran seriously behind schedule – in fact, so much that, as related in the memoirs of Vlaeriy Ye. Menitskiy, Merited Test Pilot and Hero of the Soviet Union, by the time when the testbed started flying at long last, all the tests and live missile firing trials, as well as drops of laser- and TV-guided bombs, had already been conducted on the actual fighter-bomber. Flights within the framework of the *Kaira*'s test programme were performed by a crew captained by NII RP (Weapons Research Institute?) project test pilot L. Tetsman; the Mikoyan OKB was represented by test navigators Leonid S. Popov and V. Zaïtsev. The *Kaira* system was adopted for service introduction. In addition to the MiG-27K, it was used on the Su-24M tactical bomber (the latter had a version of this system designated LTPS-24).

An-26K (*Kaplya*) avionics testbed
After the completion of flights associated with the *Kaira* programme the An-26K was used for other work. Within the framework of the *Kaplya* (Drop [of liquid]) research programme Soviet designers created an optical correlation guidance system for air-to-surface missiles, development of which also involved the use of the suitably re-equipped An-26K; the K now conveniently stood for *Kaplya*.

In March 1989 the An-26K crashed, killing the crew captained by LII test pilot I. V. Borisov. During a night test flight at low altitude over the Azov Sea the aircraft collided with a wild goose. The big bird took out the entire windscreen, the pilot was wounded by the flying splinters and involuntarily pushed the control column forward…

An-26 *Polyot* avionics testbed
The 1960s saw the beginning of the introduction of the Unified state system of air traffic control in the USSR. For this system Soviet designers developed the *Polyot* (Flight) navigation suite based on the KSB navigation/attack system of the ill-starred M-50 supersonic bomber created by Vladimir M. Myasishchev's OKB-23. Several dozen aircraft were involved in the development of this system; one of them was a testbed based on the An-26.

Test flights of this machine within the framework of the *Polyot* programme started at LII in 1968. The work on the KSB and *Polyot* systems resulted in the development of the TKS-P precision compass system, a vertical gyro of the TsGV family, the TGV-P precise vertical gyro, the SVS-72 air data system, the *Strela* (Arrow) Doppler speed/drift sensor, the Koors-MP and RSBN-2 SHORAN, the SOM-64 ATC/SIF transponder, the NV-PB navigation computer, the SAU-1T automatic control system and other items of equipment. The *Polyot* system found wide use on aircraft of all categories.

Subsequently the same flying laboratory was used for testing the BNK-1P basic navigation instrument set for civil aviation. This work was conducted as a joint effort of the OKB developing the equipment, the Antonov Design Bureau and LII; S. Yu. Garnayev was the programme's project test pilot.

An-26 ALS components testbed
When all the tests of the first prototype An-26 (c/n 0201) had been completed, the aircraft was converted into a testbed used in 1982-1993 for developing elements of an automatic landing approach system (ALS). This included the first automated landing approach instrument set involving the use of GPS. The flights were performed with the participation of test pilot Ye. A. Lebedinskiy, test navigators Yu. M. Goobarev and N. I. Anisimov. The results obtained were used for perfecting the avionic suites of the Yak-40 and Yak-42 aircraft.

An-26LL ecological survey aircraft
This An-26LL was created in 1995 within the framework of a programme of rehabilitation of environment at former Soviet military bases. The aircraft (identity unknown) was fitted with equipment for aerial photography and multi-spectrum sounding of the Earth's surface.

An-26 avionics testbed
The assorted fleet of Elf Air, the commercial flying division of the NPO Vzlyot avionics house, included an all-white An-26 with the non-standard registration RA-13398 (c/n 2607). A close look at this aircraft revealed an elongated fairing immediately aft of the rudder, the absence of the first two windows on each side (these were faired over) and an elongated metal plate just aft of the entry door. This plate was clearly intended to reinforce the skin where some item of equipment had previously been installed.

An-26 avionics testbed (?)
Sometime in the 1980s LNPO Leninets obtained an early-production An-26. Registered CCCP-26648 (c/n 06-09; the c/n is actually painted on with a dash!), the aircraft was possibly a navigation systems testbed – or yet another flight checker. Outwardly it was distinguishable by a dorsal strake aerial on the forward fuselage (as on An-26ASLK CCCP-26642) and two small natural metal fairings located in tandem beneath the centre fuselage, offset to port. The aircraft is still in use by the Leninets Holding Co. as RA-26648.

Foreign Versions

An-26Z-1 ELINT aircraft
An indigenous ELINT version of the An-26 was created in Czechoslovakia where a production Czechoslovak Air Force An-26 serialled 2904 (c/n 12904) was fitted with equipment supplied by the Czechoslovak Tesla company. The machine received the designation An-26Z-1 (Z = *zastavba*, retrofit). The aircraft, which was operated by the 344th Transport and Reconnaissance Air Regiment based at Pardubice, was instantly identifiable

by the two big dielectric fairings on the centre fuselage sides and a smaller fairing just aft of the nose gear unit.

An-26SM ELINT aircraft

One of the 12 East German Air Force An-26s ('373 Black', c/n 14208) delivered in August 1985 was immediately converted locally to an ELINT aircraft bearing the unofficial designation An-26SM (*Sondermaschine* – 'special aircraft'). Its mission equipment was capable of detecting and intercept the signal of not only VHF and UHF radios but also of radios with pencil-beam antennas and determine the working frequencies of the adversary's air defence radars.

The An-26SM was officially declared operational on 20th December 1985. It operated in the interests of the East German MoD's Intelligence Department, performing once-weekly or twice-weekly flights along the West German border. These missions proceeded in utmost secrecy and were codenamed *Diskant* (Treble). The mission equipment was worked by eight operators assigned to the aircraft from the East German Army's 3rd ELINT Regiment in Dessau. On 30th September 1990 the aircraft was stripped of its mission equipment and returned to TS 24 as a regular transport.

An-26M navaids calibration aircraft

Another EGAF An-26 ('369 Black', c/n 11402) was converted locally into a flight checker for testing the ILS at Laage AB where MiG-29 fighters were stationed. The base was equipped with a Soviet-supplied instrument landing system which needed to be checked from time to time.

This East German counterpart of the An-26KPA was known unofficially as the An-26M (*Messflugzeug* – lit. 'measurement aircraft'). The aircraft remained in service long

A Yugoslav Air Force An-26 serialled 71371. Only the last three digits are carried visibly. Most of these aircraft were inherited by the Serbian Air Force after the break-up of Yugoslavia.

Above: The original caption to this publicity picture does not reveal whether these People's Liberation Army Air Force aircraft are An-26s or Chinese-built Y7Hs.

The An-26 was used a lot by the United Nations for peacekeeping operations in such places as former Yugoslavia, Ethiopia and Eritrea etc. Here is one of these aircraft, RA-26664 (c/n 97307905) leased from the Kirov State Air Enterprise, seconded to the UNPF contingent in Bosnia-Herzegovina in 1994.

enough to see the reunification of Germany and become Luftwaffe 52+09 on 3rd October 1990. However, on 20th June 1994 the An-26M was retired and sold to Luftwaffenmuseum Uetersen.

Xian Y-7H military transport

The experience accumulated by the Chinese aircraft industry in copying and building – without the benefit of a license – the An-24 airliner, coupled with the availability of the An-26s delivered from the USSR, enabled Chinese engineers to successfully copy this machine as well. The aircraft intended for use by the PLAAF was originally designated Y14-100.

The prototype took to the air for the first time at the end of 1988. After the completion of the test programme the reverse-engineered An-26 entered production as the Y7H (Hao = cargo). The aircraft was introduced into the PLAAF inventory in 1992; twelve such machines were delivered to service units by 1997.

Xian Y7H-500 and Y7H-500A transport/cargo aircraft

On 24th March 1992 tests began of a civil version of the Y7H designated Y-7H-500. The aircraft entered low-rate production, receiving its type certificate in December 1993. At present the customers are offered a somewhat more expensive variant, the Y7H-500A equipped with Western avionics. The Y7H and Y7H-500 are powered by uprated Dong'an WJ5E engines (a Chinese version of the AI-24VT) and by the Baoding J16-G10A auxiliary engines (a counterpart of the Soviet RU19A-300). The performance of these aircraft differed little from that of their Soviet counterparts.

No information concerning the number of Y7Hs and Y7H-500s built has ever been published. According to the fragmentary information available, by 1995 only two such aircraft (!) were built at the Xian aircraft factory; one of them, serialled '4520 Red', was fitted with equipment for dispersing clouds and was delivered to the air force; the other was delivered to Mauritania in 1997.

Xian Y7H-300 transport/cargo aircraft

The export version of the Y-7H military transport aircraft is designated Y7H-300.

Above: Aeroflot An-26s were often used for paradropping teams of firefighters in areas affected by forest fires. Here one of these teams is about to board An-26B CCCP-26022 (c/n 10202).

An-26 '1403 Black' (c/n 1403) was one of 12 supplied to the Polish Air Force's 13th Airlift Regiment (13. PLT) at Krakow-Balice.

Chapter 3

An-24/An-26 in Detail

The An-24 in Detail

The following structural description applies to the basic An-24B. Details of other versions are indicated as appropriate.

Type: Twin-engined short-haul airliner (An-24 *sans suffixe*/An-24A/An-24B/An-24V/An-24RV). The An-24T and An-24RT transport aircraft are intended for the transportation and landing/paradropping of troops and materiel, as well as for medevac duties. The airframe is of all-metal riveted and bonded construction, being chiefly made of aluminum and magnesium alloys, with steel and glassfibre used for some components. Rivets with lentil-shaped heads are used on the fuselage, with flush riveting on the wings and tail.

The aircraft features a classic aerodynamic layout with a conventional tail unit. Normal stability and controllability can be ensured at centre of gravity (CG) positions varying from 15 to 33% mean aerodynamic chord (MAC).

Fuselage: Semi-monocoque structure of beam-and-stringer type. Its cross-section changes from quasi-circular (formed by two arcs of different radii with the larger radius at the bottom) for most of the length to elliptical with the longer axis vertical at the rear. Maximum fuselage width 2.9 m (9 ft 6⅛ in); maximum cross-section area is 5.9 m² (63.5 sq.ft), fineness ratio 9.0.

The fuselage structure comprises 49 frames and 74 stringers, plus girders. Stringers 13L and 13R are the fuselage chines at the places where the two arcs forming the fuselage cross-section intersect. Chemically milled skin panels are utilised; the thickness varies from 1 to 1.5 mm (0.039 to 0.059 in) on most of the structure, reaching 2.5 mm (0.098 in) in the most heavily stressed areas.

Structurally the fuselage is divided into three sections: the forward fuselage (frames 1-11), centre fuselage (frames 11-40) and rear fuselage (frames 40-49). The sections are joined by fittings, with bands and overlapping cover plates. The fuselage is pressurised within the space between frames 1-40 to a pressure differential 0.3 kg/cm² (4.28 psi).

The *forward fuselage (Section F1)* includes the flightdeck (frames 1A-7) separated from the rest of the pressurised cabin by a rigid bulkhead with a door and the forward baggage compartment. Frame 1 is the forward pressure bulkhead mounting the weather radar dish; the fibreglass radome of honeycomb construction with four external reinforcing ribs opens upward and is secured by four tension locks. The nosewheel well is located below the flightdeck floor immediately aft of the pressure bulkhead. It is flanked by two avionics bays with upward-opening access covers between frames 2-4.

The flightdeck glazing features a one-piece frame with three windscreen panels, five side windows (three to port and two to starboard) and two eyebrow windows. The left and right windscreen panels located directly in front of the pilots are made of birdproof triplex silicate glass and feature electric de-icing. All other flightdeck windows have Perspex glazing 10-12 mm (0.39-0.47 in) thick. The foremost pair of side windows are sliding direct vision windows which can be used for emergency evacuation on the ground. There is also an escape hatch in the flightdeck roof frames 5-7; on some aircraft it is replaced by a transparent blister (astrodome). A circular window of 390 mm (15½ in) diameter with single Perspex glazing 10 mm thick is provided on the starboard side between frames 5-6 to provide natural lighting for the navigator and radio operator, if any.

There is a rectangular baggage/cargo door measuring 1.2 x 1.1 m (3 ft 11¼ in x 3 ft 7⅜ in) to starboard between frames 7-10, opened by pushing inwards and sliding upwards into the roof. Duralumin reinforcement plates are attached to the fuselage sides in the propellers' plane of rotation between

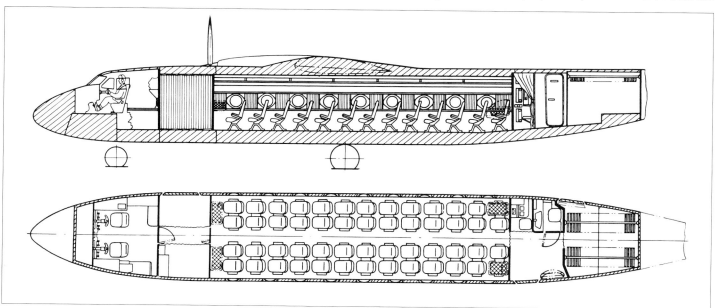

This drawing depicts the interior layout of the baseline 50-seat version of the An-24A.

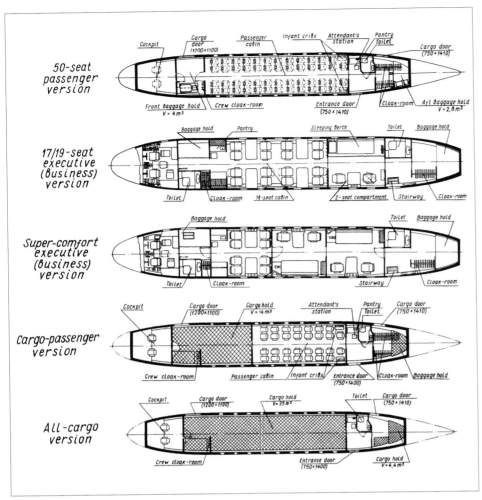

These drawings from an Aviaexport advertising brochure illustrate the An-24's possible interior layouts. The 'super-comfort' bit is obviously salesmen's pep talk...

frames 10-11 to protect the skin against pieces of ice breaking away from the propeller blades and increase fatigue resistance in the area.

The *centre fuselage (Section F2)* accommodates the passenger cabin(s) and the entry vestibule. On each side of the cabin there are nine circular windows of 390 mm diameter featuring double Perspex glazing, the inner and outer panes being 3 mm (0.12 in) and 4 mm (0.15 in) thick respectively. Rectangular emergency exits measuring 0.5 x 0.6 m (1 ft 7⅝ in x 1 ft 11⅝ in) are found between frames 14-15 to port and frames 23-24 to starboard. The inside of fuselage sections F1 and F2 is covered with heat- and soundproofing mats.

A plug-type entry door measuring 0.7 x 1.4 m (2 ft 7½ in x 4 ft 7⅛ in) is located on the port side between frames 31-33. It has a quasi-oval shape (the aperture is 'flattened' at the bottom to provide a wide threshold) and is opened by pushing inwards and sliding aft. It is equipped with manually operated two-section airstairs which fold away against the forward bulkhead of the entry vestibule. A 0.7 x 1.41 m (2 ft 7½ in x 4 ft 7½ in) service door/emergency exit of similar design is located on the starboard side between frames 34-36 (in the wardrobe area). All doors have rain gutters above them.

The *rear fuselage (Section F3)* is unpressurised. It incorporates attachment points for the tail surfaces at frames 40, 43 and 45 and mounts the ventral fin (or twin fins from Batch 29 onwards).

Wings: Cantilever shoulder-mounted wings of trapezoidal planform. Span 29.2 m (95 ft 9½ in), total wing area 72.46 m² (779.14 sq.ft) on batches 00 through 25 or 74.98 m² (807.2 sq.ft) from Batch 26 onwards. Aspect ratio 11.37, taper 2.92 (on batches 00 through 25) or 3.2 (from Batch 26 onwards); wing chord 3.5 m (11 ft 6 in) at the roots and 1.094 m (3 ft 7 in) at the tips. Zero sweepback and zero dihedral on the inner wings; the detachable outer wings are swept back 6°50' at quarter-chord and have 2° anhedral.

The wing centre section features a TsAGI S-5 airfoil with a thickness/chord ratio of 18%. The outer wings use the S-3 airfoil with better lifting properties and a thickness/chord ratio of 13%. The chosen airfoils provide high lift properties at speeds up to Mach 0.7 while

offering low drag and good stability and handling within a wide range of angles of attack. Wing camber −3° at the tips, incidence +3°.

The wings are a two-spar structure with 23 ribs in each wing; the spars and ribs are of a girder type. The wing spars are mated to fuselage mainframes 17 and 20. The variable-thickness extruded wing skin panels are of a slab type; the stringer webs were formed in the process of pressing the panels. The detachable wing leading edges have a double skin, incorporating the air ducts of the de-icing system.

Structurally, the wings are built in five sections: the one-piece centre section (inner wings), which is integral with the fuselage and carries the engine nacelles, and the outer wings, each of which, in turn, is divided into two sections. The manufacturing joints are located just outboard of the engine nacelles (ribs 12L and 12R) and at about two-thirds span (ie, at half-span of each outer wing). The sections are mated with the help of fittings. The wing/fuselage joint is covered by a fairing.

Large streamlined engine nacelles of adhere to the extremities of the wing centre section from below. Apart from the engine bays (and APU bay, in the case of the starboard nacelle), they incorporate the main-wheel wells which are separated from the engine bays by titanium steel firewalls.

On batches 00 through 25 the wing centre section featured double-slotted Fowler flaps with an area of 4.9 m² (52.7 sq.ft) located between the fuselage and the engine nacelles. From Batch 26 onwards they were supplanted by simple slotted flaps having an area of 5.53 m² (59.46 sq.ft), which brought about an increase of the wing centre section chord from 3.2 m (10 ft 6 in) to 3.5 m (11 ft 5¾ in). The inner sections of the outer wings (mid-span sections) carry double-slotted Fowler flaps with an area of 9.47 m² (101.8 sq.ft); the overall flap area of late-production An-24Bs et seq. is 15.0 m² (161.5 sq.ft). The flaps are actuated by a hydraulic motor located on the rear spar via drive shafts and combined angle drives/screwjacks (one for each inboard flap and two for each outboard flap); they move on curved tracks housed entirely inside the wings. Flap settings are 15° for take-off and 38° for landing; time to full deployment is 12.5-17 seconds and retraction time is 7-11 seconds.

There are two-section ailerons on the outermost parts of the outer wings (see Control system); each aileron section is suspended on two brackets.

Tail unit: Cantilever trapezoidal tail surfaces of stressed-skin two-spar construction with a NACA-0012 symmetrical airfoil. The *vertical tail* is swept back 21.5° at quarter-chord. It comprises the fin with an area of 13.28 m² (143 sq.ft), a one-piece rudder with an area of 5.0 m² (53.8 sq.ft; see Control system), a dorsal fin with an area of 2.57 m² (27.7 sq.ft) and a ventral strake or strakes. The fin is attached to the centre and rear fuselage at frames 40 and 43. It has a detachable leading edge incorporating de-icing system air ducts; there are three rudder hinge brackets.

Aircraft from c/n 0001 through 67302810 had a single ventral strake with an area of 1.8 m² (19.4 sq.ft). From c/n 67302901 onwards it was replaced by twin canted strakes with a total area of 2.02 m² (21.7 sq.ft), set at an angle of 70°.

The *horizontal tail* consists of two stabilisers and one-piece elevators (see Control system). Stabiliser span 9.08 m (29 ft 9½ in), dihedral 9°, incidence 3°, sweepback 15°30' at quarter-chord; total area (including the part integral with the fuselage) is 17.23 m² (185.5 sq.ft). The stabilisers are attached to the rear fuselage structure at frames 43 and 45; each stabiliser has a detachable leading edge (incorporating de-icing system air ducts) and three elevator hinge brackets.

Landing gear: Hydraulically-retractable tricycle type, with free-fall extension in emergency; there is a mechanical backup to ensure the undercarriage uplocks are released in case of a failure of the hydraulic system. All three units retract forward. Wheel track 7.9 m (25 ft 11 in); wheelbase in static load condition 7.85 m (25 ft 9 in), although some documents quote a figure of 7.89 m (25 ft 10⅝ in); minimum turning radius 11.25 m (36 ft 11 in). The undercarriage permits operation from paved, unpaved, snow- and ice-covered airfields, as well as from airstrips covered with PSP.

The steerable nose unit is equipped with twin 700 x 250 mm (27½ x 9⅞ in) K2-105 non-braking wheels and a combined steering actuator/shimmy damper. It can turn ±45° for taxying and ±10° during the take-off or landing run for collision avoidance. Maximum overall compression of the nose gear strut is 290 mm (11⅜ in).

The main units retract into the engine nacelles and feature twin 900 x 300 mm (35⅞ x 11¹³⁄₁₆ in) KT-94/2A wheels equipped with multi-disc brakes (KT = *kole**so** tormoz**noye*** – brake wheel).

All landing gear struts have oleo-pneumatic shock absorbers and scissor links. Initial nitrogen pressure in the oleos is 27.0 kg/cm² (385.7 psi) for the main units and 15.0 kg/cm² (214 psi) for the nose unit. Maximum overall compression of the main undercarriage struts is 509 mm (20 in). Tyre pressure is 6-6.6 bars (85-94 psi) for the mainwheels and 4-4.5 bars (57-64 psi) for the nosewheels.

The nosewheel well is closed by twin lateral doors and a small door linked to the nose gear oleo. The main units have large

The tail unit of an Aeroflot An-24B (c/n 47301001) registered somewhere between CCCP-46747 and CCCP-46753. This view illustrates the strong tailplane dihedral. Note that the aircraft was originally an An-24A!

clamshell doors bulged to accommodate the wheels; each main door incorporates a small hinged segment in line with the gear fulcrum. The large wheel well doors open only when the gear is in transit; the hinged segments of the main gear doors open automatically when the doors shut after gear extension.

Powerplant: (An-24 *sans suffixe*/early An-24As) Two Ivchenko AI-24 Srs I turboprop engines having a take-off rating of 2,550 ehp and a cruise rating of 1,500 ehp at 6,000 m (19,685 ft) and 450 km/h (280 mph). Late An-24As, An-24Bs, early An-24Vs and An-24RVs had identically rated AI-24A (AI-24 Srs II) engines with water injection. At take-off rating, the AI-24A's engine pressure ratio

(EPR) is 6.40, the mass flow is 13.1 kg/sec (28.8 lb/sec) and the turbine temperature 1,150°K. SFC at take-off rating 0.264 kg·hp/hr (0.58 lb·hp/hr); cruise SFC 0.245 kg·hp/hr (0.54 lb·hp/hr). Engine speed is 13,900 rpm at ground idle and 15,000 rpm at all operational settings.

Late-production An-24Vs and An-24T (An-24RT) transports are powered by the AI-24T engines with a take-off rating of 2,820 ehp and a cruise rating of 1,580 ehp. The power increase was achieved by increasing the EPR to 7.05; take-off SFC 0.262 kg·hp/hr (0.57 lb·hp/hr); cruise SFC 0.242 kg·hp/hr (0.53 lb·hp/hr). Engine speed is 14,050 rpm at ground idle and 15,800 rpm at all operational settings.

The AI-24 is a single-shaft turboprop with an annular air intake, a 10-stage axial compressor, an annular combustion chamber, a three-stage axial turbine and a fixed-area jet-pipe with a conical centrebody. Bleed valves are provided at the 10th compressor stage. Power is transmitted via a planetary gearbox with a reduction ratio of 0.08255; the gearbox incorporates a torque meter. Construction is of steel and magnesium alloy. The spool rotates in three bearings: a roller bearing in the air intake assembly (with an extension shaft to the reduction gear), a ball thrust bearing and a roller bearing ahead of the first turbine disc. The air intake assembly has inner and outer cones connected by four radial struts and is de-iced by engine bleed air. The welded stainless steel combustion chamber has eight burner cones, with igniters and pilot burners in two of them. The outer casing is split vertically for access to the burner cones.

The front-mounted accessory gearbox drives the accessories mounted on the forward casing: the starter-generator and AC generator, an R-68DT-24M constant-speed regulator, the fuel, oil and hydraulic pumps, a fuel control unit, the propeller autofeathering system and an ice detector.

For all versions overall length is 2,345 mm (7 ft 8⅞ in), width 677 mm (2 ft 2⅝ in), height 1,075 mm (3 ft 6⅞ in) and dry weight 600 kg (1,320 lb). The AI-24A has a 22,000-hour service life and a 5,000-hour time between overhauls.

The AI-24 is cranked and started electrically by an STG-18TMO starter-generator using DC power from the APU or a ground power source. The pressure-feed lubrication system uses a 75/25% mixture of MK-8 grade oil and MS-20 or MK-22 grade oil. The engine has a closed circuit oil system; the oil which is in the oil tank does not circulate in the system but is a reserve which can be used to replenish the oil circulating in the engine.

The engines drive Stoopino Machinery Design Bureau AV-72 or, in the case of the An-24T/An-24RT, AV-72T four-blade variable-pitch constant-speed propellers turning clockwise when seen from the front; diameter 3.9 m (12 ft 9½ in), weight 260 kg (570 lb). The propellers are equipped with spinners. The propeller wash affects about 34% of the overall wing area, increasing wing lift by 15-20%.

To enhance flight safety the engines are fitted with safety systems for automatic, man-

Top left: The main landing gear unit with twin KT-94/2 brake wheels. The struts are slightly inclined forward when extended. Note the small doors forming sections of the mainwheel well doors which open to accommodate the breaker strut. Note also the riveted heat shield aft of the engine jetpipe.

Left: The nose gear union with K2-105 wheels.

ual and hydraulic (emergency) feathering. Besides, the propeller design incorporates protective devices: a mechanism locking the blades at an intermediate pitch, three devices for locking the propeller at a definite pitch and a throttle valve in the coarse pitch channel. Locking the blades at an intermediate pitch lessens the negative thrust if an engine cuts and prevents negative thrust when the engine is running at low rpm.

A hydraulic pitch lock automatically locks the blades in the case of a stoppage in the feed of oil into the propeller, preventing the propeller from overspeeding. A mechanical lock serves as a backup at blade pitches ranging from 8° to 50°. A centrifugal mechanism locks the blade pitch when the propeller speed reaches 1,265 rpm. A throttle valve in the coarse pitch channel slows down the turning of the blades in the direction of off-loading the propeller, thus preventing an abrupt increase of a negative thrust in the case of the engine cutting. The automatic feathering system feathers the propellers if an engine fails when running at anywhere between 70% of the nominal power and take-off power, the power output suddenly drops to less than 10% of the nominal rating. When an engine cuts at a lower setting, the system does not come into action.

The engines are mounted in nacelles attached to the undersurface of the inner wings. They are carried on V-shaped truss-type bearers via vibration dampers; the mounting lugs are placed on the forward and centre casings. The engines are installed at a 2° nose-down angle in relation to the wing centre section chord; the distance between the engine's axis and the centreline is 3.95 m (13 ft). The ground clearance to the engine's axis is 3.17 m (10 ft 5 in) and the blade tip clearance is 1.22 m (4 ft).

Each engine is enclosed by a cowling which consists of a one-piece forward fairing incorporating the oil cooler, two upward-hinged side panels and a lower panel. The jet-pipes exit on the outer faces of the nacelles and are angled downward, with heat-resistant steel plates aft of them.

For self-contained engine starting and ground power supply the An-24A/B/V/T/TV have a Kazan' Machinery Design Bureau TG-16M APU installed in the rear portion of the starboard engine nacelle. The intake louvres and the exhaust are located on the starboard side of the nacelle. The APU consists of a 100-shp GTD-16 gas turbine and a GS-24A starter-generator driven via reduction gear. Maximum continuous power is 81.6 hp and rotor speed is 24,000 rpm.

The An-24RT and An-24RV aircraft have a Tumanskiy RU19A-300 APU/booster engine rated at 900 kgp (1,985 lb st). The RU19A-300 is an axial-flow turbojet with a seven-stage

The starboard AV-72 variable-pitch constant-speed propeller of an An-24. Note the electric de-icing strips on the inboard portions of the leading edges.

compressor, an annular combustion chamber, a single-stage turbine and a fixed-area jetpipe. It breathes via a fixed-area intake on the port side of the nacelle; the exhaust is located at the tip of the nacelle. The rear end of the nacelle hinges upwards, serving as a one-piece cowling. The APU/booster is installed in the rear portion of the starboard engine nacelle on a mount attached to the rear spar and to the undercarriage mounting truss.

Control system: Conventional mechanical dual control system with push-pull rods, control cranks and levers (everywhere except for the rudder control circuit where cables and rollers are used to transmit inputs from the rudder pedals). Cables and rollers are also used actuate the elevator trim tabs; the rudder and aileron trim tabs are electrically actuated. The control rods and cables are provided with pressure seals where they exit the pressure cabin. Gust locks are provided to prevent damage to the system by high winds while the aircraft is parked.

The system includes an AP-28L1D electric autopilot. The autopilot servos controlling the tail surfaces, ailerons and elevator trim tabs are connected to the control runs in parallel and may be disengaged pyrotechnically at the push of a button if they jam. The servos feature overriding clutches, allowing the pilots to take corrective action when the autopilot is engaged.

Roll control is provided by ailerons with an overall area of 6.12 m² (65.8 sq.ft); each aileron is built in two sections geared to each other. The ailerons have internal aerodynamic

balancing, hinge balancing (29%) and mass balancing (100%). Maximum deflection is +16/–24°. The inboard sections incorporate geared servo tabs with an overall area of 0.52 m² (5.6 sq.ft) and a maximum deflection of +14°30'/–9°30'. Additionally, the port inboard aileron section has a trim tab with an area of 0.26 m² (2.8 sq.ft) and a maximum deflection of ±15°.

Directional control is provided by a one-piece rudder a hinge balance of 30%. It features a trim tab with an area of 0.375 m² (4.0 sq.ft) and a servo tab with an area of 0.371 m² (4.0 sq.ft). Maximum deflection is ±25° for the rudder and ±20° for the trim tab and the servo tab.

Pitch control is provided by one-piece elevators with a hinge balance of 28%. Total elevator area is 5.16 m² (55.5 sq.ft) and maximum deflection is +15°/–30° (some sources say ±25°). Each elevator incorporates a trim tab having an area of 0.144 m² (1.55 sq.ft); the trim tabs can be deflected ±20°.

A curious feature of the pilots' workstations on the An-24 is the horizontally placed control columns of an unusual design ensuring maximum comfort for the pilot in the chosen flightdeck layout. The rudder pedals are geared to the nose gear steering mechanism and feature brake pedals.

Mounted between the pilots' seats is the central control pedestal accommodating the elevator trim tab handwheel, rudder and aileron trim tab control switches, the flap selector, an emergency wheel braking handle and the gust lock handle. It was possible to place a removable seat for the flight engineer behind the central control panel.

Fuel system: The An-24 *sans suffixe*, An-24A and some An-24Bs have four bag-type tanks (fuel cells) made of kerosene-proof rubber housed in special containers in the inner wings and integral tanks in the inboard sections of the outer wings giving a total capacity of 5,100-5,500 litres (1,122-1,210 Imp. gal.). Some An-24Bs passenger aircraft feature four extra bladder tanks in the wing centre section increasing total capacity to 6,180 litres (1,360 Imp. gal.); these are a standard fit on the An-24T/An-24RT.

The fuel tanks are divided into three groups. Group 1 comprises the inner wing bag tanks. Group 2 is the outer wing integral tanks, portions of which are set aside as service tanks and designated as Group 3. The tanks feature ETsN-14A electric centrifugal delivery pumps (*elektricheskiy tsentrobezhnyy nasos*) and BNK-104 transfer pumps.

Single-point pressure refuelling is provided; it is also possible to fill or top up the tanks via individual filler caps on the wings' upper surface. Normally the port and starboard engines' fuel systems are isolated, but a cross-feed valve enables either engine to draw fuel from any group of tanks. Fuel grades used are Russian T-1, TS-1 or T-2 jet fuel, Western Jet A-1, DERD.2494 and DERD.2498 (NATO F35 and F43) or equivalent.

Electrics: Three subsystems using 27V DC power, single-phase 115V/400Hz AC power and three-phase 36V/400Hz power.

Main DC power is supplied by two STG-18TMO engine-driven starter-generators. Backup DC power is provided by two 12SAM-28 lead-acid batteries. The main source of 115V AC power is two GO-16PCh8 generators (*ghenerahtor odnofahznyy*); emergency supply is provided by a PO-750 Srs II AC converter (*preobrazovahtel' odnofahznyy*). 36V AC power is supplied by two 1-kW PT-1000TsS converters (main and backup) and one PT-125Ts (*preobrazovahtel' tryokhfahznyy*).

An additional source of electric power is the APU (equipped with a TS-24A starter-generator) which can be started on the ground. On An-24RT and An-24RV aircraft the TG-16 is supplanted by the RU19A-300 APU provided with an electric generator. A ground power receptacle is provided on the starboard engine nacelle.

To ensure a high level of reliability, the An-24's electrical system makes use of special insulation for the busbars transmitting the current and for the distributing devices.

Hydraulics: Two systems (main and backup). The main hydraulic system operates the landing gear, flaps, wheel brakes, nose gear steering mechanism, windscreen wipers and the emergency engine shutdown cocks and propeller feathering actuators.

The main system is powered by two constant-capacity engine-driven hydraulic pumps; nominal pressure is 150 kg/cm² (2,140 psi). The emergency hydraulic system is actuated by a pump unit driven by an electric motor; it ensures the extension of flaps and the braking of the undercarriage wheels. When a cross-feed valve is opened, the emergency system operates all hydraulically-powered equipment. The nominal pressure in the emergency system is 160 kg/cm² (2,280 psi).

De-icing system: The wing and tail unit leading edges and engine air intakes are de-iced by hot air. The de-icing system utilises the micro-ejection principle; the air is bled from the engines' 10th compressor stage and ejected through exit gills at the wing, stabiliser and fin tips. The propeller blades and spinners, pitot heads, the flightdeck windscreen and the aircraft clocks have electric de-icing. An RIO-2 radio isotope ice detector (*radiatsionnyy indikahtor obledeneniya*) is installed on the port side of the nose.

Fire suppression system: For active prevention of a fire, the engines are provided with a fire suppression system which is controlled both manually and automatically. When the temperature in a vulnerable area rises critically or the rate of its growth exceeds a certain value, flame sensors automatically trigger the fire extinguisher bottles, firing the first shot. If this proves insufficient, the pilot can activate the second shot of fire extinguisher bottles. In case of need the bottles making up the inert gas pressurisation system can also discharge their contents into the fire suppression system.

Avionics and equipment: The An-24 is fully equipped for all-weather day/night operation, including automatic flight assisted by an autopilot and landing in poor visibility conditions.

a) Navigation and piloting equipment: The navigation suite includes an RPSN-2AN Emblema or RPSN-3N Groza-24 weather radar with a secondary traffic collision avoidance system (TCAS) function.

Early production aircraft were equipped with the SP-50M Materik instrument landing system which comprised the ARK-5 ADF (later superseded by the ARK-11), the MRP-56P marker beacon receiver, the KRP-F localiser receiver, the GRP-2 glideslope beacon receiver (both served by antennas hidden inside the radome) and the RV-2 radio altimeter. Late production aircraft had the Koors-MP ILS featuring more modern subsystems and an RSBN-2S Svod (Dome) short-range radio navigation (SHORAN) system with flush antennas built into the fin. Some An-24Vs were equipped with navigation system receivers of Western manufacture.

An-24T and An-24RT transport aircraft in Air Force service are equipped with the PDSP-2M theatre navigation system for bringing the aircraft to the designated drop zone.

The AP-28L1 electric autopilot ensures automatic flight along the orthodromic line or the loxodrome; switching over from one of these modes to the other can be effected without switching off the autopilot. It also ensured such operations as making turns, climbing and descending, automatic course correction at angles up to 120°, the possibility of switching off the elevator servos and switching the pitch control channel into manual mode – for instance, during landing approach. On initial production aircraft, prior to the completion of testing, the autopilot was put into operation while still lacking some elements – it was not yet fitted with the devices ensuring elevator trimming and automatic course correction in response to inputs from the course-setting device.

b) Communications equipment: The communications suite enables the crew to carry out two-way voice or telegraph communication with air traffic control centres or other aircraft. It features a short-wave comms radio comprising an R-836 Neon transmitter and a US-8K receiver, one RSB-5 **Gheliy** (Helium) or SVB-5) medium-wave radio and one or two RSIU-5B (R-802V) VHF command link radios. Machines intended for flights on international routes were equipped with the RSIU-5G VHF radio comprising a transceiver with a power supply unit, a control unit with a memory device, a monitoring unit and a complement of spare parts and tools. Aircraft intended for operations in the High North were equipped with the SVB-5 medium-wave radio.

An SPU-7 Series B intercom (*samolyotnoye peregovornoye oostroystvo*) and an SGU-15 public address system (*samolyotnoye gromkogovoryashcheye oostroystvo*) are provided for communication between crew members and crew-to-passengers communication.

c) IFF system: SRO-2 or SRO-2M Khrom (Chromium; NATO *Odd Rods*) IFF transponder (*samolyotnyy rahdiolokatsionnyy otvetchik* – 'aircraft-mounted radar responder'). The characteristic triple IFF aerials serving one of the wavebands are located ahead of the flightdeck glazing and under the aft fuselage. The aircraft also features an ATC transponder with aerials inside the radome.

d) Data recording equipment: MSRP-64B primary flight data recorder (FDR) (later replaced by an MSRP-12-96 FDR), K-3-63 backup FDR and MS-61B cockpit voice recorder (CVR).

e) Exterior lighting: Port (red) and starboard (green) navigation lights faired into the wingtips; white tail navigation light on the tail-cone. Retractable FRS-200 landing/taxi lights built into the outer wing leading edge under-side at mid-span. Red SPM-1 rotating anti-collision beacons (*samolyotnyy probleskovyy mayak*) under the centre fuselage (between frames 56-57) and built into the fin leading edge at the fin/dorsal fin junction; the lower beacon is enclosed by a teardrop fairing with a metal front end to protect it from flying stones.

Two EKSP-39 electric flare launchers (*elektricheskaya kasseta signahl'nykh patronov*) are fitted low on the starboard side of the nose between frames 1 and 2. Each launcher fires four 39-mm (1½-in) signal flares (red, green, yellow and white).

f) Flight instrumentation: The cockpit instrumentation comprised AGD-1 gyrohori-zons, directional gyros, gyro-flux gate and magnetic compasses (GIK-1, TsGV-4 and GPK-52AP), aircraft clocks, vertical speed indicators, main and back-up altimeter and airspeed indicators, engine control instru-ments and instruments for the control of all on-board systems. Most of the instruments on the captain's console were duplicated on the co-pilot's console.

Air conditioning and pressurisation system: The An-24 features a ventilation-type pressure cabin pressurised by engine bleed air to a pressure differential of 0.3 kg/cm² (4.28 psi). In cruise flight at 6,000 m (19,685 ft) the pressurisation system automatically maintains a cabin pressure equal to 2,140 m (7,020 ft) ASL.

The ACS cools the air tapped from the engine compressors in a cooling turbine, fil-ters and dries or humidifies it. The system maintains the preset air temperature in the pressurised cabin; it also caters for maintain-ing the purity of the air, ensuring that the air is changed 25 times during every flight hour.

The heating of the passenger cabin as based on the use of heat-radiating panels. Warm air supplied through lower distributing ducts is fed into the space between the heat insulation/sound-proofing panels and the inner cabin trim panels, heating the latter and thus the cabin. Then it passes into the cabin through outlets located near the ceiling. There is a convective system used for speed-ily warming up or cooling down the cabin; it supplies the air through ventilation ducts run-ning along the cabin walls. Some aircraft have passenger service units featuring individual ventilation nozzles. The air is discharged from the cabin through outlet valves of the pres-sure controller installed beneath the floor.

Oxygen equipment: The oxygen equip-ment is intended to ensure a short-term sup-ply of oxygen for the crew for the purpose of bringing the aircraft down to a safe altitude in the case of cabin depressurisation. In addi-tion, the aircraft is provided with portable breathing apparatus intended for those pas-sengers who might feel unwell in a normal flight.

Accommodation: The flightdeck of the An-24A/B/V/RV is configured for a crew of five (two pilots, a navigator, a flight engineer and a radio operator), albeit operations with a reduced crew are possible. Cabin layouts included an all-economy layout with 50 seats four-abreast at 75 cm (29½ in) pitch for the An-24A; 50-and 52-seat all-economy versions with a miserable 72 cm (28⅜ in) seat pitch, as well as a 48-seat all-economy layout and a 40-seat tourist class layout with a 84 cm (33 in) seat pitch for the An-24B. There are also sev-eral VIP configurations, including a 20-seat 'de luxe' version with three cabins (8+8+4) and a 32-seat version (28+4).

Basic specifications of the An-24T and An-24RT

	An-24V-II	An-24RT
Crew	2-5	2-5
Powerplant	2 x AI-24 Srs II	2 x AI-24T + 1 x RU19A-300
Take-off power/thrust	2 x 2,550 ehp	2 x 2,820 ehp + 900 kgp (1,985 lb st)
Propeller type	AV-72	AV-72T
Length overall	23.53 m (77 ft 2⅜ in)	23.53 m (77 ft 2⅜ in)
Height on ground	8.32 m (27 ft 3½ in)	8.32 m (27 ft 3½ in)
Wing span	29.2 m (95 ft 9½ in)	29.2 m (95 ft 9½ in)
Tailplane span	9.08 m (29 ft 9½ in)	9.08 m (29 ft 9½ in)
Wing area, m² (sq.ft)	74.98 (807)	74.98 (807)
Wheel track	7.9 m (25 ft 11 in)	7.9 m (25 ft 11 in)
Wheelbase, m (ft)	7.89 m (25 ft 10⅝ in)	7.89 m (25 ft 10⅝ in)
Empty weight, kg (lb)	13,300	14,060-14,650
	(29,320)	(31,000-32,300)*
Maximum take-off weight, kg (lb)	21,000 (46,300)	n.a.
Payload, kg (lb)	5,500/5,700 (12,125/12,570)†	5,700 (12,570)
Top speed, km/h (mph):		
at sea level	442 (275)	n.a.
at 6,000 m (19,680 ft)	485 (301)	n.a.
at 8,000 m (26,250 ft)	452 (281)	n.a.
Rate of climb, m/sec (ft/min)	1.9 (375)	3.4 (670)
Cruising speed at 6,000 m, km/h (mph)	450-500 (280-310)	450 (280)
Unstick speed, km/h (mph)	n.a.	180 (112)
Landing speed, km/h (mph)	165 (102)	175 (109)
Time to altitude, minutes:		
6,000 m (19,680 ft)	17.5	n.a.
8,100 m (26,580 ft)	45.2	n.a.
Service ceiling, m (ft)	9,000 (29,530)	9,000 (29,530)
Maximum ferry range, km (miles)	2,970 (1,846)	2,970 (1,846)
Range, km (miles)	2,400 (1,490)	425 (264) ‡
Take-off run, m (ft)	500 (1,640)	n.a.
Take-off distance to h=15 m (50 ft), m (ft)	870 (2,850)	n.a.
Landing run, m (ft)	590 (1,935)	540-580 (1,770 –1,900)
Landing distance from h=15 m (50 ft), m (ft)	1,130 (3,710)	n.a.
Cargo hatch dimensions, m (in)	1.1 x 1.2 (47¼ x 43⅜)	1.4 x 2.8 (55⅛ x 110¼)
Maximum dimensions of cargoes, m (in)	n.a.	1.1 x 1.5 x 2.6 (43 x 59 x 102)
Capacity of the overhead hoist, kg (lb)	none	1,500 (3,300)
Capacity of the roller conveyor, kg (lb)	none	4,500 (9,920)
Cargo hold dimensions: length		15.68 m (51 ft 5⅜ in)
width		2.17 m (7 ft 1½ in)
height		1.765 m (5 ft 9½ in)
Number of seats (passenger configuration)	50	38
Number of stretcher cases (medevac configuration)	none	24
Number of sitting patients	none	37
Number of medical attendants	none	1

Different sources give different figures; † In passenger and cargo configuration respectively; ‡ With maximum payload

The An-26 in Detail

Since the An-26 was heavily based on the An-24 airframe, only the differing design details are described here as appropriate.

Fuselage: Basically similar to that of the An-24 but manufactured in four sections, with an additional production break at frame 33. Fuselage frames 2, 3, 5, 6, 15, 16, 21, 22, 34-39 and 44 are reinforced.

The *forward fuselage (Section F1)* differs in having a large hemispherical observation/bomb-aiming blister measuring 700 mm (27½ in) in diameter on the port side for the navigator between frames 5-6. A plug-type entry door measuring 0.6 x 1.4 m (1 ft 11⅞ in x 4 ft 7⅛ in) between frames 7-9 replaces the baggage/cargo door of the An-24, opening inwards and aft. A rectangular escape hatch measuring 1.155 x 0.7 m (3 ft 9½ in x 2 ft 3½ in) with a forward-hinged cover is located ventrally between frames 7-10; the cover is opened by two hydraulic rams to double as a slipstream deflector.

The *centre fuselage (Section F2)* accommodates the cargo hold, which continues all the way to frame 40, and has less than half the An-24's number of cabin windows. Four hardpoints for BD3-34 pylons are provided between frames 15-16 and 21-22.

The *aft fuselage* (it has no separate 'Section F' number) is the so-called hatch section. It is cut away from below, featuring six formers (Nos. 34-39) which rest on hefty beams flanking the cut-out. The latter is the cargo hatch. The cargo hatch aperture located between frames 33-40 has a length of 3.4 m (11 ft 2 in), its maximum width between frames 33-36 being 2.4 m (7 ft 10½ in). Further aft it tapers off symmetrically to 2.1 m (6 ft 10⅝ in) at frame 40 which is the rear pressure bulkhead.

The opening is closed by a cargo ramp. When it is fully closed, the sides of the rear fuselage 'droop' beyond the underside of the ramp, forming long shallow strakes. The ramp is actuated by the aircraft's hydraulic system which includes a manual plunger pump ensuring the ramp's operation when the engines were shut down and there was no ground power supply. The ramp is controlled from the navigator's station or from a special panel at the aft end of the cargo hold to port.

The cargo ramp can be opened in two ways, depending on the type of cargo handling operations in hand. In one position it hinges down conventionally to serve as a ramp for vehicle loading. Alternatively, the ramp can be lowered and slid forward under the centre fuselage to permit loading cargoes directly from a truck bed or paradropping troops, cargoes or vehicles. In so doing the front end of the ramp travels along a track on the fuselage centreline running all the way to frame 23, while the centre portion supports slide along hinged guide rails housed in fairings flanking the cargo hatch threshold.

The cargo hold measures 11.10 x 2.78 x 1.91 m (36 ft 5 in x 9 ft 1½ in x 6 ft 3 in) excluding the cargo ramp (frames 7-33), or 15.68 x 2.78 x 1.91 m (51 ft 5⅝ in x 9 ft 1½ in x 6 ft 3 in) with the cargo ramp. Cargo hold volume 60 m³ (2,120 cu.ft). With the aircraft empty, the threshold of the cargo hold is 1.45 m (4 ft 9 in) above the ground and the upper edge of the cargo hatch opening is 3.014 m (9 ft 10⅝ in) above the ground.

The unpressurised *rear fuselage (Section F3)* is likewise new and flattened from below to permit vehicle access; the above-mentioned strakes continue almost all the way aft, forming 'fangs' in cross-section. Frames 43 and 45 and mount the tail surfaces. The rear fuselage incorporates an avionics bay with a ventral access hatch between frames 42-43.

Wings: As for An-24s built from Batch 26 onwards (with wide-chord inner wings and simple slotted inner wing flaps.

Tail unit: Basically as for the An-24 but horizontal tail span increased to 9.973 m (32 ft 8⅝ in); horizontal tail chord 2.783 m (9 ft 1½ in) at the root and 1.13 m (3 ft 8½ in) at the tip, aspect ratio 5.0, taper 2.46. Vertical tail height

Above and below: The forward fuselage of the An-26 differs structurally from that of the An-24 in having an oval entry door on the starboard side, a port side observation/sighting blister and a ventral escape hatch.

4.90 m (16 ft 1 in), chord 3.90 m (12 ft 9½ in) at the root and 1.561 m (5 ft 1½ in) at the tip, taper 2.5, aspect ratio 1.81; sweepback at quarter chord stated as 21°73'.

Landing gear: As for An-24, except that the main gear units have 1,050 x 400 mm (41⁵⁄₁₆ x 15¾ in) KT-157 wheels.

Powerplant: Two AI-24VT engines with a take-off rating of 2,820 ehp and a cruise rating of 1,650 ehp, driving AV-72T propellers, plus one RU19A-300 booster/APU. The turbo-props' power increase was achieved by increasing the EPR to 6.40 and the mass flow to 14.4 kg/sec (31.7 lb/sec). At 1,070°K, the turbine temperature is actually lower than on previous versions, and the SFC is reduced to 0.256 kg·hp/hr (0.56 lb·hp/hr) at take-off rating and 0.239 kg·hp/hr (0.52 lb·hp/hr) in cruise mode. Engine speed is 14,050 rpm at ground idle and 15,800 rpm at all operational settings.

The AI-24VT engines retain their take-off rating in ambient temperatures of up to +30°C (86°F). The permitted percentage of hours logged by the engines at nominal power in relation to the overall engine life is as high as 40%, making it possible to operate the aircraft at high take-off weights. In addition, permitted continuous operating time at maximum power is 1.5 hours, which makes it possible to enhance the powerplant's output in the case of an engine failure.

Control system: Basically as for An-24, except that the rudder is controlled by rigid push-pull rods, too. The aircraft is equipped with an AP-28P1 electric autopilot designed to ensure automatic stabilisation and control of the aircraft following a predetermined flight path.

Fuel system: Basically as for the An-24 but with ten bag-type tanks in the inner wings instead of eight. The fuel load is 5,500 kg (12,130 lb), distributed as follows: 2,580 kg (5,689 lb) in Group 1; 1,865 kg (4,112 lb) in Group 2; and 1,055 kg (2,326 lb) in Group 3. An **inert gas pressurisation system** is provided to lessen the risk of a fire and explosion in an accident, in the event of the aircraft straying into a thunderstorm – or if the aircraft is hit by enemy fire. As the fuel is used up, the empty tanks are pressurised with carbon dioxide.

Avionics and equipment: The aircraft was provided with a compete suite of highly reliable communications/radio navigation equipment and flight instrumentation. The equipment is multiply redundant. The avionics fit enables the aircraft to operate on domestic and international air routes round

Above: Civil An-26s lack the small IFF antenna blisters just aft of the radome characteristic of Air Force examples. Note the twin EKSP-39 signal flare launchers and the RIO-2 icing detector below them.

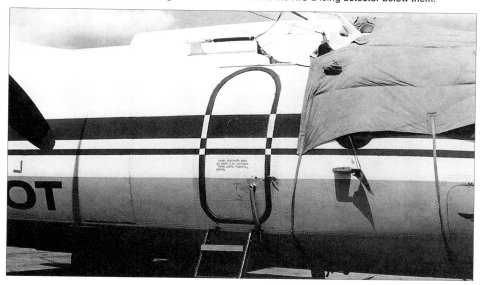
Above: The forward fuselage of An-26ASLK CCCP-26642 featuring a non-standard dorsal strake aerial. Note the improvised anti-theft lock on the entry door.

The rear fuselage of An-26 '02 Red' (c/n 1208) at Moscow-Tushino, showing the cargo ramp actuator/guide rail fairings, the ventral strakes and the reduced number of windows.

View into the An-26's cargo hold from the lowered cargo ramp. Note the rail for the overhead hoist and the tip-up seats along the sides of the hold.

The cargo ramp can be slid forward under the fuselage for loading containers etc. In this case a support is placed under the rear fuselage, passing through a door in the edge of the ramp. Note the ramp guide rails.

communications, as well as communication within the crew; to execute a landing in adverse weather conditions and at night; to scan the ground below for navigation purposes; to determine the true altitude, radio bearing, drift angle and ground speed; to warn the pilots about storm activity or intensive turbulence; and perform pinpoint paradropping, using targets with a distinct radar signature or beacons as a reference. Among other things, the aircraft is equipped with an R-836 Mikron short-wave radio, an R-802B *Baklan* (Cormorant) VHF radio, an SPU-7 intercom, an ARK-7 or ARK-15M ADF, an RV-4 radio altimeter, an RSBN-2S SHORAN, a PDSP-2S precision paradropping system and a Groza-26 radar (Thunderstorm-26, pronounced *grozah*); early production aircraft had an RPSN-3N radar.

The exterior lighting of military An-24s includes orange formation lights and small blue lights built into the undersides of the wings, stabilisers and rear fuselage. The latter are identification lights for cooperation with friendly forces on the ground (for instance, during supply operations).

Accommodation and transportation/ paradropping equipment: The An-26 is equipped with a full range of cargo handling devices and equipment for loading, unloading and paradropping vehicles, troops and cargo.

As already mentioned, the aft fuselage incorporates a unique dual-mode cargo ramp/door which can be opened conventionally, allowing motor vehicles weighing up to 1,300 kg (2,870 lb) to be driven aboard. Vehicles that are not self-propelled can be hauled aboard by means of an external tractor, a long cable and a system of pulleys, one of which is attached to the vehicle and the other two rigidly installed on the cargo hold floor at frames 10 and 22. Special flooring and wheel chocks are used in this case.

For lifting items of cargo from the ground or from a truck-bed and arranging them in the cargo cabin the An-26 is equipped with an overhead hoist. This consists of an LPG-250/500T or BL-56 winch installed at frame 28 and a carriage with a hook which travels along a monorail mounted on the cabin ceiling between frames 29-39. The electrically powered hoist can also be driven manually. As the designation implies, the selectable LPG-250/500T has a traction force of either 250 or 500 kgf (550 or 1,100 lbf), but a system of pulleys increased the lifting capacity of the hoist – originally to 1,500 kg (3,310 lb).

Tip-up seats equipped with seat belts are installed along the cargo hold walls as standard; so are 'traffic lights' and a siren for initiating the drop sequence. In paratroop

the clock and in adverse weather conditions. Among other things, the An-26 is equipped with the GMK-TG compass system and the Privod-ANE-1 command and navigation system.

The main flight instruments and engine/systems control instruments are similar to those of the An-24. Inputs to membrane and aneroid instruments are supplied by two PVD-7 pitot tubes (PVD = *preeyomnik vozdooshnovo davleniya* – air pressure sensor) and one PPD-1 pitot. The power supply of membrane and aneroid instruments is duplicated.

The An-26's avionics make it possible to maintain two-way air-to-ground and air-to-air configuration the cargo hold is rigged with static line attachment cables running from frame 11 to frame 38, and static line catchers are fitted on the insides of the ventral strakes. A jumpmaster's seat and a safety barrier are installed at frame 33.

The version configured for paradropping materiel has a P-147 chain drive conveyor built into the cargo hold floor; it enables mechanised dropping of palletised cargo and equipment items with a total weight of up to 4,550 kg (10,030 lb). It also makes it possible to mechanise loading and unloading operations. The conveyor is powered by twin electric motors, with a backup manual drive from a handcrank.

The cargo is tied down by means of special devices, including a set of detachable tie-down cleats (28 single units and 20 twin cleats), 30 tie-down belts and four tightening belts, two cargo nets and turnbuckles. The tie-down cleats are screwed into special sockets closed by plastic plugs when the cleats are not in place.

Electrics: Basically as for An-24, except that the voltage of the DC subsystem is increased to 28V, a slightly different model of generator (GO-16PCh48) supplies single-phase 115V/400 Hz AC, and the back-up source of three-phase 36V/400 Hz AC is a TS-310S04A transformer whose primary coil is fed by the starboard GO-16PCh48 AC generator.

Hydraulics: Basically as for An-24, except that the main hydraulic system is also responsible for operating the ventral escape hatch, the cargo ramp with its complex opening sequence and the APU's compressor bleed valve; it has a marginally higher nominal pressure of 155+5 kg/cm² (2,214+71 psi) and includes a manually operated pump as a further back-up source of pressure. This pump ensures the opening/closing/sliding of the cargo ramp with its associated locks and refills the hydraulic tank.

The emergency system is modified to ensure emergency actuation of the cargo ramp when the main system or the engines are inoperative. In case of need the emergency system pump can be included into the main system and used for operating the devices fed by the main system.

Fire suppression system: As for An-24.

De-icing system: As for An-24.

Oxygen system: The oxygen system is used for providing oxygen to the crew and to persons accompanying the cargo and accommodated in the cargo hold. The crew is provided with five KP-24MT breathing appa-

Loading a crate by means of the overhead hoist. Note the 'traffic lights' for paratroopers in the upper right-hand corner and the static line catchers on the insides of the ventral strakes just visible at the top.

A Polish-built Nysa 522 minibus is driven into the cargo hold. Lots of these minibuses were supplied to the Soviet Union in the 1960s and 1970s.

ratus (*kislorodnyy pribor*), two KP-21s and five KP-23 parachute-type oxygen masks.

Air conditioning and pressurisation system: As for An-24.

Armament: In case of need the aircraft can be fitted with four BD3-34 racks on the centre fuselage sides between frames 15-16 and 21-22 for use as an auxiliary bomber. The racks can carry bombs up to 500 kg (1,102 lb) calibre. For bomb-aiming and pinpoint paradropping an NKPB-7 night-capable collimator bomb sight (*nochnoy kollimahtornyy pritsel bombardirovochnyy*) is installed inside the port side blister.

Changes in the design of production An-26s

As the manufacture of production An-26s progressed, improvements were introduced into the transport's design. For example, starting with c/n 0801 (identity unknown), production An-26s featured an alteration in the ventral crew escape hatch actuation system. The emergency hydraulic system working the crew escape hatch by means of an electric pump and an electromagnetic valve was brought into play by just one shuttle valve. Previously two shuttle valves had been used, the higher complexity increasing the likelihood of a malfunction.

Starting with c/n 0901 (identity unknown), a reduction valve, a synchronisation valve, a throttle valve and a backflow cut-off valve were installed in the hydraulic circuit controlling the longitudinal movement of the cargo ramp during its stowage under the fuselage. The new features lessened the pressure fluctuations in this hydraulic circuits and ensured a shock-free opening and closing of the ramp.

An-26s from c/n 0903 (identity unknown) onwards had 1,050 x 400 mm (41⁵⁄₁₆ x 15¾ in) KT-157 wheels with low-pressure tyres on the main undercarriage units; previously stock An-24 mainwheels measuring 900 x 300 mm (35⁷⁄₁₆ x 11¹³⁄₁₆ in) had been used. This alteration gave the aircraft soft-field capability; the required specific runway strength was reduced from 7 kg/cm² (100.0 lb/sq.in) to 5 kg/cm² (71.4 lb/sq.in). With the new wheels the aircraft was allowed to operate at a weight of 24 tons (52,920 lb) when performing take-offs and landings on unpaved airfields; in contrast, the operating weight of aircraft using the older KT-94/2A wheels was restricted to 21 tons (46,300 lb).

From Batch 11 onwards the navigator's port side blister was provided with a fairing giving it a teardrop shape to reduce drag.

Electric control of the cargo ramp's lateral locks was introduced on Batch 13, starting with c/n 1301 (identity unknown), a development aircraft operated by LII. Previously these locks were actuated by the main or backup hydraulic system or by the hand-driven pump. The new design of the locks was both simpler and lighter.

Top left: The An-26's tail unit is basically similar to that of the An-24, except for the larger vertical tail area and stabiliser span (because of the wider rear fuselage). Early Soviet Air Force An-26s, like '02 Red' (c/n 1208), were delivered with a red-painted fin top.

Left. The rear portion of the starboard nacelle hinges upwards to expose the RU19A-300 booster almost completely. Early An-26s had an An-24RV-style intake on the inboard face of the nacelle, replaced by a dorsal intake on later aircraft.

Above: The starboard engine nacelle and main landing gear of An-26 '02 Red' (c/n 1208) Note the larger mainwheels and the nozzle of the RU19A-300.

Improvements in the design of the cargo tie-down belts and of their wedge locks were effected to An-26 c/n 2101 (which was then an uncoded grey-painted aircraft in Soviet Air Force insignia) in response to demands from service units. These alterations were subsequently introduced on the production line in Kiev.

Starting with An-26 c/n 2407 (identity unknown), the original PSBN-3N radar gave way to the new Groza-26 weather radar. The Groza radar family was developed at the end of the 1960s specially for the needs of commercial aviation. Unlike their predecessors created some 20 years earlier, these radar were able to determine more clearly the boundaries and intensity of storm fronts; in addition, they possessed greater accuracy in determining the coordinates of objects and were more reliable. The introduction of these avionics was welcomed by aircrews in the Air Force and in Aeroflot.

An-26 c/n 3401 (identity unknown) introduced a new reinforced cross-bar for the overhead cargo hoist featuring the LPG-250/500T or BL-56 winch. Now the loading and unloading of cargo items weighing up to 2 tons (4,410 lb) could be mechanised; up to and including An-26 CCCP-26560 (c/n

57303310) this capability had been restricted to a weight of 1.5 tons (3,300 lb). The new device used Model 29-9471-400 belts made of tough Capron (Nylon-6) as cargo slings; their fastening was also changed. (Until then, cheaper Model 24-9400-400 belts had been used.)

By the time An-26 c/n 3801 (presumably CCCP-26567) was built, changes had already been made to the forward section of the starboard engine nacelle (ie, aft of the engine firewall). The modified nacelle incorporated a variable-area dorsal air intake for the RU19A-300 booster/APU closed by an aft-hinged

The fairing of the high-powered retractable light serving for phototheodolite measurements on the An-26ASLK. Note the cover protecting the retracted light on the ground.

An-26B CCCP-26212 (c/n 14401) operated by the Kazan' Aero Engine Production Association (KMPO) on final approach. Note the lack of the port side blister characteristic of the civil version.

An-26 specifications

Powerplant	2 x AI-24VT + 1 x RU19A-300
Take-off rating	2 x 2,820 ehp + 900 kgp (1,984 lb st)
Length overall	23.8 m (78 ft 1 in)
Height on ground*	8.585 m (28 ft 2 in)
Static ground angle*	–0°40'
Wing span	29.2 m (95 ft 9½ in)
Wing area, m² (sq.ft)	74.98 (807)
Wing loading, kg/m² (lb/sq.ft)	320 (65.5)
Empty weight, kg (lb)	15,550-16,914 (34,288-37,295) †
Take-off weight, kg (lb):	
normal	23,000 (50,715)
maximum	24,230 (53,427)
Fuel load, kg (lb)	5,500/7,080 (12,127/15,610)
Payload, kg (lb)	5,500 (12,127)
Speed, km/h (mph):	
maximum	540 (336)
cruising	435-480 (270-298)
Rate of climb at sea level, m/sec (ft/min)	9.2 (1,811)
Service ceiling, m (ft)	7,500 (24,600) ‡
Range with maximum payload, km (miles)	1,100 (684)
Ferrying range, km (miles)	2,700 (1,678)

* empty aircraft

† Different documents give different figures

‡ For early production aircraft documents quote the figure of 9,000 m (29,530 ft)

door. An access panel was added on the lower part of the nacelle, and the port side featured a hatch for access to the APU's fuel filter. On early production An-26s up to and including c/n 3710 (identity unknown) the mounting hatches for the APU had been cut out in the upper and lower parts of the nacelle, and a flush fixed-area air intake had been located in the port side of the nacelle. At the same time changes were made in the coupling of the duct which supplied hot air to the de-icing system of the APU (the coupling was made telescopic), and the design of this unit was simplified. This feature was used not only on all the subsequent An-26s but also on late-production An-24s.

Starting with An-26 CCCP-26505 (c/n 3901), more dependable valves were installed in the hydraulic system. From c/n 4501 (identity unknown) onwards the caps of the landing gear retraction slide valve in the emergency gear extension mechanism were provided with a stencil reading, 'Caution! Undercarriage retraction button'. (Before that, there had been cases when the undercarriage retracted of its own accord or was retracted by mistake on a parked aircraft.)

Chapter 4

Big Head Antonov

An-24FK photo mapping aircraft prototype

The most notable specialised version of the An-24 was the An-24FK prototype intended for topographic aerial photography (FK = *fotokartograficheskiy* – photo mapping, used attributively). Design work on this version was entrusted to the Taganrog-based Beriyev OKB which was then headed by Aleksey K. Konstantinov. Previously this design team had been engaged exclusively in the design of water-borne aircraft.

Work on the photo mapping derivative of the An-24 began in the summer of 1966. The new aircraft was based on the airframe of the late-production An-24B which entered production in the second half of that year – ie, the version with wide-chord inner wings and single-slotted inboard flaps.

The An-24FK differed from the baseline model primarily in having an all-new forward fuselage ahead of the production break at frame 11, which became its main recognition feature. The entire fuselage nose where the radome used to be was extensively glazed, evoking reminiscences of the Boeing B-29 and the early Soviet post-war airliners. This 'verandah' provided accommodation for the navigator and housed equipment enabling

the aircraft to precisely follow the stipulated route with the piloting both in manual and automatic mode. Placed behind an oblique optically flat front glazing panel was an optical sight intended for determining the point for starting the photography and for monitoring the precision of maintaining the prescribed route.

All this required so much space that the flightdeck had to be raised by 410 mm (1 ft 4⅛ in) in comparison with the An-24, giving the An-24FK a distinctive 'big head' *à la* Boeing 747. The passageway to the navigator's station was on the starboard side under the flightdeck floor; even a person of rather short stature almost had to crawl on all fours to get there, as one of the authors discovered! The radio operator and the flight engineer sat in the first cabin immediately aft of, and slightly below, the elevated flightdeck; further aft, behind a partition with a door, was a cabin housing the mission equipment which featured five camera windows in the floor.

Each camera window was a fairly complex design. Its main element was a transparent panel made of special optical glass with a high degree of precision. The biggest glass

panel (in the camera window No.1) measured 890 x 865 x 40 mm (35 x 34 x 1⁹⁄₁₆ in), the actual transparency measuring 810 x 785 mm (31⅞ x 30¹⁵⁄₁₆ in). The smallest glass panels were in camera windows No.4 and No.5; they measured 340 x 340 x 30 mm (13⅜ x 13⅜ x 1³⁄₁₆ in), the actual transparency being 280 x 280 mm (11 x 11 in). Attachment fittings for the camera window transparencies ensured perfect sealing, the damping of vibrations and elimination of any additional stresses affecting the glass panels.

All camera windows were closed with covers which protected the glass panels during take-off/landing/taxying and in the course of the flight, when the cameras were switched off. The Nos. 1, 2 and 3 camera windows placed in tandem on the fuselage centreline were closed by a single large sliding metal cover; placed symmetrically further aft of it were the Nos. 4 and 5 camera windows with individual covers. The considerable size of the glass panels' attachment fittings and of the sliding cover mechanisms necessitated placing all this in special angular fairings standing proud of the flattened fuselage underside.

The 'Mother of All Tadpoles', the An-24FK prototype converted from An-24B (presumably CCCP-46797; c/n 57302003). Here the aircraft is seen in its original guise. Note the full An-24 style complement of cabin windows and the pitot probes mounted ahead of the flightdeck windscreen.

Above: The An-24FK at a later stage of the tests; the civil registration has been removed (although the CCCP- prefix still remains) and the tactical code '91 Red' has been applied on the nose.

Above and below: An-30 CCCP-30030 (c/n 0605) in 1973-standard Aeroflot colours at the 1975 Paris Air Show with the exhibit code 363. The aircraft belonged to the Ukrainian CAD/Kiev UAD/86th Flight.

The aerial camera complement could include four or five stationary cameras which were placed on the TAU-M topographic mounts (*topogra**fich**eskaya aero[**foto**]usta-**nov**ka*). The first three cameras were mounted vertically and were intended for mapping photography. The cameras placed above the Nos. 4 and 5 windows were angled out at 28° to both sides and were intended for oblique photography of the localities. One of these cameras could be replaced by an additional optical sight.

In addition to cameras and their control panels, the second fuselage compartment housed the power supply system, storage lockers for a supply of film cassettes, part of the navigation suite, comfortable seats for off-duty crew members who might wish to have a rest, a food closet with Thermos bottles and workstations for two operators of the mission equipment. The aft end of the compartment was formed by a sealed bulkhead (frame 40) which had a hatch for access to the unpressurised tail section of the fuselage.

Since the extreme nose was occupied by the navigator's workstation and by numerous items of additional equipment, the designers had to sacrifice the radar. On the other hand, the aircraft obtained other items of additional navigational equipment. One of them was the DISS-013-24FK Doppler navigator which was capable of indicating the true speed of the aircraft relative to the ground and had a degree of precision far superior to the previously used aerodynamic means of measurement.

The main items of the aircraft's equipment were the AFA-42/100 and AFA-54/50 aerial cameras (AFA = *aerofotoapparaht* – aerial camera). (Note: On Soviet aerial cameras the

numerator figure refers to the camera type and the denominator figure shows the lens's focal length in centimetres.) These cameras could be used for photography from altitudes between 2,000 and 7,000 m (6,560 and 22,970 ft), the scale of the photographs being within the range between 1:200,000 and 1:15,000,000. The aircraft was provided with one AFA-42 camera mounted above the camera window No.1 and an additional three or four AFA-54 cameras mounted above the other camera windows.

The aircraft's powerplant comprised two AI-24VT turboprops with a take-off rating of 2,820 ehp, and the RU19A-300 APU.

The prototype An-24FK was converted from a late-production An-24A built in 1965 (probably CCCP-46797; c/n 57302003). (Note: While the c/n is confirmed, the registration is not: however, CCCP-46797 is in sequence for this c/n.) The conversion took place at the experimental aircraft plant No.49 (the prototype construction shop of the Beriyev OKB) which manufactured a new 'head' and grafted it onto the 'body' of the airliner. Quite possibly the aircraft gained a new c/n (0101) after conversion.

Still wearing its basic pre-1973 standard An-24 colour scheme but sporting only the CCCP- prefix, the An-24FK took to the air for the first time on 21st August 1967 with test pilot I. E. Davydov in the captain's seat. Subsequently, wearing the tactical code '91 Red' (which again, as in the case of the 'An-24T Mk I', was painted on the forward fuselage) but still retaining the Soviet flag and prefix, the machine was submitted for State acceptance trials. These were held by GK NII VVS and GosNII GA, lasting a fairly long time. (The fact

Above: An-30 CCCP-30067 (c/n 1208) belonged to the Leningrad CAD/2nd Leningrad UAD/70th Flight based at Leningrad-Rzhevka. It was used in the Gyunesh scientific experiment of 1984.

that the State acceptance trials were held in parallel by a military and a civil organisation, may explain the prototype's 'identity crisis'.) The report on the results of flight testing the aircraft's photographic equipment was endorsed in March 1968, and in 1970 the State Acceptance trials were completed at long last. Redesignated An-30, the aircraft entered series production at the Kiev factory in 1971.

An-30 photo mapping aircraft (An-30A or An-30, version 'A')

A complete set of documents for the series manufacture of the An-30 (the so-called version 'A' for use in the Civil Aviation system)

was prepared at the Kiev Machinery Plant under the direction of V. A. Garvardt. Between 1971 and 1980 KiAPO, which was still manufacturing the An-24 and its versions in parallel, turned out 123 production An-30s for aerial photography in different versions. Batch 2 consisted of two aircraft, batches 3 and 4 had five each; subsequent batches consisted of ten aircraft, except for the 16th and final batch which had just one aircraft.

Outwardly production aircraft differed from the An-24FK prototype in having fewer windows (1+1+1+1+door to port and 1+door+1+1+1 to starboard); in contrast, the prototype had a full set of windows and exits inherited from the passenger machine.

An air-to-air shot of another Kiev-based An-30, CCCP-30022 (c/n 0404), showing the wide-chord inner wings. The unusually large Soviet flag on the tail is noteworthy.

Above: One of the very first production An-30s illustrates the pre-1973 livery originally applied to the type.
Below: This 'toad's eye view' illustrates the An-30's extensively glazed nose (dubbed 'verandah' – with good reason).

The first production An-30 with the An-24 style registration CCCP-46632 (c/n 0201) was used for certification tests at GosNII GA which ended in April 1974. However, in late 1974 a production An-30, CCCP-30028 (c/n 0510), was fitted out with test equipment for GosNII GA for holding an additional series of tests.

Most An-30s were completed in civilian configuration known as 'version A' or An-30A. (The nose titles, however, invariably read simply 'An-30'.) Of these, the biggest proportion (65 aircraft) was delivered to the Ministry of Civil Aviation, ie, Aeroflot. Six An-30s were obtained by other Soviet civil organisations.

Eighteen An-30As were purpose-built for export. China became the biggest foreign recipient, purchasing seven machines of this type, including the very last An-30 built (registration number 883 (with no B- nationality prefix), c/n 1601). Among the countries of Eastern Europe it was Bulgaria, Romania and Czechoslovakia that bought this dedicated photo mapping aircraft. Later, a few examples of the An-30 in both export and standard configuration were delivered to Vietnam, Afghanistan, Mongolia and certain other countries, reportedly including some African nations. The equipment complement was negotiated individually in each case.

Like the An-24T, production An-30s in both civil and military versions could be fitted with BD3-34 bomb racks, but initially they were not used in practice. As series manufacture progressed, the aircraft's design was subjected to the same alterations that were introduced into the design of the baseline An-24 (in particular, changes were made to the installation, mounting hatches and air intake of the RU19A-300 APU/booster).

In 1975 a freshly completed An-30 with the registration CCCP-30030 (c/n 0605) was shown for the first time at the Paris Air Show with the exhibit code 363. After this the An-30 received the NATO reporting name *Clank*.

Operational service revealed that the decision to relinquish the onboard radar was a mistake. Hence some An-30As were retrofitted with the Groza-M30 radar; its antenna was housed in a small teardrop fairing under the nose, part of which was attached to the nosewheel well doors.

Above: On most production An30s the pitots were relocated to a position low on the nose glazing frame.

Above: The Myachkovo United Air Detachment of the Central Regions Civil Aviation Detachment was the first Aeroflot detachment to include a specialised An-30 flight. Among other examples of the type, it operated CCCP-30042 (c/n 0901) depicted here. The Myachkovo UAD has since become a specialised aerial work operator called Myachkovo Air Services; the Russian version of the name – Myachkovskiye Aviauslugi – abbreviates to something that sounds like 'mouse'!

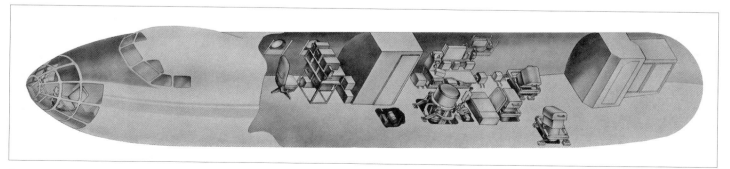

A cutaway drawing showing the location of the cameras, their controls and film storage lockers inside the An-30's cabin.

Above: Caught by the camera on short finals to Zhukovskiy, this Soviet Air Force An-30 B coded '86 Red' (c/n 0806) is operated by the Flight Research Institute (LII) and equipped with special equipment pods of unknown purpose (possibly housing a SLAR). '07 Red' (c/n 0405) was identically equipped.

This radar-equipped Russian Air Force An-30B with the out-of-sequence registration RA-30078 (c/n 0507) in basic Aeroflot colours is one of several used for Open Skies monitoring flights. It is seen here at its home base, Kubinka AB, on 8th August 1997. Note the red-painted spinner tips.

Above: Most An-30Bs delivered to the Soviet Air Force, including '06 Red', were finished in this An-26 style overall medium grey colour scheme. The forward location of the tactical code is noteworthy.

This radar-equipped Russian Air Force An-30B ('87 Red', c/n 0807) photographed at Kubinka AB on 8th August 2002 is equipped with two BD3-34 bomb racks on the fuselage sides for fitting Veyer IRCM flare dispenser pods.

The first production An-30 (c/n 0201) wore the non-standard An-24 style registration CCCP-46632 (so did the second production aircraft, c/n 0202, which was CCCP-46633). This aircraft was involved in the State acceptance trials programme.

An-30B photo mapping aircraft (An-30 version 'B')

The Soviet Air Force received 26 An-30s built as 'version B' (An-30B) which differed mainly in avionics fit (IFF, radio altimeters, communications radios etc.). For example, civil An-30s were equipped with two Landysh (Lily of the valley) radios which were absent on the military machines. The An-30Bs were usually painted light grey overall and wore full military markings; only a few were quasi-civil.

Another peculiarity of the An-30B was that it had provisions for passive infra-red countermeasures (IRCM). When An-30s engaged in combat operations in Angola and Afghanistan, man-portable air defence systems (MANPADS), such as the famous Stinger, posed a distinct threat to these aircraft. Therefore a decision was taken to retrofit most of the machines belonging to the Air Force with IRCM chaff/flare dispensers. At first, two **Veyer** (Fan) chaff/flare dispenser pods with 192 26-mm (1.02-in.) PPI-26 magnesium flares each were mounted on BD3-34 bomb racks on the centre fuselage; unlike the An-24T/An-24RT and An-26, the An-30 always carried only two such pylons at frames 21-22. The slab-sided pods had a teardrop shape in side view, and the name was obviously derived from the fact that the flares shot out in a fanlike spread.

However, the bulky pods not only led to a reduction of speed and range but also adversely affected directional stability during the photo run. To eliminate this shortcoming some machines were fitted with conformal side IRCM packs, each housing six standard UV-26 (ASO-2B) dispensers, to give a total of 384 decoy flares. (ASO = *avtomaht sbrosa otrazhahteley* – automatic chaff/flare dispenser; PPI = *peeropatron infrakrahsnyy* – infra-red [countermeasures] cartridge.) The upgrade was performed by the Soviet Air Force's aircraft overhaul plant No.308 at Ivanovo-Severnyy AB in central Russia.

The Soviet troops in Afghanistan operated three An-30Bs; these machines coded '04 Red', '16 Red' and '17 Red' were taken from various 'non-combatant' units of the Air Force and placed on the strength of the previously mentioned 50th OSAP. This made it possible to relieve the tactical aviation reconnaissance aircraft of some of the tasks that would entail wasteful use of available forces and means. Yet, the 'aerial survey aircraft' were never regarded as a universal substitute for the MiGs, Sukhoi and Yakovlev aircraft, if only because the An-30s were unarmed and their crews could not promptly deal a strike against the discovered enemy objectives before the combat aircraft or helicopters with landing parties arrived on the scene. (Speaking of which, the Yak-28R reconnaissance aircraft used on the Afghan theatre of operations was scathingly nicknamed **goloob' meera** (Dove of peace) because it was likewise unarmed.)

It took some time to arrive at a rational distribution of the workload between the combat reconnaissance aircraft and the aerial photography aircraft. The range of the An-30 crews' main tasks took shape gradually. On the Afghan TO the An-30Bs fulfilled the following missions:
- visual observation;
- guiding combat aircraft to targets in the course of large-scale operations and to targets discovered during visual reconnaissance by the An-30B crews (ie, 'attacks by request');
- photographing the areas designated for bombing and attack raids and for artillery or rocket strikes prior to and after the strike (post-attack reconnaissance);
- photographing the localities for disembarkation of helicopter-borne landing parties when preparing the 'combing' of some areas and other operations;
- photographing large areas and aerial photography along certain 'axes' for the purpose of revealing unknown targets or for the corroboration of information obtained from other sources concerning the positions, movement routes, fortified areas, strongholds and locations of various weapon elements of the Mujahideen forces;
- photographing roads and the adjoining localities during troop movements, and later, when preparations for the Soviet withdrawal from Afghanistan started, for the purpose of

discovering enemy concentrations, localities suitable for ambush operations, and also for determining alternative routes for the movement of troops and military vehicles if the main routes have to be given up;

- locating downed aircraft during search and rescue operations, etc.

The An-30B's undisputed advantage was its reasonably long range of 2,600 km (1,620 miles) at altitudes above 6,000 m (19,680 ft). Thanks to this the An-30B, operating from Kabul International airport, could reach any area in Afghanistan, fulfil its mission and return to base where just 40 minutes later specialists of the information processing section started deciphering the aerial photos. Endurance at the altitude of 6,000 m was 6 hours 10 minutes. Bearing in mind that before 1985 up to 40% of the flying time logged by the crew of a photo survey aircraft was used up by visual observation and independent search, these capabilities were a decisive factor in choosing the tasks to be tackled by the An-30Bs.

One more advantage was that virtually all members of the crew could perform visual observation. Nothing beats the proverbial Mk 1 eyeball, and an extra set of eyeballs is always welcome. The cabin glazing and camera windows afforded a view practically in all directions. Each crew member had his own designated field of view. Binoculars were always available on board, making it possible to get a detailed view of an object that had attracted attention. The aircraft's cruising speed was only half as much as that of reconnaissance versions of fighter aircraft; this increased the time available for a thorough visual examination of the locality overflown by the aircraft and for identifying the objects presenting an intelligence interest. This obviated the need for repeat passes over the targets (involving the danger of being fired upon) and gave a certain tactical advantage.

Despite its not very impressive power-to-weight ratio, the An-30B possessed reasonably good manoeuvrability. With the flaps set for landing (38°) and with 45-60° bank the turn radius was 500-300 m (1,640-980 ft). When performing aerial photography in a gorge without a through passage this property of the aircraft enabled the crew to return safely to base.

Aerial cameras were the only 'weapons' of the An-30B. Initially the aircraft was equipped with one AFA-42/100 mounted above the No.1 camera window and three AFA-54/50 cameras in a standard arrangement (one for vertical photography and two for oblique photography). However, these cameras and the A-72 long-range operations (LOROP) camera that was added later had two important shortcomings. One of them was a limitation as to the minimum altitude from which they could

Above: Ukrainian Air Force An-30B '81 Yellow' (c/n 0609) belongs to the Blakytna Stezha ('Blue Patrol' in Ukrainian) squadron based at Kiev-Borispol'. It is one of two used by the UAF for Open Skies flights.

be used (1,500 m/4,920 ft for the AFA-54/0 and 2,100 m/6,890 ft for the A-72) which was due to image shift at speeds over 300 km/h (186 mph), and to the fact that overlapping of the pictures became impossible below a certain altitude. The other shortcoming consisted in the insufficient width of the photographed area as related to the altitude (0.3H for the AFA-42/100, 0.6H for one AFA-54/50 and 0.45H for the A-72). Taking all this into consideration, a decision was taken to use the proven AFA-42/20 camera which was free from these limitations. Its range of operational altitudes included low altitudes at which the width of the photographed area was equal to the altitude multiplied by 1.5. A possible mistake in choosing the direction towards the object to be photographed was adequately compensated by the width of the photographed area which was 5 times greater as compared to the AFA42/100. However, as early as the beginning of 1984 the An-30B crews had to revert to the original camera

complement because they were compelled to raise the minimum altitude for photography in connection with more effective anti-aircraft weapons becoming available to the enemy. In 1986, when the Mujahideen came into possession of a large number of Stinger shoulder-launched anti-aircraft missiles, the photo surveyors' minimum flight altitude above the average locality plane reached 4,000 m (13,120 ft); from the spring of 1987 onwards it was further raised to 5,000 m (16,400 ft), and subsequently it became still greater.

As mentioned earlier, to provide protection against MANPADS the An-30B was fitted with ASO-2B chaff/flare dispenser packs, each containing 384 decoy flares. The main control panel for the ASO-2B was placed at the radio operator's workstation. Every crew member was allotted a definite field of view for the purpose of detecting a missile attack in time. Decoy flares were fired during take-off and landing, when the low-flying aircraft was vulnerable, in the course of flying over areas

One more Open Skies aircraft, the Czech Air Force's one-of-a-kind An-30FG upgrade ('1107 Black', c/n 1107), wears appropriate markings on the tail. Note the '80 Years of the Czechoslovak Air Force' nose titles.

Above: Five An-30s belonging to the Myachkovo UAD, including RA-30075 (c/n 1306), were converted to the An-30D *Sibiryak* long-range version equipped with external fuel tanks.

Above: The An-30Ds wore the red/white Polar colour scheme and *Sibiryak* badges.

where anti-aircraft missile launches were likely, or after an actual launch was discovered; in such cases the decoy flares were fired at six-second or two-second intervals, depending on the flight altitude.

The An-30B was also widely used in peacetime. In particular, in the 1990s such aircraft were used by Russia, the Ukraine and the Czech Republic for monitoring the military activities of other states which had signed the Open Skies Treaty in 1992 (within the framework of the first stage of the Treaty). In the second half of 1995 a special base was set up at Kubinka AB near Moscow; it had several An-30Bs on strength, including '04 Black' (c/n 0704), '87 Red' (c/n 0807) and RA-30078 (c/n 0507). In accordance with the abovementioned Treaty, during the first stage of its implementation a monitoring aircraft could be fitted with only one camera (two cameras, according to some sources); for monitoring flights during the second stage of the Treaty's

implementation (three years after the Treaty's coming into force) monitoring devices of the following categories could be used:

- optical aerial cameras for single-frame and panoramic photography with a resolution not higher than 25 cm (about 10 in) in terms of the size of objects discernible in the photos of localities;
- TV cameras with the same resolution;
- SLAR with a resolution not higher than 5 m (16 ft 6 in) in terms of the size of discernible objects on locality photos;
- infra-red line scanners with a resolution not higher than 50 cm (about 20 in).

The Open Skies Treaty contained strict provisions governing the procedure of planning and implementing the monitoring flights for all nations which were parties to the Treaty. A calendar schedule of flights over each country had to be agreed upon not later than three months prior to the commencement of the flights. Not later than 72 hours prior to the

scheduled time of arrival at the entry point the monitoring party was to inform the country to be monitored about its intention to perform a monitoring flight in accordance with the previously agreed schedule. The party to be monitored was free to choose whose aircraft – its own or an aircraft belonging to the monitoring party – would be used for the flight.

Not later than 24 hours before the commencement of a given monitoring flight the monitoring party informed representatives of the country to be monitored about the exact route and flight profile for further approval. These representatives checked whether the route was planned in conformity with the provisions of the Treaty. If not, they could suggest an alternative route so as to preclude the possibility of turning a legitimate monitoring flight into a spy mission. This additional agreement of the route was to be completed within eight hours.

As a rule, the An-30Bs chosen for performing the Open Skies mission during Stage 1 were equipped with two identical cameras (AFA-41/10s, AFA-41/20s or AFA-42/20s). The use of monitoring equipment was sanctioned only after an international verifying procedure had been completed, and the characteristics and employment modes of the devices became known to all participant nations. In fact, one of the An-30Bs involved ('04 Black') now sports a sticker on the nose reading 'Certified Open Skies aircraft'.

The installation of new navigation equipment, onboard computer and visual orientation instruments enabled the aircraft to maintain the prescribed route and the stipulated altitude with a high degree of precision. The An-30Bs participating in the Open Skies programme were fitted with the following navigation and radio equipment: an A-723 long-range radio navigation (LORAN) system, an RSBN-2S Svod SHORAN system, a TNL-100 satellite navigation system (GPS) receiver, an RV-18Zh high-range radio altimeter, an RV-UM low-range radio altimeter, a VMF-50 altimeter calibrated in feet, an ARK-11 ADF, a DISS-013-24FK Doppler speed/drift meter, a Groza-M30 weather radar, an SD-75 distance measuring equipment (DME), a Koors-MP-70 automatic approach/landing system working with VOR/ILS radio beacons, and an SO-72M international ATC/SIF transponder.

The An-30B's mission equipment had the following characteristics.

The AFA-41/10 aerial camera had an MRO-2 lens with a focal length of 100 mm and an aperture ratio of 1:8; effective shutter speeds were 1/500, 1/250, 1/120 and 1/60 of a second. The frame size was 18 x 18 cm (7 x 7 in); the resolution was 43 lines/mm in the centre and 11 lines/mm peripherally. The camera had a central shutter. The minimum operating altitude was 1,700 m (5,580 ft); the maximum interval between exposures was 90 seconds, the minimum interval being 2.25 seconds. The film cassette contained a film roll of 60 or 120 m (197 or 394 ft). The camera's weight was 49 kg (108 lb).

The AFA-41/20 had an ORION-20 lens with a focal length of 200 mm and an aperture ratio of 1:63; 1:8; 1:11; 1:16; effective shutter speeds were 1/500, 1/250, 1/120 and 1/60 of a second. The frame size was 18 x 18 cm (7 x 7 in); the resolution was 47 lines/mm in the centre and 20 lines/mm peripherally. A central shutter was used. The minimum operating altitude was 4,500 m (14,765 ft); the maximum interval between exposures was 90 seconds, the minimum interval being 2.25 seconds. The film cassette contained a film roll of 60 or 120 m (197 or 394 ft).

The AFA-54/50 had a RADON-1 lens with a focal length of 500 mm and an aperture ratio of 1:5; 1:5.71; 1:7.2; 1:9; 1:11.4; 1:14; effective shutter speeds were 1/800, 1/640, 1/250, 1/160 and 1/100 of a second. The frame size was 30 x 30 cm (11¹³⁄₁₆ x 11¹³⁄₁₆ in); the resolution was 28 lines/mm in the centre and 12 lines/mm peripherally. A baffle shutter was used. The minimum operating altitude was 5,200 m (17,060 ft); the maximum and minimum interval between exposures was 90 and 2.25 seconds respectively. The film cassette contained a film roll of 60 or 120 m (197 or 394 ft); the camera's weight was 325 kg (717 lb).

An-30B with SLAR
In the late 1980s two Soviet Air Force An-30Bs coded '07 Red' (c/n 0405) and '86 Red' (c/n 0806) were equipped with an unidentified SLAR of West German origin. The SLAR antenna arrays were housed in compact cylindrical pods on the lower centre fuselage sides; the pylons were of a different type than hitherto, with small elongated bulges on the fuselage sides immediately above them. '07 Red' and '86 Red' operated from the LII airfield in Zhukovskiy.

An-30D *Sibiryak* photo mapping aircraft
In 1990 an extended-range version of the An-30 was developed; it was designated An-30D (dahl'niy – long-range) and unofficially dubbed *Sibiryak* ('inhabitant of Siberia'). The aircraft was immediately recognisable by two streamlined external fuel tanks (of the same type as on the An-26D) scabbed onto the centre fuselage sides; this increased endurance to more than nine hours. Additionally, the aircraft wore the red/white Polar version of Aeroflot's 1973-standard livery and appropriate 'An-30D' nose titles plus 'Sibiryak' badges.

Five aircraft registered CCCP-30053 (c/n 1008), CCCP-30059 (c/n 1108), CCCP-30063 (c/n 1202), CCCP-30068 (c/n 1202) and CCCP-30075 (c/n 1306) were converted to this configuration; all five belonged to the

Central Regions CAD/Myachkovo UAD based at Myachkovo airfield near Moscow.

The An-30D was intended for patrolling the 200-mile maritime economic zone, guiding ship convoys in ice-fields, performing ice reconnaissance and for spotting fish shoals and sea animals. The An-30D's mission equipment included the Kvitok-2 LORAN (*kvitok* is a colloquial form of the word kvitahntsiya – receipt), a medium-wave radio and a data link system for transmitting pictures showing the ice situation. The aerial cameras enabled the crew to obtain photographic evidence showing a ship that was trespassing in the 200-mile zone or any other object of interest; the pictures were accompanied with the data showing geographical references, date and time of the event. The An-30D carried a set of rescue equipment on board.

An-30FG photo mapping aircraft
In 1990 the Czechoslovak Air Force acquired An-30 (presumably An-30A) LZ-AEG (c/n 1107) from the Bulgarian charter airline Hemus Air; the aircraft was properly serialled '1107 Black'. When Czechoslovakia disintegrated into two states – the Czech Republic and Slovakia, the sole An-30 remained with the Czech Air Force and was later used by the Czechs in the 'Open Skies' programme. It was retrofitted locally with a Western weather radar in a larger fairing with a hemispherical front end. The aircraft was designated An-30FG by the Czechs.

An-30M (An-30 *Meteozashchita*) meteorological protection aircraft
In the mid-1980s several Aeroflot An-30s equipped with the Groza-M30 radar were converted into a version designated An-30 *Meteozashchita* or An-30M (*meteozashchita*

means 'meteorological protection'). The No.2 camera window was turned into an outlet for a device intended for discharging granulated carbon dioxide (known colloquially as 'dry ice'); the latter was housed in eight heat-insulated containers in the cabin, each of which held 130 kg (290 lb). Two Veyer chaff/flare dispenser pods loaded with PV-26 silver iodide cartridges were carried on BD3-34 racks.

The aircraft's mission was to protect a given area from rainfall by causing rains in the adjoining areas, thereby preventing the rain clouds from entering the protected zone, or to avert an impending hailstorm which could do great damage (especially to crops). A local discharge of a large amount of carbon dioxide into the atmosphere caused the temperature to fall, and microscopic particles of silver iodide became the centres of concentration to which moisture clung, turning into raindrops. One gram of silver iodide produced on average one billion raindrops.

The 'sky cleaner' aircraft were primarily intended for ensuring good weather for conducting especially urgent and important tests of aircraft; in actual fact, however, they were mostly used in connection with various public events of a cultural character, including the MAKS aerospace exhibitions in Zhukovskiy.

The An-30M had a TOW of 22,100 kg (48,730 lb) and an operational speed of 300-350 km/h (186-218 mph); maximum endurance in operational mode was 4 hours 30 minutes at the altitude of 3,000 m (9,840 ft) and 5 hours 20 minutes at 6,000 m (19,680 ft).

An-30R chemical and radiation reconnaissance aircraft
A production An-30s operated by the Central Regions CAD/Myachkovo UAD (CCCP-30055, c/n 1101) was converted into a chemical and

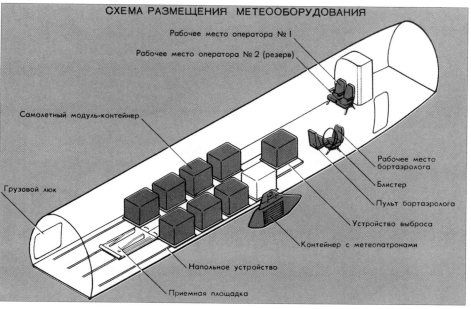

This diagram shows the An-30M's interior layout with granulated carbon dioxide containers along the cabin walls, the forward loading device, the centrally-mounted discharge device and the external flare packs.

Above: Front view of the An-30M 'sky cleaner' aircraft, showing the radar, external flare packs and the observation blister in the rearmost window.

Close-up of the port Veyer pod loaded with PV-26 silver iodide flares for making rain. The pods are carried on BD3-34 pylons; note how the pylons partly obscure the Aeroflot titles.

radiation reconnaissance aircraft similar to the An-24RR in the wake of the Chernobyl' nuclear disaster. Designated An-30R, it carried an identical pylon-mounted sensor pod on the port side (which was later removed) and two standard RR8311-100 radiation sampling canisters on shackles on the forward fuselage sides. Both the sensor pod and the port sampling canister were located further aft

than on the An-24RR, resulting in a staggered arrangement of the canisters. The cabin housed equipment for analysing the content of radionucleids in the outside air.

Another An-30R lacking the port side sensor pod is operated by the Russian Air Force. Registered 30080 (c/n unknown) and painted in an all-white colour scheme, this aircraft based near St. Petersburg was seconded to

the United Nations Peace Forces in 1996. This aircraft carried only one air sampling canister on the port side, while the starboard shackle was reserved for what was reportedly a huge flare bomb.

An-30 navigation systems testbed

Several An-30s were used by different organisations as flying testbeds and research aircraft. One of them was a grey-painted ex-Russian Air Force example coded '07 Red' (c/n 0405) which belonged to the Gromov Flight Research Institute (LII). Based at Zhukovskiy, the aircraft was used for testing new navigation systems (more exactly, the so-called correlation-type navigation systems for extreme conditions) between 1982 and 1994. The results of these tests were used for the introduction of theses navigation systems on military aircraft and for evolving the methods of testing such systems.

An-30 research aircraft (Institute of Cosmic Studies of Natural Resources)

A photo circulated by the TASS news agency in July 1981 depicted an Aeroflot (Leningrad CAD/2nd Leningrad UAD/70th Flight) An-30 registered CCCP-30067 (c/n 1208) which was described as a 'flying laboratory' (ie, research aircraft) belonging to the Institute of Cosmic Studies of Natural Resources, a division of the USSR Academy of Sciences. According to TASS, this institute was the main participant of an Industrial-Scientific Association for Cosmic Studies established under the auspices of the Academy of Sciences of Azerbaijan (then a Soviet Republic).

Presumably it was this aircraft that later took part in two so-called aerocosmic experiments involving airborne and space-based means of sampling and survey – the **Chornoye More** (Black Sea) experiment of 1983 and the *Gyunesh* (Azerbaijani for 'sun') experiment of 1984. These experiments also involved three other aircraft – an An-2, an Il'yushin IL-14 and a Mil' Mi-8 helicopter, as well as the Salyut-7 space station. They were based on correlation of data obtained simultaneously by satellites and airborne sensors. The An-30 flying laboratory used in the Gyunesh experiment was equipped with a thermal imaging device, an infra-red spectrometric suite and a VHF radiometric suite, including an East German Zeiss Ikon MKF-6M multi-spectrum aerial camera.

An-30 geophysical survey aircraft

According to a press report which appeared in 1983, a production An-30 (presumably an An-30A) was fitted with infra-red instruments for prospecting natural resources. It was used with the participation of the *Aerogheologiya* (Aerogeology) Industrial Association for studying the geological properties of rocks. It may well be the same aircraft as described above (infrared devices are mentioned in both cases).

An-30D (modified) geological prospecting aircraft

Interestingly, in 1994 An-30D RA-30053 was outfitted for off-shore oil prospecting in Norway. It was leased for this purpose by Conoco (Continental Oil Co.), operating from Kristiansund-Kvernverket airport. Outwardly the aircraft's new role was revealed by a slender wire-braced boom tipped with a sensor array protruding aft from the tailcone.

An-30 survey aircraft (Institute of Atmospheric Optics)

At the end of the 1990s an unidentified An-30 was converted into a research aircraft by the Institute of Atmospheric Optics of the Russian Academy of Sciences' Siberian Division. The institute was developing optical methods of analysing environment conditions. One of these methods involved the use of a laser locater, dubbed 'lidar' by the Russian researchers. Such a laser locater was installed on the An-30. Among other things, it could be used for spotting fish shoals for the benefit of the fishing industry.

The laser locater was also capable of measuring the degree of transparency of the upper layers of the sea amenable to quickly changing their optical properties. Exactly such measurements were conducted by the Institute with the help of the An-30 in the North Sea areas off the coasts of Scotland at the invitation of Defence Evaluation and Research Agency (DERA) of Great Britain. A published photo of this aircraft shows it has strap-on fuselage tanks – presumably this is a suitably modified An-30D.

Above: Close-up of the forward fuselage of An-30R RA-30055 (c/n 1101) radiation monitoring aircraft. Note the staggered arrangement of the air sampling canisters.

An-30-100 (An-30A-100, An-30 VIP) passenger/VIP aircraft

This is a passenger or VIP conversion of the An-30 undertaken by Aircraft Repair Plant No.410 in Kiev, the Ukraine. The refurbished cabin provides accommodation for 34 passengers with the same degree of comfort as on purpose-built airliners. Extra windows with square-shaped external reinforcement plates around them are added to provide better lighting.

The cabin is equipped with an air conditioning system catering for a comfortable microclimate during intermediate stops at airports, and with a toilet. Different layouts of the passenger cabin are offered. In case of need the aircraft can be reconverted to the aerial photography configuration.

Among the versions offered there are various VIP layouts seating up to 20 passengers; they feature, among other things, two toilets, two snack-bars with warm food, extra windows and additional emergency exits.

Conversion of An-30s to passenger/VIP configuration was authorised by resolution No.30/446-99 signed by the Ukrainian State Aviation Administration and the Antonov Aviation Scientific & Technical Complex (ANTK imeni Antonova) on 22nd July 1999. The specification for such a conversion was formulated in 2000. Shortly afterwards An-30A UR-30044 (c/n 0906) was converted into the first An-30A-100 for use by the Kiev City Administration. The aircraft has a 20-seat interior with a rigid bulkhead at frame 19 dividing the rear VIP cabin from the business class cabin for the retinue.

Wearing the full livery of ARP 410 Airlines, the flying division of Aircraft Repair Plant No.410, and the Kiev city crest on the nose, UR-30044 was in the static park at the MAKS-2001 airshow (14-19th August 2001). This aircraft is operated by the Kiev City Administration. UR-30000 (c/n 1401), another ARP 410 Airlines aircraft, was the second An-30 to be converted, becoming the first An-30A-100.

Front view of the An-30M. Following operational use over the Chernobyl nuclear power station the aircraft had to be withdrawn from use at Moscow-Myachkovo due to permanent radioactive contamination.

Above and below: Pictured at Gromovo AB, Russia, this quasi-civil Russian Air Force An-30R (30080) was seconded to the United Nations Peace Forces sometime before 1996. Note the flare bomb on the starboard shackle.

Chapter 5

'The Indian Order'

Prototype An-32 military transport

The An-24 and An-26 were widely exported and enjoyed a good reputation. By the early 1970s GSOKB-473 had established a strong partnership with India, a nation which became one of the OKB's standing customers. In particular, the Indian Air Force successfully operated the An-12 military transport. In the mid-1970s the need arose to replace the IAF's many US-built Fairchild C-119 Flying Boxcar piston-engined light transports which were getting long in the tooth. The Government of India announced an international competition for a state-of-the-art tactical transport aircraft for the IAF.

However, in actual fact the competition was a mere formality. According to some sources, Indira Gandhi, the then Prime-Minister of India, had decided to give this order to the Soviet Union from the outset. This decision was undoubtedly influenced not only by her friendship with Leonid Brezhnev, the Soviet leader, but also by the very successful use of the An-12s in the Indo-Pakistani border conflict of 1971.

The specifications outlined by India said, among other things, that the aircraft should be capable of operating from airfields situated up to 4,500 m (14,765 ft) above sea level in ambient temperatures up to +50°C (122°F).

Above: The Hindu belief about soul transition applies to aeroplanes as well, eh? Here is An-26 CCCP-83966 No.1 (c/n 1006) tucking up its undercarriage...

The An-26 was a very attractive replacement for the C-119 but it could not meet these specifications. Not wishing to lose a potentially very lucrative order, the specialists of the Antonov OKB suggested developing a derivative of the proven An-26 featuring a new powerplant of greater output. The Ivchenko AI-20D turboprop was chosen to power the An-32, as the new transport aircraft aimed at the Indian market was designated. This engine merits a few words.

The AI-20D had originally been designed with a view to installing it in the An-8 transport instead of the existing AI-20A engines. Without making any major changes to the design, the engineers of A. G. Ivchenko's OKB-478 succeeded in boosting the take-off rating of the AI-20D to 5,180 ehp from the 4,000 ehp of the AI-20A Srs 3 by means of simple adjustment. Subsequently the AI-20D was built in series for the An-8 and the Beriyev Be-12 amphibian. Now a new version of the engine,

...and look at it now! Yes, this is the same aircraft following conversion into the prototype of the An-32 developed for the Indian Air Force. The redesigned high-set engine nacelles and the enlarged ventral strakes are obvious. Note that a fairing has been added to the navigator's blister.

Above and below: An-32 CCCP-83966 No.1 cruises in the vicinity of Kiev during an early test flight. Note the so-called *ledoboy* ('ice smasher') – the fixed inverted leading edge slat on the tailplane designed to prevent icing (its shadow can be seen on the fuselage strake) – and the exhaust-blackened tailplanes.

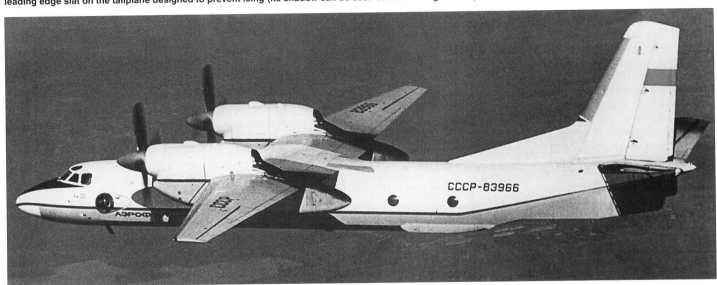

The prototype at a later stage, featuring the extended curved engine jetpipes adopted for the production model. Noted the repositioned landing lights on the sides of the nose, the bolder 'An-32' titles and the lack of a registration (the prototype was in the process of being reregistered CCCP-46961 at the time).

Above: Another view of the first prototype taxiing along a grass strip at Kiev-Gostomel'. Even at this low power the engines can be seen to emit a conspicuous smoke trail.

the AI-20D Srs 5 or AI-20DM, was created specially for the An-32; it featured alterations to the mounting lugs and relocated engine accessories.

This is where the Antonov engineers started running into problems, with the result that the An-32's outlook changed appreciably by comparison with its precursor. Firstly, the AV-72T propellers of 3.9 m (12 ft 9½ in) diameter used on the An-26 could not absorb the much higher power output, and a decision was taken to use larger propellers. The AV-68 four-blade constant-speed propeller was a logical choice, as this propeller developed by the Stoopino Machinery Design Bureau had been used successfully with the AI-20 on other aircraft types. For the An-32, however, a new version designated AV-68DM was developed, featuring a diameter increased from the usual 4.5 m (14 ft 9⅛ in) to 4.7 m (15 ft 5 in).

Secondly, the new engines were much larger and heavier than the AI-24VT; the AI-20D's external dimensions were 3,097 x 842 x 1,180 mm (10 ft 2 in x 2 ft 9⅛ in x 3 ft 10½ in) versus 2,345 x 677 x 1,075 mm (7 ft 8⅜ in x 2 ft 2⅜ in x 3 ft 6⅜ in), and dry weight was 1,080 kg (2,380 lb) versus 600 kg (1,320 lb). Thus an attempt to retain the An-26's engine placement ahead of and just below the wing leading edge would have provoked an unacceptable forward shift of the aircraft's CG. Besides, if the position of the engine axis was retained the blade tip clearance would have been reduced to a mere 0.82 m (2 ft 8¼ in), which increased the risk of damage by flying stones on dirt strips.

The solution was obvious, if not very elegant. Since the new engines would have necessitated a redesign of the engine nacelles anyway, the bulky AI-20Ds were moved up and aft to a position above the wings, the engine jetpipes pointing straight aft instead of being angled outwards and down. The lower fairing of the nacelle incorporating the oil cooler was reshaped, the finished result looking not dissimilar to the 'Andy Gump' nacelles of the Boeing B-50 Superfortress bomber. Thus the objective was attained without resorting to a radical redesign of the basic airframe. Since the new engines offered nearly twice the power of the AI-24VT, the RU19A-300 jet booster was no longer needed, and the An-32 reverted to the TG-16 APU located in the rear portion of the starboard nacelle which was borrowed completely from the An-24B.

Thirdly, the higher thrust line, combined with the much greater engine power, created a much stronger pitch-down force; also, the more powerful engines created stronger yaw in the case of asymmetric thrust. To compensate for this the designers increased the area of the vertical tail by inserting a 100-mm (4-in) 'plug' at the root; the horizontal tail area was also enlarged by increasing the stabiliser span by 225 mm (8⅞ in).

The first prototype in intermediate configuration in flight. The *ledoboy* has been replaced by conventional hot air de-icers and the tailplanes painted black to make the soot less conspicuous (see also page 87).

Above: The first prototype An-32 wearing the exhibit code 342 with which it was displayed at the 1977 Paris Air Show.

Below: A diagram showing the operational modes of the An-32's cargo ramp. Note the small hinged pressure door at the top and the hinged fairing aft of the ramp to provide an unbroken surface when the ramp is closed.

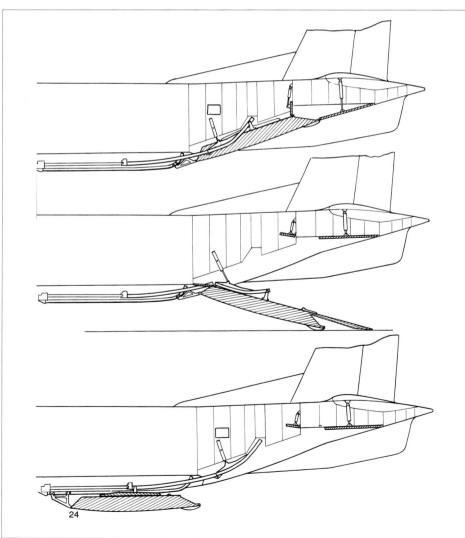

The wing high-lift devices also underwent a radical redesign: the single-slotted inner wing flaps used previously gave way to triple-slotted flaps (the double-slotted flaps outboard of the engine nacelles were retained). As the reader remembers, earlier the Antonov OKB had traded the An-24B's double-slotted flaps for single-slotted ones for the sake of structural simplicity. Now, however, the engineers had to complicate things due to the need to ensure maximum lift in the rarefied air of the mountain regions where the An-32 was to operate. The reputed Soviet (Russian) design philosophy is 'make it simple, make it strong, but make it work'; well, what's the point of keeping it simple if the darn thing doesn't work?

Finally, the vortex problem encountered on the An-26 (and cured by installing strakes on the aft fuselage sides) grew more acute on the An-32 with its stronger propeller wash. Same problem, same cure: to maintain directional stability and avoid excessive drag the downward-pointing strakes flanking the cargo hatch were substantially enlarged and recontoured. Of course, the airframe structure was suitably reinforced, and larger wheels with low-pressure tyres were fitted to the main gear units.

Otherwise, the An-32 had few external differences from the usual An-26. However, the avionics and equipment were revised. The main difference consisted in the use of the KN-32 avionics suite comprising a LORAN system, the DISS-013-26Sh Doppler speed and drift indicator, an air data system, the Groza radar and other items of equipment. The radio equipment came to include the Mikron short-wave radio and the RV-15M *Reper* (Benchmark; pronounced like the English word 'repair') radar altimeter which had been designed for fourth-generation combat aircraft. (Later the aircraft was fitted with the Western Omega LORAN system.)

Like the An-26, the An-32 featured an NKPB-7 optical bombsight for determining the point of paradropping, solving navigation tasks and dropping ordnance from the four BD3-34 bomb racks. The external fuselage hardpoints could be used for carrying up to four paradroppable containers weighing up to 500 kg (1,102 lb) apiece. The aircraft could also carry bombs of the 50- to 100-kg (110 to 220-lb) calibre, including SAB-100 flare bombs (*svetyashchaya aviabomba*). To increase the ferry range, provision was made for installing a 4,500-litre (990 Imp. gal) ferry tank in the cargo hold. In all, more than 40% of the aircraft's systems were renewed or replaced by new ones.

The first prototype An-32 was manufactured by converting an early-production An-26 with the non-standard registration CCCP-83966 (c/n 1006), retaining this registration. (As a point of interest, this registration was subsequently reused for the first prototype An-72 STOL tactical transport, formerly registered CCCP-19774.) The first post-conversion flight – the An-32's maiden flight – took place on 9th July 1976, and as early as 1977 the prototype was shown at the 31st Paris Air Show, wearing the exhibit code 342. This time the latest Soviet transport attracted much interest on the part of aviation experts and the military who were quick to sense its potential. The NATO reporting name allocated to the An-32 was *Cline*.

Curiously, the Western aeronautical press published three-view drawings of the first prototype An-32 showing a pronounced dogtooth on the outer wing leading edge at about half-span. In fact, this was a misconception caused by slightly different shades of metal at the production break between the inner and outer portions of the detachable outer wings

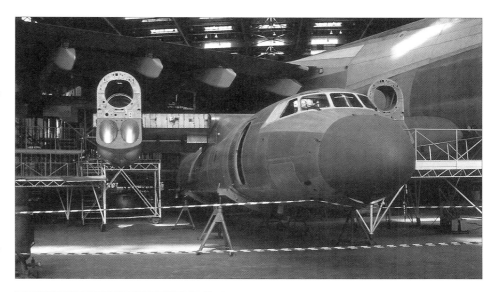

Top: A 35% complete An-32 airframe trestled in the final assembly shop of the Aviant factory at Kiev-Svyatoshino in 2000. The aircraft is dwarfed by the last An-124 Ruslan (f/n 03-03) still awaiting completion as of this writing.

Above: The second prototype (first pre-production) An-32 with the non-standard registration CCCP-380122 (c/n 001) built in 1982 was the first example to be painted in 1973-standard colours.

Below: The third prototype (second pre-production) An-32, CCCP-380322 (c/n 003), was used for paradropping tests. Note the cine camera 'egg' ahead of the cargo ramp to record load separation.

Above: Indian Air Force An-32 K2754, coded 'N'; interestingly, the code is carried both on the tail and the fuselage. Note that the red outline around the emergency exit suggests it is much larger than it really is.

which someone mistook for a dogtooth; no An-32 ever featured a wing dogtooth.

Initially the first prototype featured inverted fixed leading-edge slats on the horizontal tail (they can be seen on early photos of this machine). This design feature developed and patented by the Antonov OKB was the so-called *ledoboy* (lit. 'ice smasher') organising the airflow in such a way as to preclude stabiliser icing. Eventually, however, the engineers decided to leave well enough alone and CCCP-83966 No.1 reverted to hot air de-icing on the stabilisers. Still, the *ledoboy* did find use on the tiny An-28 feederliner.

This was not the only design change to be incorporated during trials. Soon after the beginning of flight tests the engine nacelles, which originally were cut away from above immediately after the engine jetpipes, were altered to feature long gently curving exhaust pipes running all the way to the tips of the nacelles à la IL-18. This feature was incorporated on all subsequent examples.

In 1982 the first prototype was joined by two prototypes, or maybe rather pre-production aircraft – the first of many to be manufactured at Kiev-Svyatoshino. They were registered CCCP-380122 (later CCCP-21508 No.1, c/n 001 – ie, Batch 0, 01st aircraft in the batch) and CCCP-380322 (later CCCP-21132 No.1, c/n 003). The highly unusual six-digit registrations encountered on some Antonov development aircraft are explained as follows. The first and the last digits correspond to the aircraft type: 3+2 = An-32; cf. An-74 CCCP-780334 and An-71 CCCP-780151. (However, this does not work with all Antonov types; cf. An-124 CCCP-680125 and An-225 CCCP-480182!) The meaning of the second digit, which is always an 8, remains unknown; this may be a code for the OKB's experimental shop. The next two are the sequence number of the airframe built: CCCP-380122 is No.1 and CCCP-380322 is No.3 (it is presumed that the second new-build An-32 airframe, c/n 002, was used for static tests). Finally, the last-but-one digit shows the year of manufacture (2 = 1982).

The testing of the An-32 was conducted very thoroughly and lasted for a fairly long time because of development work and the subsequent certification of the machine. The Indians watched the testing with a keen interest. The An-32's productivity in hot-and-high conditions proved to be 50% higher and the transportation costs were 40% as compared to the An-26.

Upon completion of the tests in October-November 1985 Antonov OKB test pilots Yuriy V. Koorlin, A. V. Tkachenko and P. K. Kirichuk established 14 world altitude records in the class of aircraft with a weight of up to 25,000 kg (55,125 lb) on this aircraft. These included a maximum altitude of 12,010 m (39,405 ft) with no payload and 11,230 m (38,846 ft) with a payload of 5,000 kg (11,020 lb).

An-32 tactical transport

The contract for the series production of the An-32 for India was signed in 1980. Initial plans called for the production of 95 aircraft, most of which were to be manufactured in India under licence by Hindustan Aeronautics Ltd. (HAL) at the company's plant in Kanpur, Uttar Pradesh; only the first batch was to be produced in Kiev. However, it was not before 1982 that the decision was taken to launch full-scale series production of the An-32 at the Kiev Aircraft Production Association (plant No.473). It may well be said here that the licence production plans never materialised; in the 1980s India fell into the grips first of a political, and then also an economic crisis which led to the cancellation of several military programmes, including the programme which called for the licence manufacture of the An-32.

Wearing full Indian Air Force markings and the serial AJ301, the first production example (c/n 0101) took to the air on 23rd June 1983, and the same year saw the commencement of export deliveries. Up to 1994 a

One more Indian Air Force An-32, K2745 (c/n 0901); the code 'E' is just visible on the fuselage. All IAF An-32s were delivered in this grey/white colour scheme. Note the unswept blade aerials above the flight deck and under the centre fuselage associated with a Western radio.

Above: Two An-32Bs at Kiev-Svyatoshino awaiting delivery to the Sri Lankan Air Force; the one nearest to the camera is serialled CR 866. The aircraft were delivered as attrition replacements after two of the SLAF's original three An-32s had been shot down.

total of 214 new and used aircraft had been sold to Afghanistan, Angola, Bangladesh, Colombia, Croatia, Ethiopia, India, Mexico, Nicaragua, Panama, Peru, Saudi Arabia, Sri Lanka, Tunisia, Swaziland and – reportedly – Cuba, Cabo Verde and Zambia.

The biggest recipients of the An-32 were India, which took delivery of 123 machines (some sources say 118) and Afghanistan with 49 examples. There is positive evidence that the bulk of the first nine production batches and of Batch 12 went to India. The new aircraft also evoked considerable interest on the part of Peru which had begun buying aircraft of Soviet manufacture on advantageous terms in the 1970s. A batch of 15 An-32s was built for that country to replace the An-26 which was ill-suited to operating in the extremely difficult conditions of the Andes.

The first An-32 arrived in India on 11th July 1984; it was taken on charge by the transport squadron which catered for the needs of the Airborne Forces School at Agra, Uttar Pradesh. Gradually several transport squadrons of the Indian Air Force re-equipped with the An-32, retiring their aged C-119s. The IAF has a habit of giving popular names to the aircraft it operates – even to those that have one already; the An-32 is known locally as Sutlej after a river in Punjab.

In 1991 the Soviet Air Force, having by then gained considerable experience of 'hot and high' warfare in Afghanistan, also took an interest in the An-32. Presumably the Air Force command believed that an aircraft capable not only of landing on small airstrips, but also of zooming to altitude out the reach of the enemy's MANPADS, might be useful for assault troops and *spetsnaz* (commandos) units. However, the nearly 50 An-32s that had been completed for the VVS by the time of the Soviet Union's dissolution proved to be no longer needed by the customer and were gradually sold off – mostly to small air carriers, both in the CIS republics and further abroad.

Some of the production An-32s built for the home market were powered by 4,250-ehp AI-20M engines which were intended for operation in a moderate climate and traded a slightly lower rating for a longer service life. Another advantage of these engines consisted in lower fuel consumption per hour at take-off rating. Apart from the engines, these machines also differed in being equipped with the SRO-1P *Parol'* (Password) IFF system, new radios and other equipment items. In all, 357 An-32s had been built in Kiev by 2000 and at least eight Batch 36 machines in varying degrees of completion were still on the assembly line in September 2002; judging by a pencilled inscription on the nose, one of them (c/n 3602) was earmarked for a customer in Italy!

The demise of the Soviet Union placed the Kiev Aircraft Production Association, which had already changed its Soviet-style name of Trood (Labour') to the more appealing Aviant (a contraction of 'Aviation' and 'Antonov', since it had manufactured exclusively Antonov types for the last 50 years), into a difficult situation. Selling the new aircraft met with ever-increasing difficulties under the conditions when they were not needed by the

Ukrainian Air Force, and Russia was unable to pay for most of the aircraft that had been ordered for her Air Force and had already been manufactured.

An-32A cargo aircraft

This was the first civil version of the An-32 intended for the home market – specifically, for the air transport divisions of major heavy industry enterprises. The An-32A differed from the export An-32 *sans suffixe* mainly in IFF and communications equipment. Interestingly, the nose titles invariably read simply 'An-32' – without the A, just as in the case of the An-30A.

Starting in 1987, about three dozen such aircraft were delivered to various MAP and MOM enterprises and design bureaux; the earliest known example is CCCP-48974 No.3 (c/n 1404; the registration had been used twice before by other aircraft). Operators included the aircraft factories in Gor'kiy (No.21, now called NAZ 'Sokol'), Komsomol'sk-on-Amur (No.126, currently KnAAPO) and Ulan-Ude (No.99, currently U-UAPO), the aero engine factories in Kaluga (now Kadvi) and Ufa (UMPO), MAP's Transport Aviation Production Association, the Beriyev OKB in

The Bangladesh Air Force's second An-32, S3-ACB/1701 (c/n 1701). The An-32s were delivered as replacements for three An-26s which did not have the required hot-and-high performance.

Above: An-32A RA-48090 (c/n 2601) belonging to the Beriyev OKB (TANTK Beriyev) was operated for the UNPF in 1993. It was sold to the Moldovan cargo carrier Renan in 2001 as ER-AWA.

An An-32B with the non-standard An-26 style registration RA-26222 (c/n 2301) operated by Aerolit (aerolith, an old word for meteorite) seen at Moscow-Tushino on 9th May 1995. Tragically, on 8th January 1996 this aircraft (by then sold to Moscow Airways) crashed at Kinshasa-N'dolo, killing 297 persons.

Taganrog and the Myasishchev Experimental Machinery Plant in Zhukovskiy – and, of course, the manufacturers (KiAPO and the Antonov OKB).

An-32B cargo aircraft

In 1995 the Antonov OKB completed certification tests of a new purely commercial version, following the example of the An-26B, was designated An-32B. It was intended primarily for operation on short- and medium-haul routes. The efficient high-lift devices and the good power/weight ratio (this version also used the 5,180-ehp AI-20D engines) made it possible to operate this machine from airfields with short runways (the take-off run was just 760 m/2,500 ft), from airfields high up in the mountains, and perform flights with steep paths of climb and descent. The An-32's special undercarriage with low-pressure tyres and the high-set engines enabled it to operate from unpaved and snow-covered airfields in Siberia. The cargo hold measuring 12.48 x 2.78 x 1.84 m (40ft 11⅜ in x 9 ft 1½ in x 6 ft) could accommodate various civil cargoes, including passenger cars, with a total weight of 6.7 tons (14,770 lb). Provision was made for the transportation of people (up to 50 persons); bulky cargoes could be air-dropped on special platforms etc.

A small number of such aircraft were acquired by several Russian airlines and institutions. According to information available in the Ukrainian Ministry of Industrial Policy, 41 An-32Bs were sold between 1992 and 1997. Four examples of this version outfitted as VIP transports were acquired by the Ministry of State Security of North Korea. These aircraft were obtained illegally through bogus firms in third countries.

An-32B-100 cargo aircraft

The An-32B-100 is a version of the production An-32B with enhanced transport capacity and improved performance. The aircraft features an airframe of greater structural strength, which has made it possible to increase the maximum take-off weight to 28.5 tons (62,840 lb) and the payload to 7.5 tons (16,540 lb). To enhance operational safety at the maximum take-off weight, the An-32B-100 is powered by AI-20D Srs 5M engines with a longer service life. The engines are derated to 4,200 ehp for take-off, but to ensure safe operation of the aircraft at a maximum weight a contingency power setting is available. The new engines

proved to possess fairly good service life characteristics: the service life until the first overhaul is 4,000 hours, and the designated service life is 20,000 hours. The cargo hold volume is 60 m³ (2,120 cu.ft); An-32B-100 has a 800 kg (1,674 lb) higher payload and a 600 km (373 miles) longer range. Like all preceding versions, it has a crew of three.

An-32V-200 cargo aircraft/ tactical transport

The next step resulted in the creation of the An-32V-200 version. The modifications consisted in fitting the aircraft with new equipment (first of all, with Collins avionics) which made it possible to operate the aircraft with a crew of two, dispensing with the navigator and the radio operator, while the flight engineer (or, more exactly, the cargomaster/dropmaster) was included into the crew only in the military version. Onboard sets of navigation aids and communications equipment with modern data processing and presentation systems made it possible to keep the crew's psychological and physiological load at an acceptable level and ensured interaction with a wide range of traffic control means of both Russian/Ukrainian and foreign manufacture. The onboard equipment complement could be tailored to the customer's requirements.

The fuel tankage was supplemented by two external tanks with a total capacity of 3,000 litres (660 Imp. gal) which are mounted on the fuselage sides. With these tanks, the range with a 2,800-kg (6,170-lb) payload rose to 3,200 km (1,990 miles); in this case the aircraft retained an emergency fuel reserve for 45 minutes' flight.

An improvement of the airframe's fatigue resistance, the powerplant (the An-32B-200 is powered by AI-20D Srs 5M engines) and aircraft systems have made it possible to go over from the established system of maintenance schedules and pre-planned preventive repairs to maintenance as per necessity, which reduced operating costs. At the same time the machine's initial calendar service life was extended to 25 years.

The aircraft can be delivered in both civil and military configuration. In the paradropping version it is intended to carry up to 7,500 kg (16,540 lb) of cargo, or 42 fully equipped troops, or 38 paratroopers, or 24 stretcher cases and one medical attendant. The built-in hoist and detachable roller conveyor make it possible to air-drop cargo platforms weighing up to 3 tons (6,615 lb). In the civil version the machine can transport standard cargo containers and pallets. The maximum all-up weight is increased to 28,500 kg (62,840 lb), the maximum fuel tankage in the wing amounting to 7,100 litres (1,562 Imp. gal), supplemented by 3,000 litres (660 Imp. gal) in the strap-on tanks. The aircraft's performance includes a cruising speed of 500-530 km/h (310-330 mph), a ceiling of 9,400 m (30,840 ft), a take-off run of 950 m (3,120 ft) and a landing run of 600 m (1,970 ft).

In 1999 the An-32V-200 was offered to the Greek Air Force and negotiations started on the delivery of 15 machines of this type. There were plans for fitting the aircraft with a new Rockwell-Collins targeting and navigation avionics set, with new communication equipment and with IFF transponders meeting the NATO standards. On 31st August 1999 an official delegation from the Ministry of National Defence of Greece headed by Minister of Defence A. A. Tzohadzopoulos visited the Antonov Design Bureau and the production plant in Kiev. The guests familiarised themselves with a number of development projects, including the An-70, but they paid special attention to the An-32V-200. The members of the delegation watched with great interest a demonstration flight of the aircraft which included impressive vertical manoeuvres, a flight with one engine inoperative, a landing approach with a 7° glideslope angle and other manoeuvres. At the end of the visit Tzohadzopoulos emphasised that he had gained a personal impression of the aircraft's capabilities. Still, the negotiations failed to result in a deal – the Greeks opted for the Italian/US Alenia/Lockheed Martin C-27J Spartan STOL tactical transport.

As of this writing, Brazil and Bolivia have also displayed interest in the An-32V-200.

An-32P Firekiller water bomber

The An-24LP and An-26P water bombers intended for fighting forest fires worked up a

Above: The An-32P prototype, UR-48004 (c/n 1306), minus water tanks at Kiev-Gostomel' on 14th September 2002 during the Aviasvit-XXI airshow.

fairly good track record, but the operators were dissatisfied with their payload capacity. Hence in the mid-1980s a fire-fighting version of the Il'yushin IL-76 heavy transport (the IL-76P, aka IL-76TDP or IL-76MDP) made its appearance, but the 190-ton (418,870-lb) aircraft required a long paved runway which might not be available. In many cases potential customers could quite as well do with a lighter aircraft that would happily combine sufficient cargo-carrying capacity, fuel efficiency and flight safety.

This was exactly the solution that the Antonov Design Bureau specialists found. The company's new 'fire fighter' was based on the An-32 with its 'mucho machismo' engines. Designated An-32P by analogy with its precursor, the new firebomber featured much larger water tanks holding 8 tons (17,640 lb) of water or fire retardant. The tanks had a conformal shape to minimise drag while

maximising internal volume; the aircraft so equipped had a range of 330 km (205 miles) with 30-minute emergency fuel reserves. As was the case with the An-26P, the two tanks scabbed onto the fuselage sides left the whole of the cargo hold free for a team of fire-fighters to be paradropped at the fire site. The aircraft could also carry dispensers loaded with cloud-seeding chemicals for inducing rain.

Tests showed that the discharge of 8 tons of fluid from both tanks at an altitude of 40-50 m (130-165 ft) and a speed of 240-260 km/h (149-162 mph) doused an area 120-160 m (390-525 ft) long and 10-35 m (33-115 ft) wide. The concentration of fluid in this area was relatively high – more than 1 litre per square meter. The fluid could be discharged in a salvo or consecutively from two sections of each tank with an automatic delay. The AI-20D engines made it possible to operate the aircraft in mountainous areas, using flight

An-32P UR-48086 (c/n 2901) sporting Firekiller titles and the logo of the Aviant factory which owns it, makes a water bombing demonstration at one of the many airshows in which it participated.

Towards the end of its flying career the first prototype (by then reregistered CCCP-46961) was converted into the An-32LL propfan technology testbed.

This propeller was presumably a technology demonstrator for the Stoopino Machinery Design Bureau SV-36 contra-rotating propeller used with the Lotarev (ZMKB) D-236T experimental propfan engine. An eight-blade propeller of similar design formed the front stage of the SV-36, the aft stage having six blades. The D-236T/SV-36 combination was envisaged for the An-70 military transport. On the actual aircraft, however, more powerful Muravchenko (ZMKB) D-27 propfans driving SV-27 contraprops of similar design had to be used because of the much-increased gross weight.

An-32 testbed/research aircraft
A photo published in the Western aeronautical press showed an example of the An-32 fitted with streamlined wingtip containers. This was allegedly a flying laboratory. No further information on it is available.

An-32 maritime patrol upgrade
According to press reports dated October 1997, the US company Heli-Dyne based in Hurst, Texas, outfitted two Mexican Navy An-32s (identities unknown) with quick-change maritime patrol equipment packages.

An-32 export version for Peru
Western reports indicate that the An-32 transports delivered to the Peruvian Air Force (the nation's first operator of the type) in 1987 were equipped with the Litton Omega navigation system.

An-32 versions – unbuilt projects
According to articles published by the well-known French aviation historian Jacques Marmain in 1988 after his visit to the Antonov Design Bureau, the OKB's designers were working on several versions of the An-32, including a fishery spotting aircraft, a flying hospital and – oddly enough – an agricultural aircraft. Nothing has been heard about these projects ever since; presumably they were abandoned at an early stage.

An-32 re-engining project
At the MAKS-99 aerospace show in Zhukovskiy (17th-22nd August 1999) the Antonov Design Bureau presented a model of a projected version of the An-32 with a new powerplant. Unlike the baseline An-32, the engines were placed under the wings in compact An-24/26/30 style nacelles, driving six-blade low-noise propellers with scimitar-shaped blades. No information is available on this version, but it may well be presumed that the intention was to make use of a Western engine, probably the Allison GMA2100. The model could be identified as an An-32 derivative (as distinct from the very similar An-26) by the deeper aft fuselage ventral strakes characteristic of the An-32.

paths with a high gradient. The aircraft could operate from semi-prepared unpaved airfields lacking ground power supply, compressed air chargers, centralised refuelling and other amenities.

In the early 1990s two production aircraft were converted into the An-32P prototypes. As early as the autumn of 1993, when the flight tests had just begun, the machines had their 'baptism of fire'; in October the two machines were used for extinguishing a forest fire in the mountains near the famous Yalta health resort on the Crimea Peninsula. The crews performed nearly 100 flights and demonstrated a high degree of efficiency of the winged fire fighters. In May 1994 the testing of the aircraft was completed, and as many as three machines were sent for operational trials to Portugal. In the course of very intensive work (every machine performed up to 10 to 12 flights per day) the group made 545 fire-fighting sorties. Performance characteristics and efficiency of this aircraft as a means of combating fires were appraised very highly by specialists who took part in the operational trials.

The An-32P was demonstrated several times at various air shows. Thus, the first An-32P (UR-48004, c/n 1306) bearing the proud name Firekiller was shown at the MAKS-93 aerospace exhibition in Zhukovskiy on 31st August – 5th September 1993. On 19-24th August 1997 An-32P UR-48086 (c/n 2901) was demonstrated in flight at that year's MAKS show in Zhukovskiy, sporting the new colour scheme of the Aviant factory which owns it; the same aircraft had been presented at the MAKS-95 air show on 22nd-27th August 1995. Its cargo hold was equipped with stretchers for the wounded, and the ventral strakes flanking the cargo hatch were equipped with special devices intercepting

the extractor cords during the air-dropping of fire-fighters. Other known examples were registered UR-48108 (c/n unknown), UR-48083 (c/n 3001) and UR-48093 (c/n 0703)

The An-32P successfully demonstrated its abilities during demonstration flights in Malaysia and at aircraft exhibitions in the Philippines and in Australia (Airshow Down Under). Tragically, one of the cases when the An-32P was used for fighting real-life forest fires ended in the loss of the aircraft. On 6th July 1994 UR-48108 crashed in the Sierra Mariola Mountains near Alicante, Spain, killing the crew. Investigation showed that the aircraft had stalled and collided with the ground; apparently the pilots had put the machine into an all-too-steep climb, losing visual reference when the aircraft entered a pall of smoke after dropping the load of water.

On 10th March 1995 the An-32P obtained a supplementary type certificate in a special category issued by the Air Register of the CIS Interstate Aviation Committee. The Kiev-based Aviant plant completed all the necessary preparations for the series production of this special-purpose aircraft, but, unfortunately, no orders were placed for this machine, despite the obvious need for it.

An-32LL propfan technology testbed
Receiving the non-standard (for an An-32) registration CCCP-46961, the original prototype (ex-CCCP-83966 No.1) was converted into a testbed for an advanced eight-blade propeller initially fitted instead of the port AV-68DM four-blade propeller. The blades of the development propeller featured straight trailing edges and scimitar-shaped leading edges. Later in the course of testing, an identical eight-blade propeller was also fitted to the starboard engine. The aircraft has been referred to as the An-32LL.

Chapter 6

In Local Airline Service

Civil-registered An-24s, An-26s, An-30s and An-32s have been around for decades at airports in many countries. The largest number of the 'species' was found in the Soviet Union, of course, where these types could be seen both at airports run by the Ministry of Civil Aviation (MGA – *Ministerstvo grazhdahnskoy aviahtsii*), as well as at airfields belonging to different Government agencies (MAP, MOM etc.). After the demise of the Soviet Union many of these aircraft are still around, sporting new or altered registrations with the new nationality prefixes of the CIS republics and other nations that have sprung up in the post-Soviet area. In fact, at some locations these aircraft are far more common than other types!

The prelude to Aeroflot's An-24 operations was in 1960 when the prototypes took part in the State Acceptance trials with the participation of Aeroflot personnel. Operational evaluation started in April 1962; logically enough, the first Aeroflot division to take delivery of the new airliner was the Ukrainian Civil Aviation Directorate (CAD) which was the

OKB's home ground, allowing any technical problems to be rapidly resolved. The first route proving flight was performed in October 1962 by a Kiev United Air Detachment (UAD) An-24A from Kiev (Zhulyany airport) to Kherson. Among those on board were the chief of the Ukrainian CAD, crew captains and air hostesses.

It has to be said that Aeroflot's organisation closely resembled an air arm's order of battle – which is hardly surprising, considering that the Soviet civil air fleet constituted an immediately available military reserve (and considering the militarisation of the Soviet economy at large). There was a number of Civil Aviation Directorates (UGA – *oopravleniye grazhdahnskoy aviahtsii*), several of which were in the Russian Federation and one in each of the other Soviet republics. These were broadly equivalent to the air forces of the USAF or the air armies of the Soviet Air Force. Each CAD consisted of several United Air Detachments (OAO – *obyedinyonnyy aviaotryad*) based in major cities or airports; these were equivalent to an

air group (USAF) or an air division (SovAF). Each UAD had several Flights (LO – *lyotnyy otryad*) similar to an air wing (USAF) or an air regiment (SovAF). Finally, a Flight comprised up to four, or maybe more, squadrons (yes, squadrons – *aviaeskadril'ya*!); not infrequently different squadrons of the same Flight operated different aircraft types.

After a brief period of service on mail and cargo routes the An-24 soon began performing scheduled passenger services. The type was delivered to virtually all of the Soviet Union's Civil Aviation Directorates, as well as the Training Establishments Directorate (UUZ – *Oopravleniye oochebnykh zavedeniy*) controlling the civil aviation flying and technical schools. As early as the mid-1960s it had taken over a substantial share of the traffic on commuter routes from the IL-14, although piston-engined aircraft (even the last surviving Li-2Ps!) soldiered on until the early 1980s on Aeroflot's domestic services.

Table 1 illustrates known civil aviation units operating the An-24 in Soviet times.

Table 1. An-24 operators within the Aeroflot 'order of battle' (in Soviet times)

Civil Aviation Directorate	United Air Detachment & constituent Flight	Home base	New (CIS) airline name
Arkhangel'sk CAD	2nd Arkhangel'sk UAD/392nd Flight	Arkhangel'sk-Vas'kovo	AVL Arkhangel'sk Airlines
Azerbaijan CAD	Baku UAD/360th Flight/1st and 3rd Squadrons *	Baku-Bina	AZAL (no An-24s)
Belorussian CAD	Gomel' UAD/105th Flight/1st Squadron	Gomel'	Gomel'avia
	1st Minsk UAD/353rd Flight	Minsk-Loshitsa (Minsk-1)	Belavia; Minsk-Avia
	Mogilyov UAD	Mogilyov	Mogilyov-Avia
Central Regions CAD	Belgorod UAD	Belgorod	Belgorod Air Enterprise (no An-24s)
	Bryansk UAD	Bryansk	Bravia (Bryansk-Avia)
	Bykovo UAD/61st Flight	Moscow-Bykovo	Bykovo Avia
	Ivanovo UAD	Ivanovo-Yoozhnyy (Zhukovka)	IGAP (Ivanovo State Air Enterprise)
	Kostroma UAD	Kostroma	Kostroma Air Enterprise
	Kursk UAD	Kursk	Kurskavia
	Ryazan' UAD	Ryazan'	Ryazan'aviatrans
	Tambov UAD/169th Flight	Tambov-Donskoye	Aviata (Avialinii Tambova)
	Tula UAD/294th Flight	Tula	Tula Air Enterprise
	Voronezh UAD/243rd Flight	Voronezh	Voronezhavia
	Vladimir UAD	Vladimir	Vladimir Air Ent./Avialeso'okhrana
East Siberian CAD	Bodaibo UAD	Bodaibo	Bodaibo Air Enterprise
	Chita UAD/136th Flight/1st Squadron	Chita	Chita Avia
	Irkutsk UAD/134th Flight	Irkutsk-1	Baikal Airlines
	Ust'-Ilimsk UAD	Ust'-Ilimsk	Ust'-Ilimsk Air Enterprise
	Ust'-Kut UAD	Ust'-Kut	Ust'-Kut Air Enterprise
	Ulan-Ude UAD/138th Flight	Ulan-Ude/Mookhino	Buryatia Airlines
Far Eastern CAD	Sakhalin CAPA/Yuzhno-Sakhalinsk UAD/147th Flight/1st Squadron	Yuzhno-Sakhalinsk/Khomutovo	Sakhalinskiye Aviatrassy
	1st Khabarovsk UAD/289th Flight	Khabarovsk	Dalavia Far East Airlines Khabarovsk

97

Kazakh CAD	Chimkent UAD/158th Flight	Chimkent	Kazakstan Airlines; Chimkent-Avia
	Goor'yev UAD/156th Flight	Goor'yev	Kazakstan Airlines; Atyrau Air Ways
	Karaganda UAD/14th Flight	Karaganda	Kazakstan Airlines
	Kustanay UAD/155th Flight	Kustanay	Kazakstan Airlines
	Tselinograd UAD/239th Flight	Tselinograd	Kazakstan Airlines; Air Astana
Kirghiz CAD	No data available (all aircraft transferred to other directorates before 1987)		
Komi CAD	Syktyvkar UAD/366th Flight	Syktyvkar	Komiavia; Komiinteravia
Krasnoyarsk CAD	Abakan UAD/130th Flight	Abakan	Khakassia Airlines (Abakan A. E.)
Latvian CAD	Riga UAD/106th Flight/2nd Squadron	Riga-Spilve	Latavio
Leningrad CAD	Pskov UAD/320th Flight/2nd Squadron	Pskov	
Lithuanian CAD	Vilnius UAD/277th Flight/4th Squadron	Vilnius	Lithuanian Airlines
Magadan CAD	Anadyr' UAD	Anadyr'-Oogol'nyy	Chukotavia
	Chaunskoye UAD/6th Flight	Chaunskoye	Chaunskoye Air Enterprise
	1st Magadan UAD/185th Flight (1st or 3rd Squadron)	Magadan-Sokol	Kolyma-Avia
Moldavian CAD	Kishinyov UAD/407th Flight	Kishinyov	Air Moldova
North Caucasian CAD	Astrakhan' UAD/110th Flight	Astrakhan'-Narimanovo	Astrakhan' Airlines
	Krasnodar UAD/241st Flight/3rd Squadron	Krasnodar	ALK Kuban' Airlines
	Makhachkala UAD/111th Flight/1st Squadron	Makhachkala	Daghestan Airlines
	Stavropol' UAD	Stavropol'	SAAK (Stavropol' Joint-Stock AL)
	Taganrog UAD	Taganrog	Tavia
Tajik CAD	Leninabad UAD/292nd Flight/2nd Squadron	Leninabad	Tajikistan Airlines
Training Establishments Directorate	Kirovograd Civil Aviation Higher Flying School (KVLUGA)	Kirovograd	Ukraine State Flight Academy
Turkmen CAD	Ashkhabad UAD/165th Flight/1st Squadron	Ashkhabad	Turkmenistan Airlines/Akhal
	Krasnovodsk UAD/360th Flight/1st Squadron *	Krasnovodsk	Turkmenistan Airlines/Khazar
	Maryy Composite Independent Air Squadron	Maryy	
	Tashauz UAD	Tashauz	
Tyumen' CAD	Salekhard UAD	Salekhard	Tyumen'AviaTrans
	Surgut UAD/358th Flight	Surgut	Surgut Avia
Ukrainian CAD	Donetsk UAD	Donetsk	Donbass – East Ukrainian Airlines
	Kiev UAD/86th Flight/2nd Squadron	Kiev-Zhulyany	Air Ukraine/Avialiniï Ookraïny
	Kirovograd UAD	Kirovograd-Khmelyovoye	Air URGA
	L'vov UAD/88th Flight	L'vov	Lviv Airlines
	Simferopol' UAD/84th Flight	Simferopol'	Aviakompaniya Krym/Crimea AL
	Voroshilovgrad UAD	Voroshilovgrad	
Urals CAD	Izhevsk UAD	Izhevsk	Izhavia
	Kirov UAD	Kirov	**Kirov Air Enterprise (no An-24s)**
	Magnitogorsk UAD	Magnitogorsk	Magnitogorsk Air Enterprise
	1st Perm' UAD	Perm'-Bol'shoye Savino	Perm Airlines
	1st Sverdlovsk UAD	Sverdlovsk-Kol'tsovo	Ural Airlines **[Yekaterinburg]**
Uzbek CAD	Samarkand UAD/163rd Flight	Samarkand	Uzbekistan Airways
	Tashkent UAD/160th Flight	Tashkent-Yoozhnyy	Uzbekistan Airways
Volga CAD	Cheboksary UAD	Cheboksary	Cheboksary Air Enterprise
	Cheboksary UAD/Nizhnekamsk Independent Air Squadron	Nizhnekamsk	Nizhmekamsk Air Enterprise
	Gor'kiy UAD	Gor'kiy-Strigino	Nizhegorodskie Airlines (sic)
	Tatar CAPA/1st Kazan' UAD/408th Flight	Kazan'	Tatarstan Airlines
	Orenburg UAD/195th Flight/2nd Squadron	Orenburg-Tsentral'nyy	Orenburg Airlines
	Penza UAD/396th Flight	Penza	Penza Air Enterprise
	Saransk UAD	Saransk	
	Saratov UAD	Saratov	
	Ufa UAD/415th Flight	Ufa	BAL Bashkirian Airlines
	Yoshkar-Ola UAD	Yoshkar-Ola	
West Siberian CAD	Kemerovo UAD/196th Flight	Kemerovo	
	Kolpashevo UAD/237th Flight	Kolpashevo	
	Novosibirsk UAD/6th (?) Flight	Novosibirsk-Severnyy	2nd Novosibirsk Air Enterprise
	Tolmachovo UAD/448th Flight	Novosibirsk-Tolmachovo	Sibir'
	Novokuznetsk UAD/184th Flight	Novokuznetsk	Aerokuznetsk
	Omsk UAD/365th Flight/2nd Squadron	Omsk	Omsk-Avia
	Tomsk UAD/119th Flight	Tomsk	Tomsk Avia
Yakutian CAD	Yakutsk UAD/271st Flight	Yakutsk	Sakha Avia
	Mirnyy UAD	Mirnyy	Almazy Rossiï – Sakha (Alrosa)
GosNII GA		Moscow/Sheremet'yevo-1	

(Note: The 360th Flight appears to have been bodily transferred from the Azerbaijan CAD (which thus relinquished its An-24s) to the Turkmen CAD in 1987.)

Until the mid-1970s Aeroflot's colour schemes were as disparate as the aircraft it operated. Each type had its own livery, and some had two, but the An-24 had no fewer than seven – yes, SEVEN liveries (true enough, not all of them were equally widespread). The white top of the fuselage was accentuated by a silver or tan belly; the cheat line was red (with very 1950s style 'feathers'), orange or blue (single or double); even the graphic presentation of the Aeroflot titles and varied. The aircraft type was marked on the airframe in a 'handwritten' style with a heavy flourish; early production An-24As had it painted on the nose, while later machines, starting with the An-24B, carried it on the rudder. Some examples airliners wore the smart-looking logo of the Antonov Design Bureau which is in use to this day.

The new aircraft outperformed the slower IL-14 and Li-2 by a wide margin – it had a top speed of 500 km/h (310 mph) and a cruise altitude of 6,000 m (19,685 ft); also, normal seating capacity was 50 passengers versus 32. The runway length required for landing was little more than 500 m (1,640 ft), while the take-off required some 600 m (1,970 ft). The navigation, communications and flight instrumentation suite was quite advanced by the standards of the day, enabling the aircraft to fly under adverse weather conditions in the day and at night.

At Bykovo airport near Moscow the flight crews were not alone in preparing for the introduction of the An-24. All the ground support services were also heavily involved: the passenger and cargo handling personnel, the radio communication specialists, the maintenance department and the weathermen. The inauguration of the first passenger services operated by the An-24 to the regional centres of Central Russia (Moscow-Voronezh and Moscow-Saratov) proved to be a real festive occasion. The first scheduled flights were started on the autumn morning of 23rd September 1963. In addition to the Aeroflot top brass, the invited guests included representatives of GSOKB-473, specialists from the State Civil Air Fleet Research Institute (GosNII GVF and other agencies, and the omnipresent newspaper, radio and TV journalists. Suffice it to say that journalists from virtually all the central newspapers – *Pravda*, *Izvestiya*, *Trood*, *Sovetskaya Rossiya*, *Moskovskaya Pravda*, *Komsomol'skaya Pravda*, as well as correspondents of the main TV channel and the *Yoonost'* (Youth) radio broadcasting station were among the passengers on board the aircraft that took off on their first flights to Voronezh and Saratov. But what really mat-

tered was, of course, the opinion of the passengers. Many of them frankly said that flights in the An-24 to Voronezh and Saratov became a great surprise for them.

Following the example of their Voronezh and Saratov colleagues, the civil aviation workers of Ivanovo, Bryansk, Kursk, Belgorod, Kostroma started preparing to receive the An-24. Locally funded new airport buildings based on standard models were built there, supplemented by dozens of new rooms for passenger accommodation in existing airports on local routes to which the new Antonov airliner might eventually find its way.

A memorable event for Bykovo airport was the opening of scheduled An-24 services from Moscow to the North Caucasus. The best crews of the oldest Russian airport took the new machines on their flights first to Makhachkala (the capital of the Daghestan ASSR), then to Vladikavkaz (North Ossetian ASSR) and Groznyy (Chechen-Ingush ASSR). Flights to these cities were very popular among passengers, as were the frequent flights to Kiev-Zhulyany. They could be rivalled in popularity possibly only by the route from Tula to the Black Sea (to Gudauta airport near Sukhumi). Tickets for these flights to a summer resort were sold out many days in advance.

The advent of the An-24s on local routes contributed to a speedier solution of various tasks associated with raising the catering levels for passengers. This included the delivery of passengers to and from the airport; to this end roads were built and regular bus routes from the city to the airport were organised. Advance sales of air tickets were organised at hotels, railway stations and bus stations in every regional centre (ie, major town). Joint transport agencies were set up for the first time in Kursk, Ivanovo, Voronezh, Yaroslavl' and other cities of Central Russia; they sold tickets to all kinds of transport. In short, the advent of the turboprop-powered An-24s placed high-speed means of passenger transport within reach of the multi-million population of the central area of Russia.

By the early 1970s the airline's management rightly decided that having such a motley collection of colour schemes was no good. Hence a common fleetwide standard livery was developed and endorsed by MAP and MGA in March 1973, but it was a while before the now-familiar blue/white livery began appearing on actual aircraft. Most An-24s were progressively repainted as they underwent a major overhaul; Kiev-built An-24RVs from approximately Batch 88 onwards wore the new colours from the start.

Speaking of which, it was common practice in the Soviet Union that a single aircraft overhaul plant would repair all aircraft of a given type, regardless of where they were

based (including export aircraft). If the aircraft was produced in large numbers, several plants would be assigned. Thus, ARZ No.403 at Irkutsk-1 airport, ARZ No.410 at Kiev-Zhulyany and ARZ No.412 in Rostov-on-Don handled the An-24/An-26/An-30/An-32 family.

At the peak of their popularity, in the late 1970s, the An-24s served almost a thousand destinations in the country, catering for almost a third of all the passenger traffic of Aeroflot, which was at that time the world's biggest airline.

From the first days of its service the new comfortable airliner enjoyed well-deserved respect on the part of the pilots and the ground personnel. It was reliable and undemanding to operate and had a reasonably long service life. In the mid-1960s the An-24's designated service life was set at 30,000 hours. This parameter was corroborated by thorough service life tests of a specially allocated aircraft which was subjected to stresses that were equivalent to 75,000 flights. Preservation of the aircraft's long service life was facilitated by a system of registering operational stresses. All An-24s were equipped with automatic flight data recorders ('black boxes') making it possible to take into account the excessive stresses suffered by the aircraft as a result of errors and breaches committed by the crews, or as a result of being operated under extreme conditions.

The early 1970s were marked by a spate of fatal crashes of An-10 airliners and An-12 transports, with disastrous consequences for the former type. The cause of the crashes was traced to a fatigue failure of the wing structure. In 1972 the An-10 medium-haul airliners were grounded and eventually retired altogether in accordance with MGA order No.032 dated 27th August 1973; aircraft of other types, including the An-24 and its versions, were placed under strict control. Investigation of the crashes revealed not only design errors but also grave breaches of the operational rules committed by Aeroflot personnel with the connivance of the airline's leaders.

The structural strength team of the Antonov OKB led by Ye. A. Shakhatooni performed an enormous amount of work; this made it possible to guarantee reliable operation of the entire An-24 fleet. In the 1970s the overall service life of this aircraft was extended to a gigantic figure of 65,000 flying hours.

Even though some measures intended to enhance the aircraft's fuel efficiency were not implemented, the An-24 was one of the best among Aeroflot's turbine-powered airliners as far as fuel efficiency was concerned. It was expected to be profitable even with a load factor of 40-45%. Of course, these figures were somewhat over-optimistic, yet the An-24 proved to be up to the mark, being appreciably superior to the Tupolev Tu-124 and

Tu-134 twinjet medium-haul airliners with regard to seat-mile costs.

Pre-flight preparation of the machine could be done, using mainly the equipment that was already available at the airports. The aircraft had relatively small dimensions and its maintenance did not call for the use of excessively high stepladders; at the same time the engine air intakes, propellers and the bottom of the fuselage were placed high above the ground and did not suffer damage from dirt and foreign objects.

Passengers boarded the aircraft through a door in the aft fuselage measuring 1.4 x 0.75 m (55.1 x 29½ in). When entering you had to stoop a good deal, but that was the order of the day at that time. The aircraft was provided with integral folding airstairs.

The An-24 could easily take off from a paved runway, an unpaved airstrip or a strip covered by packed snow. The designers guaranteed normal operation of production aircraft even from ice-field airstrips without additional modifications. Since both propellers had the same direction of rotation (clockwise when seen from the front), this caused a slight yaw to the right which the pilot usually countered with rudder input. Once airborne, the aircraft accelerated even during initial climb. Retraction of the flaps did not affect the aircraft's pitch trim. To reduce noise pollution the pilot was permitted to perform a turn at an altitude as low as 200 m (650 ft) in the initial climb mode so as to avoid passing over a residential area.

If an engine cut during the take-off run, right up to the moment when unstick speed was attained, the take-off was to be aborted if the remaining runway length was around 1,500-1,600 m (4,920-5,250 ft). If the aircraft had already attained a speed of 215 km/h (134 mph) and the propeller of the inoperative engine was feathered, the power of one engine was sufficient for continuing the take-off and climbing with a vertical speed of 1.2-1.4 m/sec (236-275 ft/min). While doing this, the pilot prevented the machine from banking, using the control surfaces. On aircraft equipped with the RU19A-300 APU, in the event of one engine cutting the flight engineer pushed the APU throttle to the maximum power setting and switched off the non-essential electric equipment.

The powerplant of the An-24 was very reliable, but it did have an 'Achilles heel' – the propeller feathering system. Despite all efforts of the designers, it did not function quite as planned, and there were cases during operational service when the propeller of the inoperative engine entered the autorotation mode. The drag caused by the autorotating propeller created a strong yaw. For this reason the restarting of an engine in flight after a successful response of the autofeathering system was permitted only for training purposes or in the case of an engine being shut down in error.

Occurrences when both engines cut in flight were not frequent, but even in such cases the crew could save their own lives and the lives of the passengers by acting in a competent way. Thus, in 1963 such a double engine flameout happened in one of Aeroflot's training units. Flying at 3,000 m (9,840 ft), the aircraft was 22 km (14 miles) from the nearest airfield at the time, but the crew succeeded in gliding to a safe landing. From an altitude of 6,000 m (19,685 ft) one could, in theory, make it to an airfield situated some 100 km (62 miles) away.

One more trouble that plagued Antonov's regional turboprop was icing. It could occur in cruise flight at altitudes up to 5,000 m (16,400 ft). This posed a danger of the aircraft assuming a high angle of attack and stalling due to the formation of ice layers distorting the wing airfoil. When flying in the conditions of light or moderate icing, the de-icing system should be permanently activated after the throttles had been set to nominal power; in the case of severe icing the de-icing system should be activated periodically – this facilitated the removal of the so-called 'barrier' ice that formed accretions aft of the heated leading edges of the wings and tail surfaces. The micro-ejector de-icing system used on the An-24 proved to be far from 'economical'; to ensure its functioning at full intensity, it was necessary to tap 5% of the air supplied by the engine compressors, which entailed a 15% drop in power output. Hence on aircraft lacking the RU19A-300 turbojet the flight manual expressly forbade switching on the hot air de-icing system during take-off.

This problem was further aggravated by the imperfect design of the RIO-2 radio isotope icing sensors. When the skin temperature was within 0° to –3°C (32-26°F), ie, within the range when icing was particularly probable, these sensors had a too high sensitivity threshold and could not signal in time the onset of icing. Other sensors had shortcomings of their own, so it proved fairly difficult to select a substitute.

In order to conduct a thorough investigation of the aircraft's de-icing system and evolve recommendations for the crews, special tests were conducted in the High North, but even that proved insufficient to tackle the problem fully. Thus, it proved impossible to ensure the full-scale use of the system during take-off (limitations were placed on its operational use even for aircraft with a turbojet APU); efforts to ensure reliable operation of the RIO-2 and SO-4A icing sensors were of no avail. As a result, to ensure the timely heating of the propellers and elements of the airframe, the crews had to maintain visual control of the icing or assess it on the basis of indirect indications and make use of a manually actuated emergency system. To this end characteristic black or red 'zebra stripes' were painted on the wing and stabiliser leading edges of many An-24s et seq.

For any aircraft, landing is one of the most critical stages of flight when the risk of an emergency situation occurring is at its highest. For An-24 crews, landing in instrument mode was the order of the day; one of the crew called out the current altitude, and the captain shifted his gaze from the instrument panel to the runway only when the aircraft had passed the decision altitude, if there was no need to make a go-around. During descent the flight engineer had to extend the undercarriage at a speed of not less than 300 km/h (186 mph) at the crew captain's command. True, the crews sometimes tended to do this immediately prior to touchdown, being more concerned about fuel economy than flight safety. The flight manual required the flaps to be deployed just before the turn onto the final approach – first to a setting of 15°; the aircraft reacted by 'flaring up', which had to be countered by a commensurate movement of the control column. Before entering the glideslope the flaps were further deployed to the full setting of 38°; in this case the machine did not flare up quite so much, yet the crew captain had to push the control column slightly forwards.

When performing a landing, it was necessary to avoid abrupt movement of the engine controls. The system of reversing the thrust of the AV-72 propellers proved to be sufficiently effective, and it was recommended to make use of wheel brakes only at the final stage of the landing run. The aircraft was equipped with automatic anti-skid units enhancing the effectiveness and safety of the brakes.

The tough airframe structure ensured a safe belly landing or an emergency landing when one or two undercarriage legs failed to extend or lock down. In that case the crew was obliged to take measures so as to shift the aircraft's CG as far aft as possible; as the aircraft came to a halt after landing, the crew would have to ensure the speedy evacuation of the passengers.

For overwater flights at distances of more than 100 km (62 miles) from the coast the An-24 was equipped with 12-man life rafts and an emergency supply of food. Recommendations were drawn up for crews permitting them to ditch the aircraft, depending on the circumstances. After ditching the aircraft usually assumed a considerable angle of bank, and the captain had to choose correctly the route for guiding the passengers and the crew out of the cabin onto the life rafts. Before a flight above the sea a cabin attendant was obliged to give the passengers instructions what to do in the event of ditching.

By the early 1970s the An-24 had become one of Aeroflot's most widely used and most reliable aircraft. Yet, no aircraft type is immune against attrition, and the An-24 had its share of fatal and non-fatal accidents. In most cases such tragic events were caused by the tell-tale human factor (ie, crew or ATC error and breaches of discipline), or by adverse weather.

On 28th January 1970 a Yakutian CAD An-24B (CCCP-47701, c/n 59900202) coming in to land to Batagai descended prematurely and crashed into mountains 40 km (25 miles) out, killing all six crew and 28 passengers. On 17th December 1976 a Ukrainian CAD/Kiev UAD/86th Flight An-24A (CCCP-46722, c/n 37300302) came in too low and hit an embankment on short finals to Kiev-Zhulyany in foggy weather; six of the 50 passengers and one of the five crew members survived.

While we are on the subject of crew error, trainees were often responsible for accidents. On 1st June 1971 the flight engineer of an East Siberian CAD/Ulan-Ude UAD/138th Flight An-24B (CCCP-47729, c/n 69900902) shut down the live engine by mistake during a single-engine training session at Ulan-Ude/ Mookhino. The aircraft was damaged beyond repair in the ensuing crash landing – luckily with no fatalities.

Some accidents were caused by design faults, including the tendency to pitch down suddenly on landing approach in icing conditions. For instance, on 15th January 1979 a Ukrainian CAD An-24B (CCCP-46807, c/n 57302109) lost control and dove into the ground on finals to Minsk-1 (Loshitsa) airport, killing all five crew and eight passengers. It turned out that the de-icing system had been switched off prematurely. Three months earlier, on 23rd October 1978, both engines of a North Caucasian CAD An-24B (CCCP-46327, c/n 97305504) flamed out with a 14-second interval at 2,400 m (7,870 ft) – presumably due to ice ingestion. The aircraft crashed into the Gulf of Sivash, a boggy branch of the Sea of Azov; there were no survivors among the five crew and 21 passengers.

Sometimes air traffic controllers were to blame. On 17th November 1975 a North Caucasian CAD An-24RV (CCCP-46467, c/n 27307905) hit a mountain 2,400 m (7,874 ft) above sea level while 2 km (1.2 miles) from Sukhumi-Babushara airport; all five crew and 38 passengers were killed. Gross ATC incompetence was the cause this time; the approach controller had instructed the crew to descend prematurely. On 9th September 1976 a Belorussian CAD An-24RV (CCCP-46518, c/n 37308504) and a Yak-40 (CCCP-87772, c/n 9030713) collided at 5,700 m (18,700 ft) near the resort city of Anapa. Negligence on the part of the crews and gross miscalculations committed by air traffic con-

An-24A CCCP-46758 (c/n unknown) in pre-1973 colours about to touch down at one of the Soviet Union's northern airports, with five Mil' Mi-4A helicopters, a Mi-6 heavylift helicopter and a Mi-10K flying crane helicopter. The latter suggests the scene may be Syktyvkar (Komi CAD).

trollers resulted in the loss of 90 human lives (5+47 on the prop-liner and 4+14 on the jet).

A rather unusual accident took place in Luxor on 30th September 1966 when An-24V SU-AOM (c/n 67302809?) of the Egyptian airline Misrair struck a camel on take-off! The aircraft flew on to Cairo as if nothing had happened but was damaged beyond repair in the ensuing belly landing.

Another accident which drew attention to the appallingly low flight safety standards in Russia in the mid-1990s occurred on 18th March 1997 near Cherkessk in southern Russia. An-24RV RA-46516 (c/n 37308502) belonging to the Stavropol'-based carrier SAAK (*Stavropol'skaya aktsionernaya aviakompahniya* – Stavropol' Joint-Stock Airline) crashed en route from Trabzon, Turkey, to Stavropol', killing all on board. The 'tin kickers' quickly discovered that the aircraft had broken up in mid-air; the entire aft fuselage and tail unit were discovered about 5 km (3 miles) from the main wreckage in almost undamaged condition. The big question was, why? The fuselage had disintegrated near frame 40 (the rear pressure dome), and the investigation focused on a bomb planted in the rear baggage compartment. An act of terrorism seemed a distinct possibility, considering the close proximity of the rebellious Chechnya and the fact that the Chechen separatists had many sympathisers in Turkey. However, analysis of the wreckage proved beyond doubt that the catastrophic structural failure had been provoked by advanced corrosion resulting from a previous lease to an operator in South-East Asia. This crash led the Russian Civil Aviation Authority to set about improving maintenance standards.

One more tragic episode in the An-24's biography occurred in 1970 – although the aircraft itself was definitely not to blame. A father and son by the name of Brazinskas

hijacked an Aeroflot aircraft on a scheduled flight from Batumi to Sukhumi, Georgia, forcing the crew to fly to Turkey and killing air hostess Nadezhda Koorchenko in the process. The Turkish government refused to extradite the terrorists on the grounds that they would have been executed (although the Soviet Union was not the only country by far to impose the death penalty for hijacking, especially compounded with first-degree murder). Afterwards the hijackers moved to the USA which, understandably enough, was not going to extradite them either. Several years later, however, Brazinskas Jr. killed Brazinskas Sr. Call it fate's revenge, if you like.

In the 1970s new-generation feederliners – the Soviet Yak-40 and the Czechoslovak Let L-410 Turbolet – began to make their appearance en masse on the Soviet Union's domestic air routes. Their distinctive features were enhanced comfort, lower cabin noise levels and good fuel efficiency. However, these machines proved incapable of supplanting the An-24 in commuter air traffic. At the end of the decade Aeroflot began taking delivery of new, more modern Yak-42 short/medium-haul trijets, but they, too, failed to completely oust the An-24s.

The An-26 freighter was operated by Aeroflot in far smaller numbers than its 'elder brother' which had acquired a firm foothold on the domestic air routes. Nevertheless, every now and then you would encounter these 'flying lorries' with civil registrations in various airports of the huge country. In addition to ordinary Aeroflot units, the An-26 made up an important part of the aircraft fleets of various MAP, MOM and MRP divisions; it was an ideal 'cargo taxi' for uplifting urgent cargoes such as spare parts.

Apart from airlifting small amounts of regular or urgent cargo, Aeroflot An-26s rendered invaluable service during search and rescue (SAR) operations in the High North and Soviet Far East. This was quite probably because even on a 'purely civil' An-26B the cargo ramp could be slid open in flight, allowing rescue means to be dropped to people in distress. In areas such as those, with their harsh climate, prompt delivery of aid could literally make the difference between life and death.

Table 2 lists the Aeroflot units known to have operated the An-26 in Soviet times.

Unfortunately, unscrupulous people tend to use the An-26's capabilities so recklessly in pursuit of their own goals that it often led to incidents. Quite apart from the tendency to overload the aircraft, often the 'cargo' consisted of 'unofficial' (ie, illegal) passengers who were in a hurry to reach their destination by whatever means available. Worst of all, more often than not such passengers flew together with cargoes in extremely uncomfortable conditions, putting themselves at risk.

The An-26 also suffered from accident attrition – for various reasons. Sometimes crashes were caused by adverse weather conditions. For example, 36 persons died when a passenger-configured An-26 of the North Caucasian CAD/Krasnodar UAD/241st Flight crashed into a river on approach to the Armenian town of Gyumri (formerly Leninakan) on 26th December 1993. The crew had lost their bearings in dense fog during the landing approach.

Table 2. An-26 operators within the Aeroflot 'order of battle' (in Soviet times)

Civil Aviation Directorate	United Air Detachment & constituent Flight	Home base	New (CIS) airline name
Azerbaijan CAD	Baku UAD/360th Flight/1st and 3rd Squadrons	Baku-Bina	AZAL (no An-26s)
Belorussian CAD	Gomel' UAD/105th Flight (2nd Squadron?)	Gomel'	Gomel'avia
	1st Minsk UAD/353rd Flight/2nd Squadron	Minsk-Loshitsa (Minsk-1)	Belavia; Minsk-Avia
Central Regions CAD	Bykovo UAD/61st Flight/4th Squadron	Moscow-Bykovo	Bykovo Avia
	Kursk UAD	Kursk	Kurskavia
	Tula UAD/294th Flight	Tula	Tula Air Enterprise
East Siberian CAD	Chita UAD/136th Flight/1st Squadron	Chita	Chita Avia
	Irkutsk UAD/190th Flight	Irkutsk-1	Baikal Airlines
Far Eastern CAD	1st Khabarovsk UAD/289th Flight	Khabarovsk	Dalavia Far East Airlines Khabarovsk
	Kamchatka CAPA/Petropavlovsk UAD	Petropavlovsk-Kamchatskiy	Petropavlovsk-Kamchatskiy A.E.
	Sakhalin CAPA/Yuzhno-Sakhalinsk UAD/147th Flight	Yuzhno-Sakhalinsk/Khomutovo	Sakhalinskiye Aviatrassy
Komi CAD	Pechora UAD	Pechora	Komiavia; Komiinteravia
Krasnoyarsk CAD	Igarka UAD/251st Flight	Igarka	
	2nd Krasnoyarsk UAD/126th Flight	Krasnoyarsk-Severnyy	Kras Air
	Khatanga UAD/221st Flight/2nd Squadron	Khatanga	
Leningrad CAD	2nd Leningrad UAD/70th Flight	Leningrad-Rzhevka	Rzhevka Air Enterprise
	Pskov UAD/320th Flight/2nd Squadron	Pskov	Pskov-Avia
Lithuanian CAD	Vilnius UAD/277th Flight (1st Squadron?)	Vilnius	Lithuanian Airlines
Magadan CAD	Anadyr' UAD/150th Flight/2nd Squadron	Anadyr'-Oogol'nyy	Chukotavia
	1st Magadan UAD/185th Flight	Magadan-Sokol	Kolyma-Avia
	Seymchan UAD	Seymchan	NW Aerial Forestry Protection Base
Moldavian CAD	Kishinyov UAD/407th Flight	Kishinyov	Air Moldova
North Caucasian CAD	Krasnodar UAD/241st Flight	Krasnodar	ALK Kuban' Airlines
	1st Krasnodar UAD/406th Flight	Krasnodar	
Tajik CAD	Leninabad UAD/292nd Flight/2nd Squadron	Leninabad	
Training Establishments Directorate	Kirovograd Civil Aviation Higher Flying School	Kirovograd	Ukrainian State Flight Academy
Turkmen CAD	Krasnovodsk UAD/360th Flight	Krasnovodsk	Turkmenistan Airlines/Khazar
Tyumen' CAD	Salekhard UAD/234th Flight/5th Squadron	Salekhard	
	2nd Tyumen' UAD/357th Flight	Tyumen'-Roschchino	Tyumen'AviaTrans (UTair)
Ukrainian CAD	Dnepropetrovsk UAD/327th Flight	Dnepropetrovsk-Volos'ke	Dniproavia
	Kirovograd UAD	Kirovograd-Khmelyovoye	Air URGA
	Simferopol' UAD/84th Flight	Simferopol'	Aviakompaniya Krym/Crimea AL
Urals CAD	Izhevsk UAD	Izhevsk	Izhavia
	Magnitogorsk UAD	Magnitogorsk	Magnitogorsk Air Enterprise
	1st Perm' UAD	Perm'-Bol'shoye Savino	Perm Airlines
	1st Sverdlovsk UAD	Sverdlovsk-Kol'tsovo	Ural Airlines [Yekaterinburg]
Volga CAD	Penza UAD/396th Flight	Penza	Penza Air Enterprise
	Saransk UAD	Saransk	Saransk Air Enterprise
West Siberian CAD	Barnaul UAD/341st Flight	Barnaul	Barnaul Air Enterprise
	Kemerovo UAD/196th Flight	Kemerovo	
	Novokuznetsk UAD/184th Flight	Novokuznetsk	Aerokuznetsk
	Omsk UAD/365th Flight	Omsk	Omsk-Avia
	Tolmachovo UAD/448th Flight	Novosibirsk-Tolmachovo	Sibir'
	Tomsk UAD/119th Flight	Tomsk	Tomsk Avia
Yakutian CAD	Kolyma-Indigirka UAD	Cherskiy?	
	Mirnyy UAD/190th Flight	Mirnyy	Almazy Rossiï – Sakha (Alrosa)
	Yakutsk UAD/139th Flight/3rd Squadron	Yakutsk	
GosNII GA		Moscow/Sheremet'yevo-1	

Incidents and accidents plagued the civil An-26 fleet especially in the 1990s, when the machines were already well-worn. Remember that many of these aircraft had been transferred to civil operators from the VVS after the demise of the Soviet Union. Also, in the 1990s many aircraft wet-leased from CIS air carriers operated in African countries and other places of the world characterised by non-existent infrastructure and incessant armed conflicts – which certainly does not improve your chances of getting home unscathed.

Thus, an An-26 with the non-standard Yak-40 style registration RA-88286 (c/n 0802) belonging to the airline KiT (Kosmos i Transport – Space & Transport) was lost on 6th November 1994. The crew had become disoriented in poor weather en route from Okhotsk to Susuman and eventually the aircraft ran out of fuel, making an emergency landing on the frozen Omulyovka River 65 km (40.3 miles) south of Zyryanka town, Yakutia. An-26 UR-26197 (c/n 12609) belonging to the Ukrainian carrier Khors Aircompany crashed at Cafunfo, Angola, on 24th June 1996 while operating for the local airline Air Nacoia. On 25th January 1997 An-26 RA-26541 (c/n 47302106) belonging to Kolymaavia touched down on the uneven runway shoulder at Chokurdakh, Yakutia, after a messed-up landing approach and was damaged beyond repair. On 4th February 1999 An-26 EL-ANZ (c/n 13906) operated by AirAngol landed long at Luzamba (Angola) and overran into a ravine, breaking in two and bursting into flames. Two of the 36 passengers died.

Not much will be said in this chapter about the civil operation of the An-30, as its military biography is much more interesting. Nevertheless, a few facts deserve mention. The An-30 (then still referred to alternatively as An-24FK) was officially cleared for service with Aeroflot by MGA order No.87 signed by Minister of Civil Aviation Boris P. Boogayev on 20th April 1974. The first An-30s delivered to the Ministry of Civil Aviation were based at Leningrad-Pulkovo airport. In 1975, however, a specialised flight of An-30s – the first of its kind in the USSR – was set up within the Central Regions CAD/ Myachkovo UAD and the Leningrad-based examples were transferred there. (Myachkovo is a specialised airfield south-east of Moscow which hosts a jack-of-all-trades unit performing all manner of special air services. Few people realise that the IL-14s supporting the Soviet Arctic and Antarctic research stations, the Mi-8MT helicopters supporting the Soviet coal mining community on Spitsbergen etc. belonged to the Myachkovo UAD.)

The An-30 quickly supplanted the geriatric IL-14FK photo mapping machines operated by the Myachkovo UAD's 229th Flight. During the first five years of operation alone

In post-Soviet times An-24s and An-26s owned by CIS airlines were actively leased abroad. This An-24RV (TC-JUZ, c/n 37308902) operated by Turkish carrier Sultan Air is ex-Bykovo Avia RA-46636 leased in 1993.

the new machines photographed an area totalling more than 28 million square kilometres (10,810,800 square miles). Later, after one of the many reorganisations, some of the An-30s returned to the Leningrad CAD/2nd Leningrad UAD/70th Flight based at Rzhevka airport. In the course of operation these aircraft were retrofitted with the Groza-M30 radar. In addition to these units, Aeroflot An-30s also saw service with the Kazakh CAD/Burundai UAD/242nd Flight, the Ukrainian CAD/Kiev UAD, the West Siberian CAD/Novosibirsk UAD and GosNII GA. The latter operated a single An-30A (CCCP-30028, c/n 0510) which was an instrumented test aircraft used for developing improved operational procedures. In the course of operation the civil An-30s were retrofitted with the Groza-M30 radar.

Compared to its older transport stablemates, the An-32 aircraft distinguished itself with the highest degree of comfort and the lowest accident rate. (True, this type also had its share of crashes, but mostly through no fault of the machines themselves.) This is due first and foremost to the difference in technology – for all practical purposes, the hunchbacked An-32 represents a later generation of light transport aircraft.

In the Soviet Union the An-32 saw service exclusively with the transport elements of major industrial enterprises within the MAP and MOM frameworks; it was not until the

break-up of the USSR that 'normal' airlines, such as Sibaviatrans, obtained a few such aircraft. It is exactly during the post-Soviet period, when a multitude of small cargo transport companies were formed in Russia and other CIS countries, that the An-32s have had to shoulder the biggest volume of cargo and passenger traffic. In many cases these aircraft were used outside CIS in 'friendly' countries; they were flown and serviced both by Russian crews and by hired foreign crews. For example, in the course of 28 months of hostilities in Angola a huge volume of air transportation work was performed by pilots of Executive Outcomes, a South-African proactive security (read: mercenary) organisation. Dubbed 'the Diamond Dogs of War', EO operated, among other things, An-32 aircraft leased from Russian private firms.

Following the pattern of this chapter, we will note several accidents involving this last representative of the family of Antonov's light transport aircraft. On 28th September 1989 An-32A CCCP-48095 (c/n 1705) belonging to MAP's 'Transport Aviation' Production Association crashed near Semyonovka village in the Chernigov Region of the Ukraine. It was established that the autopilot had failed, causing the aircraft to enter a descending spiral and break up in mid-air after exceeding the design speed limit.

On 25th October 1995 An-32A RA-48981 (c/n 1601) belonging to the Ufa Engine Pro-

One of Aviatrans Cargo Airlines' An-32As at Moscow-Myachkovo. This aircraft is unusual in having an all-white colour scheme. The airline was renamed Atran in 1997.

duction Association (UMPO) crashed on final approach to Maksimovka airfield, inbound from Urai (Tyumen' Region). When making the approach in a heavy snowfall, the pilots misjudged their altitude and came in too low; seven of the 13 occupants were killed in the ensuing collision with trees.

One of the worst accidents in aviation history occurred on 8th January 1996 when Moscow Airways An-32B RA-26222 (c/n 2301) failed to become airborne at Kinshasa-N'dolo due to extreme overloading. Crashing through the perimeter fence, the aircraft ploughed through the crowded Simba Zikita market, killing 297 persons. The airline was already under close scrutiny due to unsatisfactory operational standards, and the crash was the last straw; Moscow Airways' operating licence was withdrawn. Some sources, however, claim *it had already been suspended at the time of the crash* and the aircraft had no business being there in the first place!

It is worth recalling that the use of the An-32P water bomber for putting out a series of major fires was an important stage in the An-32's civil operations. As noted in the preceding chapter, two An-32Ps were used for fighting a forest fire in the mountains near Yalta in October 1993. Operational experience showed the firebomber's high efficiency.

Approaching the end of this chapter, we have to say that by the end of the 20th century the venerable An-24 ranked an honourable third among Soviet-built airliners still present in the world airliner fleet. With 472 aircraft remaining operational, this aircraft was surpassed only by the Yak-40 and the Tu-154. Among transport aircraft the An-26 was numerically second only to the IL-76 (268 and 294 respectively). 70 An-32s were listed in airline fleets all over the world.

Some start-up (or upstart?) airlines experiencing a shortage of funds for purchasing equipment took the veteran An-24s out of storage and put them on international routes again! However, the An-24 is facing ever-increasing difficulties in keeping a presence on international air routes – having invested a lot of money in the requisite modern avionics and new interiors, re-training of crews and refurbishing the maintenance facilities, CIS air carriers have encountered new problems. At the end of the 1990s ICAO introduced a series of new regulations concerning passenger aircraft; airliners failing to meet them will be barred from operating in Europe and the USA. These requirements concern first and foremost noise and pollution levels and installation of traffic collision avoidance systems (TCAS) in order to maintain reduced vertical separation minima (RVSM). And TCAS are expensive – in the case of cheap second-hand aircraft, expensive to the point of being economically unviable.

Several ways were tried in an effort to remedy the situation. As early as 1965 a team headed by M. T. Shinkarook took on these problems in the Antonov Design Bureau. A task was set to reduce the cabin noise level by 10-15 dB. Propellers of smaller diameter were considered; they solved the noise problem but could not guarantee the necessary thrust.

One of the ways tried was to install extra soundproofing mats between the fuselage skin and the cabin trim panels. However, it turned out that installing an additional 60-110 kg (130-360 lb) of soundproofing reduced the noise level by a mere 3-5 dB. Special chemical coatings were developed for the aluminium skin panels to reduce their own vibrations.

The best results were obtained by synchronising propeller rotation. The use of FSA-2 propeller synchrophasers on the An-24 made it possible to reduce the acoustic impact on the environment and the occupants with no loss of thrust. However, the speed governors of production engines could not maintain the correlation between the port and starboard propellers' angles of orientation with sufficient accuracy at any given time. As a result, further studies in this direction were discontinued. To test all these innovations. A production An-24A (registration unknown, c/n 37300403) was allocated for these experiments but the modifications were not implemented in production.

Within the same period, an attempt was made at Bulgaria's request to reduce the An-24V's cabin noise by means of the so-called high-volume soundproofing panels developed in the OKB. However, calculations showed that 150-200 kg (330-440 lb) of such panels would be needed to cut noise by 7-10 dB. There were plans to test them on An-24A c/n 37300405 (identity unknown). Nevertheless, a radical reduction of noise in the cabins of production An-24s was never achieved.

To this day the Antonov Design Bureau, in parallel with its work on transport and special modifications of the An-24, continues working on improving the passenger version, keeping a close check on its present operational use. Attempts are being made to certify the aircraft as meeting current noise requirements. Besides, new versions are being created with a view to upgrading the existing fleet. Recently Aircraft Repair Plant No.410 in Kiev offered its own version of an executive aircraft equipped with air conditioners, TV sets, personal satellite communication systems, a portable toilet and other modern innovations. At the Civil Aviation 2002 airshow held at Moscow-Domodedovo on 14-18th August 2002 the same plant unveiled an upgraded An-24V, UR-47297 (c/n 17306610) featuring rectangular windows and a stylish interior equipped with pop-out oxygen masks, an IFE system and extra soundproofing claimed to reduce cabin noise levels by 20 dB.

Today the 'provincial turboprop' looks definitely outdated and is running short of service life. Still, it has had its day, proving indispensable in the 1960s to 1980s. The An-24 and An-26 have transported millions of passengers and an enormous quantity of cargo defying statistics. These humble toilers of the sky have left a good memory of themselves in nearly 30 countries all around the world.

A Soviet-built aircraft in the house colours of DHL Worldwide Express would have been unthinkable only ten years ago. Since the mid-1990s, however, DHL operates a selection of An-26s, including SP-FDR (c/n 11305) leased from the Polish airline Exin (note logo on the aft fuselage) in 1999.

Chapter 7

Antonov Twins at War

The main recipients of the An-24T, An-26 and An-30B, as well as a certain number of VIP-configured An-24Bs and 'RVs and various special mission versions, were the Armed Forces of the Soviet Union and the air forces of friendly nations. In the Soviet Union these aircraft were normally delivered to Independent Composite Air Regiments (OSAP) which supported the operation of large army formations, of the command of Defence Districts (DDs) into which the country's territory was divided and of the Soviet troops stationed abroad. Usually such air regiments, in addition to the Antonov light twins, had assorted transport/special-purpose aircraft and helicopters of other types on strength, hence the 'composite' in the designations of these units.

Light transport aircraft were also operated by search and rescue units, in the aviation element of the Border Guard troops of the State Security Committee of the USSR (KGB), and in the Army Aviation. Many regiments, independent squadrons and air detachments using Antonov light transport aircraft had a glorious combat history and had been awarded honorary titles and Government decorations. For example, the headquarters of the 24th Air Army, which in Soviet times was located in Vinnitsa, relied on the services of the 456th Volgogradskiy Independent Red Banner Guards Composite Air Regiment (OGSAP) based at Gavryshevka AB; the title reveals that the unit had participated in the defence of Stalingrad (now Volgograd) in 1942-43. In addition to the An-24 and An-26 aircraft, it operated An-12 medium transport aircraft, as well as Mil' Mi-8 utility helicopters and Mi-22 (Mi-6AYa) airborne command post helicopters. In 1992 the regiment became a part of the Ukrainian Air Force; at present it caters for the needs of the Supreme Command of the Armed Forces.

The command of the 8th United Anti-Aircraft Defence Army headquartered in Kiev had at its disposal the 223rd OSAP which was based at Zhulyany airport. It also had An-24 'Salons', An-26 transports and Mi-8 helicopters on strength. In the Red Banner Odessa DD there were two independent composite air squadrons (OSAE – *otdel'naya* **smesh**annaya aviaeskadril'ya) with unknown numbers which had roughly the same complement of aircraft. Based in Odessa itself

was a squadron equipped with An-26s, Tu-134 Balkany airborne command posts and Mi-8MT choppers; the squadron based in Tiraspol', apart from An-24s, An-26s, Tu-134s and Mi-8MTs, operated a few Mi-8PSs with VIP interior and a few Mi-9 ABCPs. Similar regiments and squadrons were stationed in virtually all defence districts. Several air squadrons had on strength special-purpose versions of the An-24. Among these squadrons were the 5th and the 86th independent long-range reconnaissance air squadrons (ODRAE – *otdel'naya* **dahl**'nyaya raz**ved**yvatel'naya avi-aeskadril'ya), based at Belaya AB (Irkutsk Region, Transbaikalian DD) and Chernovtsy AB (Western Ukraine, Carpathian DD) respectively.

The 16th Air Army of the Western Group of Forces (ZGV – **Zah**padnaya **groop**pa voysk) stationed in East Germany (and called GSVG, **Groop**pa so**vet**skikh voysk v Ghermahnii – Group of Soviet Forces in Germany until 1989), was numerically the largest air formation of the Soviet Air Force based abroad. Its command had at its disposal the 226th OSAP stationed at Sperenberg airfield. As of 1991, its aircraft complement included two Ulan-Ude built An-24B 'Salons', ten An-26s (including one navaids calibrator and one An-26RT ELINT aircraft), 13 An-12s and one Tu-134 *Balkany*, the latter being the personal aircraft of the ZGV Commander-in-Chief. The 226th OSAP was the last among the units of the 16th Air Army to leave Germany, redeploying to Kubinka AB west of Moscow. Later, in the course of reforming the Air Force and the Air Defence which was conducted in 1997-1998, the regiment was disbanded.

The 4th Air Army of the Northern Group of Forces (SGV – **Severnaya** groopa voysk) stationed in Poland included one such squadron – the 245th OSAE at Legnica AB. As of 1991, it operated six An-26s in addition to other types. In the early 1990s the squadron was also withdrawn to the Russian territory.

The Southern Group of Forces (YuGV – **Yoozhnaya groop**pa voysk) stationed in Hungary also had its own staff air squadron based at Tököl. It also operated several An-24s and An-26s. The same types were also on the strength of the OSAP supporting the command of the Central Group of Forces (TsGV – *Tsentrahl'naya* **groop**pa voysk) in Czechoslo-

vakia stationed at Mladá-Milovice AB near Mladá Boleslav. These units remained at their bases as long as their respective Groups of Forces were still in existence, and were among the last units to be withdrawn to Russia.

Antonov transports also saw service with the Naval Air Arm (AVMF – *Aviahtshiya voyen-no-morskovo flota*). For example, the headquarters of the Black Sea Fleet relied on the services of the 917th OSAP based at Kacha airfield in the Crimea. In 1992 the regiment had one An-24 and nine An-26s, in addition to other aircraft. Curiously, AVMF transports usually had yellow tactical codes.

Even some Air Force formations at the division level had their own An-24s and An-26s; these were formations that were considered to be of particular strategic importance. These were first and foremost the Long-Range Aviation (ie, strategic bomber arm) divisions, one of then being the Engels-based 22nd Guards Heavy Bomber Air Division of the 37th Air Army. At present, in addition to the two bomber regiments equipped with Tu-160 and Tu-95MS missile strike aircraft, the division has at its disposal a few An-24s in ordinary passenger configuration; these are intended to carry the ground personnel as the unit redeploys to forward bases in the case of an exercise – or, God forbid, an outbreak of hostilities.

Usually light transport aircraft were also operated by military colleges which used them for transporting the trainees to firing ranges, training airfields etc. The Balashov Military Pilot College (VVAUL – **Vys**sheye voyennoye aviatsionnoye lyotchikov) actually used such aircraft for flight training purposes in conformity with the specialisation of this college. The An-26Sh navigator trainer found active use in military navigator colleges; such aircraft were operated by, for example, the 44th Training Air Regiment (UAP – oochebnyy aviapolk) of the Lugansk Military Navigator College (VVAUSh – **Vys**sheye voyennoye aviatsionnoye oochilishche **shtoor**manov). Many aviation colleges had their own transport aircraft detachments, but these were usually small; for instance, the Armavir VVAUL had only two An-26s.

An-24s and An-26s have been used extensively – and still are – for SAR operations.

Thus, an independent SAR air squadron of the Pacific Fleet based at Yelizovo airport, Petropavlovsk-Kamchatskiy, had six An-26 transports in the early 1990s. One more SAR squadron stationed in the Far East operated from Anadyr'; it also had An-26 aircraft on strength.

Not infrequently military An-26s were used alongside An-12s and IL-76s for delivering food supplies, medicines, diesel generators, tents and other essential items to areas ravaged by natural or man-made disasters. Thus, when an earthquake hit the Kurile Islands in October 1994, VTA crews flying An-12s and An-26s delivered supplies for the stricken garrisons on Iturup Island.

An-24s and An-26s were also used by many air units of the Border Guard troops, alongside the ubiquitous Mi-8 helicopters; that was the case, for example, in a regiment of the Border Guard troops stationed on Dixon Island in the Kara Sea. One more Border Guards regiment based at Vladivostok-Knevichi airport has An-24 and An-26 aircraft at its disposal in addition to helicopters. A Border Guards air regiment based at Sadgorod has a similar complement of aircraft.

The Ministry of Defence being the main customer for the An-24T transport/assault aircraft, by far the majority of machines of this first military version of the An-24 was operated by air units of almost all arms and services of the Armed Forces. In addition to the transport role, the military used the An-24T for training purposes; the Balashov VVAUL operated several such aircraft for training VTA pilots.

As is generally the case with any type of aircraft, the An-24T and An-26 were not immune to accidents and incidents. Thus, in May 1972 a Naval Air Arm An-24T (tactical code unknown, c/n 9911302) struck treetops and then fell on a building near Solnechnogorsk (Kaliningrad Region), killing all six crew members. The accident was due to the crew's lack of experience in flying at low altitude. A year later one more An-24T (tactical code unknown, c/n 8910702) belonging to the Balashov VVAUL crashed on landing following a birdstrike. Yet, generally the light transports from the Antonov stable, especially the 'trimotor' versions equipped with the RU19A-300 jet booster, proved their worth in military service, earning a reputation for reliability. In most cases the aircraft could reach a suitable spot for an emergency landing with one engine inoperative, but, of course, a lot depended on the crew's level of training. The following case can be cited a an example,.

Lt. Col. Aleksey Semikov, a Military Pilot 1st Class (this is an official grade) of the Russian Federal Border Guards, had acquired a wealth of flying experience in the course of the 15 years that he had served in the Arctic regions of the country. Many a time he had received recognition and rewards from his command for the high skill and bravery he displayed when fulfilling special missions in complicated conditions on the An-26. On 30th April 1997 Semikov and his crew took off on their An-26 for a flight from Mys Kamennyy ('Stone Cape') to Vorkuta. There were 17 passengers and nearly two tons (4,400 lb) of cargo on board.

Eight minutes after take-off the starboard engine cut. As it turned out later, the incident was due to the failure of an electric actuator controlling the oil cooler shutter; the thing failed to open, causing an abrupt rise in oil temperature (far in excess of the permissible value). Semikov gave the order to start up the jet booster and shut down the crippled engine with a simultaneous feathering of its propeller. Now he had to choose between making an emergency landing at Mys Kamennyy or pressing on towards the destination. Being aware that the airfield at Mys Kamennyi had an uneven dirt strip which was poorly cleaned of snow into the bargain, the crew captain elected to continue the flight, knowing that the destination airfield offered all the conditions for a safe landing. Soon he landed at Vorkuta airport, covering the entire distance with one engine inoperative.

Brothers-in-arms

A few words should be said about the use of the An-24 and An-26 in the air forces of Eastern Europe. The aircraft earmarked for the air forces of Hungary, Romania, Bulgaria, Czechoslovakia, Poland and East Germany (the German Democratic Republic) were delivered almost concurrently with the procurement of these aircraft for the Soviet Air Force. Thus, the An-26s made their appearance in Poland in 1972, equipping a single unit of the the Polish Air Force (PWL – *Polskie Wojsko Lotnicze*), namely the 13th Transport Regiment (13. PLT – *Pulk Lotnictwa Transportowego*) based at Kraków-Balice airport. They were used for carrying cargoes and for training the troopers of the 6th Airborne Division (6. PDPD). From the autumn of 1974 onwards these aircraft were used for delivering mail within the Post-LOT system. The mail was delivered from far-off districts (wojewodstwo) to Warsaw and the other way round. The mail flights were performed at night.

When Poland, Hungary and Czechoslovakia joined the NATO, this led to an increase

The burnt-out hulk of a Soviet Air Force An-26 (note overall light grey camouflage) at Bagram AB in Afghanistan. When hit by a Mujahideen Stinger missile, the aircraft managed a forced landing but was totally gutted by the ensuing fire. It was subsequently stripped of all salvageable items, including the outer wings.

in the volume of transport services performed by the An-26 belonging to these countries' air forces. The An-26s carried the 'NATO freshmen' to many airbases in Europe, notably to bases where various airshows or joint exercises were staged; from the mid-1990s Antonov machines became regular participants of such exercises. For example, on 28th June 1997 two Slovak Air Force Mikoyan MiG-29 fighters and one An-26 support aircraft arrived at RAF Waddington in Great Britain; the An-26 sported the new white/grey/black camouflage which was eventually adopted as standard for the transport aircraft of the Slovak Air Force.

Even before these countries actually gained NATO membership, plans were in hand to modify the An-26s to bring them up to NATO standard. Thus, following refurbishment at ARZ No.410 in Kiev, Polish An-26s were additionally fitted with radio navigation equipment at the PWL's aircraft repair plant No.3 in Deblin (WZL-3 – *Wojskowie zaklady lotnicze*).

Prior to the introduction of new Spanish CASA C.295M transports into PWL service the An-26 was the only Polish Air Force aircraft that could perform troop landing operations and support the activities of Polish troops abroad. In 1998 Polish An-26s were retrofitted with Garmin 155XP and IPG-100F GPS receivers. In the spring of 1999 two machines which took part in the NATO operation in ex-Yugoslavia, operating from Naples, were equipped with the Unimor RS-6106 radio.

Workhorse becomes warhorse

The war in Afghanistan marked the height of the combat career of the An-24 and its derivatives. Several composite air units were formed expressly for supporting the activities of the 40th Army (the Soviet task force in Afghanistan); they were equipped with various types of aircraft, including the Antonov-designed light transport aircraft. It was the 10th Composite Air Regiment (SAP) equipped mainly with An-26s that catered for the needs of the 40th Army's command element. In 1984-88 this regiment with a mixed bag of aircraft types was based at Bagram airfield.

Among the 'Afghan' regiments of the Soviet Air Force the 50th OSAP became one of the most renowned. Although it was intended only for supporting the activities of Soviet military advisors, the crews of the regiment directly took part in virtually all major operations conducted by the 40th Army. During the initial period of the war the regiment had four An-26s, an equal number of An-12s, 12 Mi-8s, an equal number of Mi-24s assault helicopters and 16 MiG-21 fighters on strength. The regiment was based at Kabul International airport. Gradually changes occurred in its

complement, and the regiment came to include several An-24s. The crews flying the Antonov transports carried various cargoes, and performed courier flights. It was also their dreary duty to deliver coffins with the remains of servicemen killed in action to the homeland. During the ten years of the Afghan War the An-24s and An-26s of the 50th OSAP visited all of the permanent airbases of that country.

Of the Antonov aircraft described in this book it was the An-26 that suffered the highest attrition during the Afghan War, primarily because An-26s were more numerous than the An-24s and An-30s. Disregarding the risk of retribution, fanatically minded Mujahideen guerrillas opened fire on Soviet aircraft right from the outskirts of the airfields. Thus, one night in late October 1987 they succeeded in shooting down a 50th OSAP/2nd Squadron An-26 when it was coming in to land at Jalalabad. A few months later the same fate befell an An-26 captained by Maj. V. A. Kovalyov, Commander of the same unit. The shootdown occurred over Bagram airfield as the aircraft was making a second ascending turn, climbing out on the way back to Kabul after bringing 40th Army Commander Boris Gromov to Bagram.

Flights to airbases located near the borders with Pakistan and Iran posed one more danger. From the beginning of 1987 Pakistani F-16 pilots became particularly keen in their hunt for Soviet military aircraft operating in Afghanistan. The town of Khost, the centre of an Afghan province of the same name bordering with Pakistan, was completely surrounded by the Mujahideen, managing to hold its own only thanks to an 'air bridge' maintained by An-12 and An-26 transports. The airfield of Khost, surrounded by mountains on three sides, was situated a mere 15 km (9 miles) from the Pakistani border – and the valley which was the only avenue of approach pointed in the direction of Pakistan. Hence Soviet crews had no choice but to keep close to the border when coming in for landing, presenting themselves wide open for an attack. On 30th March 1987 the leader of a pair of F-16s (the Commander of the Pakistani Air Force's 9th Air Squadron) shot down an Afghan An-26 over Chamkani; the transport was coming in to land at Khost with 39 (some sources say 40) persons on board. Islamabad asserted that this aircraft had been on a spy mission over the borderside area. Some time later a bulletin issued by the Afghan Bakhtar news agency carried a news item according to which two more An-26s and four transport helicopters had fallen victim to PAF fighters near Khost by May 1987. In August the Afghan side reported the wanton destruction of another An-26 by the F-16s in the same area, again with a large loss of life. However,

the Pakistanis did not confirm their victory, and this information cannot be regarded as reliable.

Generally, however, the chief danger for transport and special-mission aircraft cruising towards their destination was the predilection for 'mountaineering' displayed by the industrious Mujahideen. On these 'mountain trips' they lugged lots of heavy materiel, including heavy machine-guns (HMGs) and MAN-PADS. To minimise the risk of unpleasant surprises, two simple rules were evolved for the An-26 crews: firstly, try to stay as high as possible; secondly, do not follow the same route. A flight later in the day should deviate some 1.5-2 km (1-1.25 miles) from the route that had been used in the morning to avoid the risk of ambush. In that case the 'mountaineers' would have to make do with curses and go empty-handed.

The aircraft designers also learned a few lessons from the Afghan War. First of all, they fitted all VTA aircraft operating into Afghanistan with IRCM flare dispensers; next, the aircraft were retrofitted with an inert gas pressurisation system (the IL-76M and IL-76MD, which already had it, were given a more powerful version). The frequent take-offs and landings with a steep gradient entailed increased stress and strain on the airframe, particularly the flaps; this required the flap attachment fittings to be reinforced.

In addition to the 50th OSAP, the 528th OSAE also operated in support of Soviet military advisors in Afghanistan. These two units operated regular An-26 transports, the An-26RT comms relay and the An-26RT (An-26RTR) ELINT aircraft, plus one to three An-30B photo mapping (photo reconnaissance) aircraft, as well as Mi-8MT helicopters.

When describing the combat career of the 'An-24 & Co.', special mention should be made of the use of various special-mission versions in numerous local armed conflicts, especially in Afghanistan.

Initially it was presumed that the Air Force's An-30B aircraft would perform such missions as photo mapping, post-attack reconnaissance to check the results of military exercises and so on. However, when the first machines were delivered to service units the military radically altered their plans concerning the use of these aircraft. Their crews began to receive training for reconnaissance missions which unit then had been the domain of dedicated reconnaissance aircraft derived from combat machines. Apparently this was due to the constant shortage of reconnaissance aircraft in the Soviet Air Force. These tasks even included spotting the mobile launchers of Pershing intermediate-range ballistic missiles (IRBMs) and Tomahawk strategic cruise missiles deep in the enemy's rear area. The views concerning the use of relay aircraft and ELINT aircraft based on the An-24 also underwent a revision. All these machines were destined to take part in a series of regional conflicts, of which the Afghan War was but the first.

One An-30B from the 86th ODRAE was seconded to the group of Soviet military advisers in Afghanistan as early as 1981; in November it was put on the strength of the 1st Air Squadron (AE) of the 50th OSAP. The first task posed for the crews that had arrived together with the machine was the mapping of the territory of the country because most of the available maps proved to be hopelessly outdated. Little by little, however, the An-30B got involved in the fulfilment of other tasks, such as spotting the enemy's weapon emplacements, ambushes, depots, guerrilla concentrations etc. As already noted, the number of An-30Bs on the Afghan TO fluctuated from one to three in the course of war.

One more special-mission aircraft also found extensive use. It was the An-26RT (An-26RTR) ELINT aircraft equipped with the highly classified Taran avionics suite enabling it to discover and pinpoint the enemy's field radio communication means and record their traffic. Normally the crew of the An-26RT (RTR) included interpreters, which made it possible to promptly take decisions about attacking the Mujahideen groups whose bearings had been taken. On one occasion, as related earlier, the crew of the electronic eavesdropper saved the crew of an An-30B operating in the same area near the border south-east of Jalalabad by giving timely warning of an impending attack by Pakistani fighters.

In the mountainous terrain of Afghanistan restricting the range of portable or vehicle-mounted radios, summoning help or directing attack aircraft to provide close air support (CAS) proved virtually impossible without the use of the An-26RT comms relay aircraft. Hence at least one such aircraft had to be kept constantly airborne in the combat area. On some days the crew of an An-26RT logged up to ten hours in the air per day. Thus, in the course of 1980 the relay aircraft performed 620 flights for the purpose of ensuring control of the troops, logging a total of 2,150 hours. On 1st March 1980 an An-26RT flying a mission at an altitude of 6,000 m (19,680 ft) east of Jalalabad was attacked by Pakistani fighters. A pair of Soviet MiG-21 scrambled from Bagram airfield to ward off the attackers, but the incident ended without losses for either side.

Combat experience in Afghanistan quickly revealed not only deficiencies in the training of personnel of various Soviet Army units but also the shortcomings of military hardware, including aircraft, as well as faults in the organisation of maintenance work in the air units. For example, during the initial period the aviation group seconded to the 40th Army lacked storage battery chargers, and the batteries had to be taken 'Unionside' for recharging! Nor did the 40th Army have the specialists required for servicing the mission avionics installed in the An-26RT relay aircraft and the Mi-9 ABCPs.

In 1986 the An-26RT relay stations and the An-30Bs of the 50th OSAP were merged into the 2nd Special-Purpose Aircraft Air Squadron. Together with the 528th OSAE this squadron took part in all major operations undertaken by the ground troops right to the moment of the Soviet pullout from Afghanistan.

Combat losses among the special-mission aircraft proved to be relatively low. On 11th March 1985 an An-30B from the 50th OSAP was hit by a shoulder-launched anti-aircraft missile over the Panjshir Valley. The captain ordered the other crew members to bail out; then, together with the co-pilot, he attempted to land the burning aircraft at Bagram but missed the approach. When attempting a go-around the aircraft lost control and crashed. On 26th December 1986 an An-26RT relay aircraft from the same regiment was hit consecutively by two missiles. Only the flight engineer was unable to bail out; the rest of the crew parachuted to safety. The machine was hit at an altitude of 8,000 m (26,250 ft) which hitherto had been considered to be absolutely out of reach of the enemy's primitive anti-aircraft weapons.

Generally speaking, the Antonov aircraft put up an excellent show in Afghanistan, earning a reputation of veritable 'workhorses'.

African tussles – and war on the home front

Concurrently with the epic story of the war in Afghanistan, the crews of the 86th ODRAE got a chance to gain combat experience almost on the other side of the globe – in Angola. Mikhail S. Gorbachov's *perestroika* (restructuring) and 'new thinking' policy initiated in the USSR in the mid-1980s led to a drastic curtailment of Soviet military activity abroad; nevertheless, the An-24T/An-26 transports and the special-mission aircraft took a most

In the mid-1990s the dump at Kandahar AB was littered with the remains of Soviet-built military hardware, including at least two An-26s in Democratic Republic of Afghanistan insignia.

Above: The spoils of war. Hostilities in Afghanistan continued unabated after the Soviet pullout and the fall of Najibullah as the local warlords fought for power. This An-26 and two An-32s (including '353') were appropriated by the Taliban militia but then captured intact by the Northern Alliance at Bagram.

active part in virtually all armed conflicts which, sadly enough, had flared up on the territory of the former Soviet Union in the course of its dissolution. These machines belonged both to the Soviet Air Force (or the CIS republics) and to civil organisations and private firms.

In the course of preparations for the operation intended to restore constitutional order in Chechnya (more commonly known as the First Chechen War which officially started on 1st December 1994), a heavy burden was shouldered by the transport aircraft, which included a good many An-26s, and the Army Aviation helicopters. In the course of transporting personnel and materiel to the Chechen TO via Mozdok (Ingushetia) and later Groznyy-Severnyy when the capital of the breakaway republic had been seized, aircraft and helicopters performed a total of 4,089 flights, logging 4,272 hours in all; 272 flights (241 hours) were performed for the purpose of redeploying units and formations, and a further 2,112 flights (2,455 hours) were used for the air support of the troops' advancement.

Much attention was paid to providing the necessary information back-up for the operation; allotted for this purpose, among the various items of materiel, was one An-30B aircraft which was ferried from Voronezh (the 5th ODRAE had its base there by then) to an airfield in Rostov-on-Don, reporting directly to the Commander of the North Caucasian DD whose forces were committed in this operation. Proceeding from Afghan experience, the crews of the An-30B fulfilled mostly tasks of an auxiliary character, while the reconnaissance was the responsibility of the Su-24MR and MiG-25RB tactical reconnaissance aircraft respectively from the 11th and 47th ORAP. The main burden of procuring information for the ground troops lay on the Su-24MR tactical PHOTINT/ELINT aircraft because they pos-

sessed more modern and specialised equipment which enabled them to conduct reconnaissance irrespective of weather conditions. However, the An-30B had a considerable advantage as far as the time on station was concerned. Its crews were tasked with visual reconnaissance, which usually resulted in summoning the Army Aviation or Tactical Aviation aircraft immediately, while a strike against targets discovered by the Su-24MRs or MiG-25RB reconnaissance aircraft was dealt only after the information obtained by them had been processed on the ground, which meant a considerable delay.

The An-26RT relay aircraft proved to be a veritably indispensable machine for waging warfare in a mountainous area. The command of the North Caucasian DD had several such machines at its disposal, and they were operated with an extremely high degree of intensity throughout the campaign. From the very first day of the war arrangements were made for three An-26RT to maintain a round-the-clock patrol (the number of aircraft corresponded to the number of directions from which the Russian government troops moved in). They ensured stable radio communication at all levels on the VHF band, maintaining interaction with field radios: the medium-power R-161A2M and the low-power R-111 and R-130 which were equipped with scramblers. In addition, two parallel lines of satellite communication were put into operation; relay work was also performed by the Mi-9 ABCPs.

During the first two or three days of the offensive which was launched on 11th December 1994, the An-26RT aircraft proved to be the only means capable of ensuring communication with the marching units in narrow valleys and mountain gorges. Thanks to their intensive work it proved possible to preserve control over all this huge mass of troops during the first and the most compli-

cated period of advancement. Subsequently the An-26RT aircraft were tasked with ensuring communication with Russian Army reconnaissance and sabotage parties, summoning close air support for the units engaged in battle etc. In all, during the First Chechen War of 1994-96 the communications relay flights totalled 262, the number of hours logged being 401. These missions were flown for the most part by the An-26RTs.

Combat operations also revealed a number of problems, concerned primarily with the (un)stable functioning of the mission equipment. Later, much harsh criticism was voiced in connection with the fact that the Federal troops in Chechnya did not have at their disposal the An-26RT (An-26RTR) ELINT aircraft that had acquitted itself fairly well during the war in Afghanistan. The use of the IL-20M for ELINT missions over Chechnya was not quite justified (these aircraft had been developed as a counterpart to the powerful Army radios of Western manufacture).

Open Spies... sorry, Open Skies duty

As early as the 1950s, when it became obvious that the USA's nuclear monopoly had come to an end, the USA proclaimed the so-called 'Open Skies' programme which envisaged unhindered flights of reconnaissance aircraft for the purpose of monitoring the implementation of eventual treaties on the reduction of armaments. For a long time the Soviet Union refused to join the 'Open Skies' programme, justifiably believing that such flights would boil down to legalised espionage. However, times were changing, and in the 1990s first the USSR and then Russia and the Ukraine agreed to give the 'aerial inspectors' access to their territories.

For the purpose of performing monitoring flights over NATO countries within the 'Open Skies' framework, Russia and the Ukraine

Above: More dead metal at Bagram, including An-32 '297' cannibalised for spares. The aircraft wears DRA Air Force roundels, suggesting it has never been used by the Taliban, and the standard Afghan tan/brown camouflage. A derelict An-12BP and an IL-28 bomber serialled '155 Black' are visible in the background.

made use of the same An-30B aircraft from the 5th ODRAE and 86th ODRAE which had become part of the Russian and Ukrainian Air Forces respectively. The Ukrainian unit soon received the poetic name Blakytna stezha ('Blue Patrol' in Ukrainian).

An-32s in action

The combat biography of the An-32, the last of Antonov's light transport aircraft family, is not so eventful as that of its elder stablemate, the An-26. Relatively few reports appeared in the press concerning its operation in the air forces of Afghanistan, India, Sri Lanka, as well as various African and Latin American countries. Only a few, mostly sorrowful pages of the type's operational biography came to our knowledge.

The Sri Lankan Air Force ordered an initial three An-32Bs to replace Avro 748s lost in the course of the prolonged and bitter civil was between the Government and the rebel Liberation Tigers of Tamil Eelam (LTTE) striving to establish their own independent state in northern Ceylon. The aircraft were operated by the 1st Transport Wing/2nd Heavy Transport Sqn at Ratmalana AB. With the fighting

being as fierce as it was, two of the three SLAF An-32Bs were shot down by MANPADS by the end of 1995, killing all aboard. CR860, the only survivor of the original three, was hastily retrofitted with Western active infra-red jammers on the fuselage sides.

More aircraft were hastily ordered; however, one of them was again lost to hostile action and another (CR865) was written off in a fatal accident at Ratmalana AB on 21st February 1997 caused by crew miscommunication (the co-pilot retracted the landing gear too early on take-off).

Misfortunes also befell some of the Indian Air Force An-32s. Thus, on 7th March 1999 at 08:23 local time An-32 K2673 (c/n 0108?) crashed 3 km (1.86 miles) from New Delhi's Indira Gandhi International airport. During approach the aircraft struck a high-voltage power line, caught fire and fell on a house where one woman and two children were killed on the ground. All 23 persons aboard were also killed.

The An-32s of the Bangladesh Air Force, painted in grey/green camouflage, figured prominently in various flights outside the borders of the country. These aircraft frequently

flew to foreign destinations (China, Malaysia, Singapore, India, Turkey etc.). They also took part in joint exercises with other countries (for example, with the Lockheed C-130s of the USAF/Maryland Air National Guard).

Winding up this chapter, the last in the book, it is worth while to remind readers that to this day the An-24, An-26 and An-30B are the main light transport aircraft of Russia and most of the CIS countries. The more modern An-72 twin-turbofan STOL transports available to the air forces of Russia and the Ukraine are not numerous, and their number is unlikely to increase in the nearest future due to funding shortages.

Bearing in mind the need for a replacement for the ageing Antonov aircraft, the Russian MoD and some other government agencies are viewing the Sukhoi Su-80 twin-turboprop utility transport aircraft which first flew in early 2002 and is undergoing tests at present. However, until production of this machine and especially of its special mission versions has got fully under way, the An-24, An-26 and An-30B aircraft will have to soldier on for quite some time.

This quasi-civil Chad Air Force An-26 registered TT-LAN (c/n 14308) has had quite a chequered career. Originally delivered to the East German Air Force as '384 Black' in 1985, it consecutively became 52+12 with the Luftwaffe, RA-49274 and RA-26234 with Komiinteravia and was sold to Chad in 2001 as surplus.

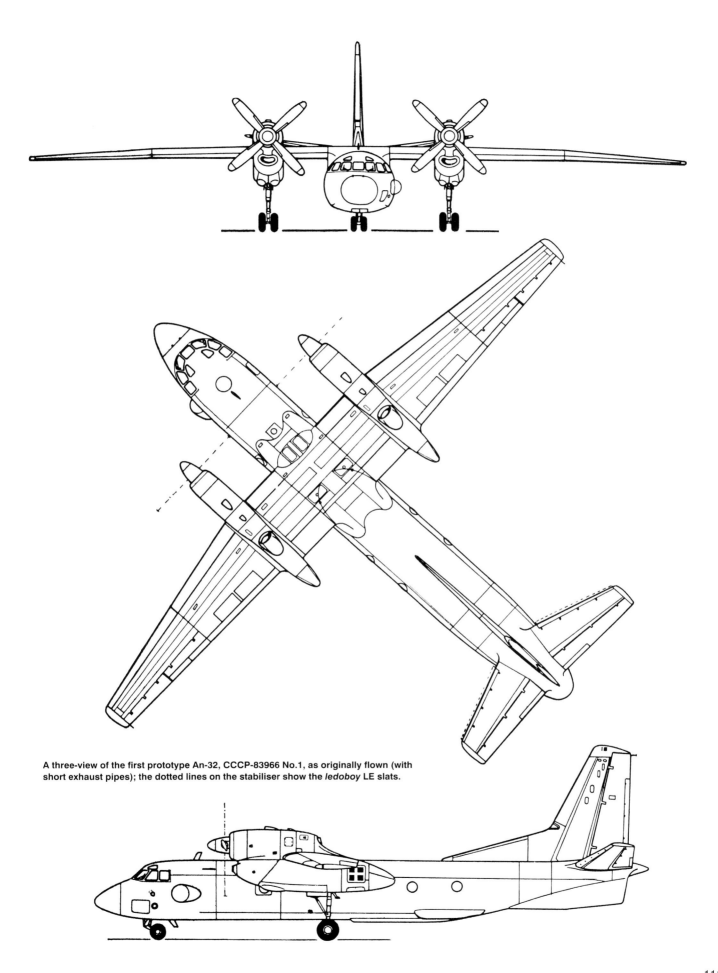

A three-view of the first prototype An-32, CCCP-83966 No.1, as originally flown (with short exhaust pipes); the dotted lines on the stabiliser show the *ledoboy* LE slats.

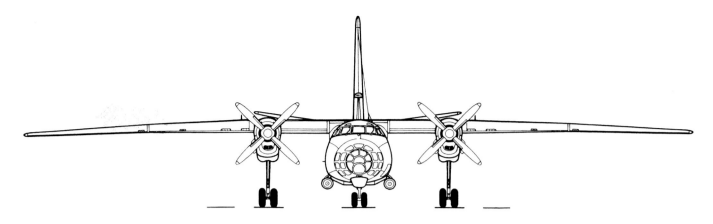

Above and below: front and starboard views of An-30R 30080, showing the RR8311-100
air sampling canister to port and a flare bomb to starboard.

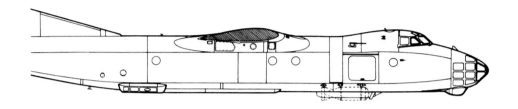

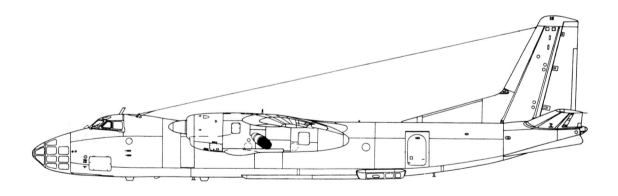

Above: A typical radarless An-30A.
Below: Port side view of An-30R CCCP-30055 in late configuration with the sensor pod removed.

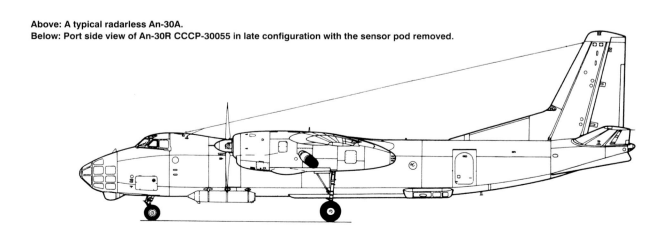

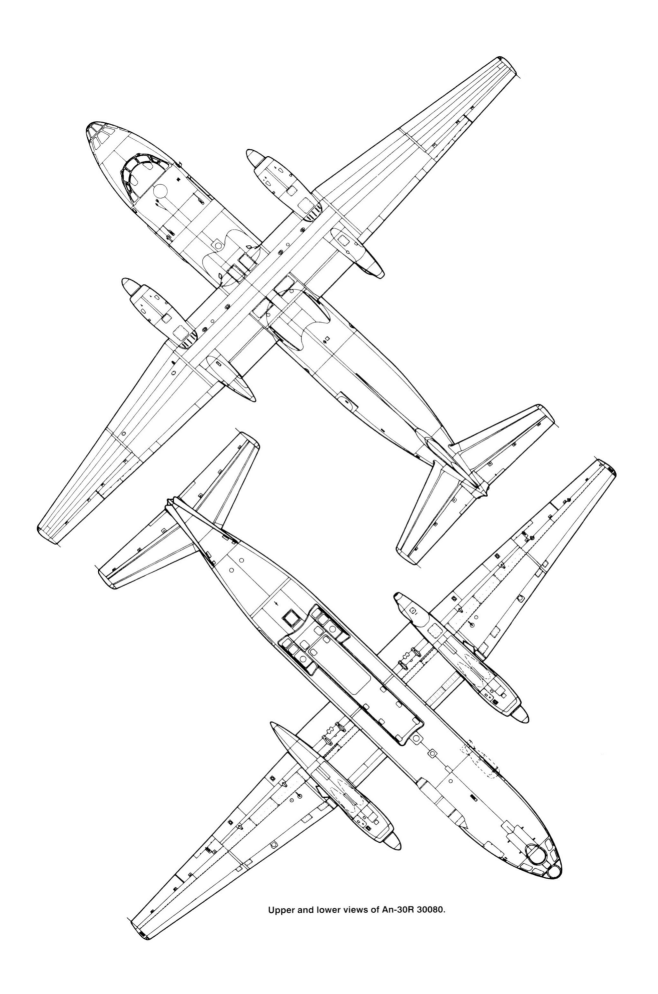

Upper and lower views of An-30R 30080.

Above: An-24 CCCP-Л1960 (in updated form) takes off from the grass strip at Kiev-Gostomel' with the starboard engine shut down and the propeller feathered to simulate an engine failure. Note the instrument probe on the nose and the cine camera fairings on the fin, at the wingtips and aft of the nose gear unit.

An-24RV UR-46838 (c/n 17306805), an updated An-24B, displays the minimalistic livery of Med Air. What is interesting about this aircraft is the interior refurbishment which includes the insertion of metal plugs into the normally circular windows to make them rectangular and thus add passenger appeal!

Above: An-24RV RA-46673 (c/n 47309605) still wears full Aeroflot colours but is operated by Baikal Airlines, the former Irkutsk United Air Detachment of the East Siberian Civil Aviation Directorate (this specific aircraft belonged to the 134th Flight).

An-24RV RA-47264 (c/n 27307806), a converted An-24B, displays the all-white colours of the Russian charter carrier Karat at Moscow/Vnukovo-1 on 18th June 2002.

Above: An-24B 'Salon' '101 Red' (c/n 59900201) in its original livery. This aircraft belonged to the 226th Mixed Composite Air Regiment of the 16th Air Army stationed in East Germany; operating from Sperenberg AB near Berlin, and was the mount of Air Marshal Ivan I. Pstygo.

One of the two An-24RR NBC reconnaissance aircraft operated by the 226th OSAP from its current base, Kubinka AB. The RR8311-100 air sampling canisters have been removed but the shackles remain. The nose titles read 'An-24B'.

Above: The other An-24RR based at Kubinka, '03 Blue' (c/n 89901901). This aircraft took part in radiation level monitoring missions over the devastated Chernobyl' nuclear power station. By 1992 it had been withdrawn from use as *dirty* (ie, permanently contaminated) and was eventually scrapped in 1996.

The sole An-24LR Nit', RA-47195 (c/n 07306202), sits on a rain-lashed hardstand at Pushkin on 8th August 2001 during the Business Aviation 2002 show. The aircraft not only wears the Polar version of Aeroflot's 1973-standard livery but has a Polar Aviation badge on the forward fuselage.

Above: '57 Red', one of the eleven An-24PRT search and rescue aircraft based on the An-24RT transport. The huge observation blister and the large ventral strake aerials characteristic of this version are clearly visible.

Hungarian Air Force An-24V 'Salon' '908 Black' (c/n 77303908) preserved at Tököl, Hungary, in post-Communist era insignia. Unlike sister aircraft '907 Black', it wears a blue cheatline. Interestingly, the aircraft actually wears 'An-24V' nose titles.

Above: Xian Y7-100C RDPL-3.4119 (c/n 10707) taxies in at Vientiane, displaying the stylish current livery of Lao Aviation.

An-24B UR-46305 (c/n 97305205) on finals to Moscow-Vnukovo's runway 24 in September 1998. At this stage it still belongs to the L'vov branch of Air Ukraine (ex-Ukrainian CAD/L'vov UAD/88th Flight). By 2000 it was repainted in the full colours of Lviv Airlines. Note that the titles are Cyrillic (Avialiniï Ookraïny).

Seen here at its home base of Kubinka on 8th August 1997, An-26 '15 Red' (c/n 9303) of the Russian Air Force's 226th OSAP used to be stationed at Sperenberg AB near Berlin.

This Russian Air Force An-26 coded '01 Red' (c/n unknown) wears a Russian flag on the tail instead of the customary star insignia. This practice was fairly common in the early 1990s but was eventually abandoned, the Russian Air Force deciding to retain the Soviet-style red stars as instantly recognisable.

Above: This Russian Air Force An-26 coded '09 Red' (c/n unknown) wears an unusual three-tone camouflage. The white radome is equally unusual for an Air Force example.

An-26 '04 Blue' in an Aeroflot-style colour scheme at its home base (Kubinka AB). On 13th July 1994 a disgruntled technician stole this aircraft and crashed it, committing suicide in this fashion.

Above: Close-up of the external tanks on the An-26D prototype, '21 Yellow' (c/n 13806), at Zhukovskiy during the MAKS-97 airshow.

The yellow tactical code on this An-26 wearing standard grey camouflage reveals that the aircraft is operated by the Russian Navy.

Above: An Aeroflot An-26, CCCP-26558 (c/n 3305), pictured during a foreign trip.

This Russian Air Force An-26 wears a highly unusual civil-style colour scheme with Rossiaya (Russia) titles and the Russian double-headed eagle on the nose. However, the red tactical code discernible under the engine nacelle reveals this aircraft does *not* belong to the Russian government flight.

Above: Polish Air Force/13.PLT An-26 '1310 Black' (c/n 1310) in original grey camouflage; it was later repainted in three-tone green camouflage. In the Polish Air Force the An-26 was nicknamed *Smok* (Dragon) because a dragon reputedly lived near Wawel Castle not far from Kraków where the An-26s are based.

Three Polish Air Force An-26s were briefly leased to LOT Polish Airlines in 1989-96 for cargo and mail flights, gaining civil registrations and LOT colours. This is SP-LWB (ex/to '1603 Black', c/n 1603).

Above: Lately some Ukrainian Air Force An-26s, including '22 Blue' (c/n unknown), have exchanged their original grey colours for a two-tone green camouflage.

Czechoslovak Air Force An-26 '2506 Black' (c/n 12506) in original guise. It is now operated by the Slovak Air Force in a black/grey/white 'splatter camouflage'.

Above: Myachkovo Air Services An-30D Sibiryak RA-30063 (c/n 1202) sits on an apron displaying signs of a recent rainstorm at Moscow-Myachkovo. Most Myachkovo Air Services aircraft still wear Aeroflot titles.

Russian Air Force An-30B '04 Red' (ex-RA-30037, c/n 0704) in typical overall grey camouflage.

Above: Beriyev OKB An-32A RA-48090 (c/n 2601) operated by the United Nations Peace Forces at Sarajevo-Butmir; the airport is surrounded by tall mountains, often plagued by bad weather and is beastly to use. Most UNPF aircraft were painted in all-white colours; the retention of the blue cheatline is thus unusual.

Bangladesh Air Force (Biman Bahini) An-32s, including S3-ACB/1702 (c/n 1702), wear this two-tone green camouflage.

We hope you enjoyed this book . . .

Midland Publishing titles are edited and designed by an experienced and enthusiastic team of specialists.

We always welcome ideas from authors or readers for books they would like to see published.

In addition, our associate, Midland Counties Publications, offers an exceptionally wide range of aviation, military, naval and transport books and videos for sale by mail-order worldwide.

For a copy of the appropriate catalogue, or to order further copies of this book, and any of many other Midland Publishing titles, please write, telephone, fax or e-mail to:

Midland Counties Publications
4 Watling Drive, Hinckley,
Leics, LE10 3EY, England

Tel: (+44) 01455 254 450
Fax: (+44) 01455 233 737
E-mail: midlandbooks@compuserve.com
www.midlandcountiessuperstore.com

US distribution by Specialty Press –
see page 2.

Vol.1: Sukhoi S-37 & Mikoyan MFI
1 85780 120 2 £18.95/US $27.95
Vol.2: Flankers: The New Generation
1 85780 121 0 £18.95/US $27.95
Vol.3: Polikarpov's I-16 Fighter
1 85780 131 8 £18.95/US $27.95
Vol.4: Early Soviet Jet Fighters
1 85780 139 3 £19.99/US $29.95
Vol.5: Yakovlev's Piston-Engined Fighters
1 85780 140 7 £19.99/US $29.95

Red Star Volume 6
POLIKARPOV'S BIPLANE FIGHTERS

Yefim Gordon and Keith Dexter

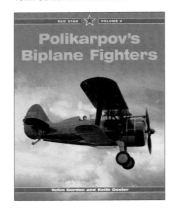

The development of Polikarpov's fighting biplanes including the 2I-N1, the I-3, and I-5, which paved the way for the I-15 which earned fame as the Chato during the Spanish Civil War and saw action against the Japanese; the I-15*bis* and the famous I-153 Chaika retractable gear gull-wing biplane. Details of combat use are given, plus structural descriptions, details of the ill-starred I-190, and of privately owned I-15*bis* and I-153s restored to fly.

Softback, 280 x 215 mm, 128 pages
c250 b/w and colour photos; three-view drawings, 60+ colour side views
1 85780 141 5 **£18.99/US $27.95**

Red Star Volume 7
TUPOLEV Tu-4 SOVIET SUPERFORTRESS

Yefim Gordon and Vladimir Rigmant

At the end of WW2, three Boeing B-29s fell into Soviet hands; from these came a Soviet copy of this famous bomber in the form of the Tu-4. This examines the evolution of the 'Superfortresski' and its further development into the Tu-70 transport. It also covers the civil airliner version, the Tu-75, and Tu-85, the last of Tupolev's piston-engined bombers. Also described are various experimental versions, including the Burlaki towed fighter programme.

Softback, 280 x 215 mm, 128 pages, 225 black/white and 9 colour photographs, plus line drawings
1 85780 142 3 **£18.99/US $27.95**

Red Star Volume 8
RUSSIA'S EKRANOPLANS
Caspian Sea Monster and other WIG Craft

Sergey Komissarov

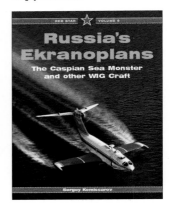

Known as wing-in-ground effect (WIGE) craft or by their Russian name of ekranoplan, these vehicles operate on the borderline between the sky and sea, offering the speed of an aircraft coupled with better operating economics and the ability to operate pretty much anywhere on the world's waterways.

WIGE vehicles by various design bureaus are covered, including the Orlyonok, the only ekranoplan to see squadron service, the Loon and the KM, or Caspian Sea Monster.

Softback, 280 x 215 mm, 128 pages
150 b/w and colour photos, plus dwgs
1 85780 146 6 **£18.99/US $27.95**

Red Star Volume 9
TUPOLEV Tu-160 BLACKJACK
Russia's Answer to the B-1

Yefim Gordon

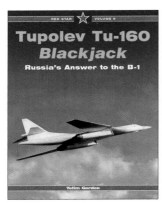

How the Soviet Union's most potent strategic bomber was designed, built and put into service. Comparison is made between the Tu-160 and the Sukhoi T-4 ('aircraft 100', a bomber which was ahead of its time), the variable-geometry 'aircraft 200' – and the Myasishchev M-18 and M-20.

Included are copies of original factory drawings of the Tu-160, M-18, M-20 and several other intriguing projects. Richly illustrated in colour, many shots taken at Engels.

Sbk, 280 x 215 mm, 128pp, 193 col & b/w photos, dwgs, colour side views
1 85780 147 4 **£18.99/US $27.95**

Red Star Volume 10
LAVOCHKIN'S PISTON-ENGINED FIGHTERS

Yefim Gordon

Covers the formation and early years of OKB-301, the design bureau created by Lavochkin, Gorbunov and Goodkov, shortly before the Great Patriotic War.

It describes all of their piston-engined fighters starting with the LaGG-3 and continues with the legendary La-5 and La-7. Concluding chapters deal with the La-9 and La-11, which saw combat in China and Korea in the 1940/50s.

Illustrated with numerous rare and previously unpublished photos drawn from Russian military archives.

Sbk, 280 x 215 mm, 144pp, 274 b/w & 10 col photos, 9pp col views, plus dwgs
1 85780 151 2 **£19.99/US $32.95**

Red Star Volume 11
MYASISHCHEV M-4 and 3M
The First Soviet Strategic Jet Bomber

Yefim Gordon

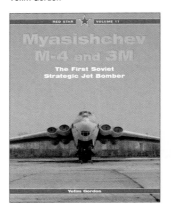

The story of the Soviet Union's first intercontinental jet bomber, the Soviet answer to the Boeing B-52. The new bomber had many innovative features (including a bicycle landing gear) and was created within an unprecedentedly short period of just one year; observers were stunned when the aircraft was formally unveiled at the 1953 May Day parade. The M-4 and the much-improved 3M remained in service for 40 years.

Softback, 280 x 215 mm, 128 pages, 185 b/w, 14pp of colour photographs, plus line drawings
1 85780 152 0 **£18.99/US $29.95**

Red Star Volume 13
MIKOYAN'S PISTON-ENGINED FIGHTERS

Yefim Gordon and Keith Dexter

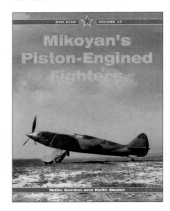

Describes the early history of the famous Mikoyan OKB and the aircraft that were developed. The first was the I-200 of 1940 which entered limited production in 1941 and was developed into the MiG-3 high-altitude interceptor. Experimental versions covered include the MiG-9, the I-220/225 series and I-230 series. A separate chapter deals with the I-200 (DIS or MiG-5) long-range heavy escort fighter.

Softback, 280 x 215 mm, 128 pages
195 b/w photos, 6pp of colour artwork, 10pp of line drawings
1 85780 160 1 **£18.99/US $29.95**